Madhu Tandan left Delhi in her mid-twenties with her husband to settle in a remote Himalayan ashram. Her life there, threaded by her dreams, inspired her first book, *Faith & Fire: A Way Within* (1997). She has since written three more, *Dreams & Beyond: Finding Your Way in the Dark* (2009), *Hemis: A Novel* (2018) and *The Logic of Dreams* (2022) to wide acclaim.

Madhu has contributed short stories and essays to anthologies, presented papers on religious dreaming at several international conferences, including the Nouvelle Sorbonne in Paris, and Wasan Island in Canada. She was awarded a writing fellowship at Hawthornden Castle, Edinburgh.

She and her husband have made the hills of Sattal their home.

A WAY WITHIN

Seven Years in a Himalayan Ashram

Madhu Tandan

SPEAKING TIGER BOOKS LLP
125A, Ground Floor, Shahpur Jat, near Asiad Village,
New Delhi 110049

First published as *Faith & Fire: A Way Within* by
HarperCollins Publishers in 1997
This revised and expanded version published by
Speaking Tiger Books 2023

Copyright © Madhu Tandan 2023

ISBN: **978-93-5447-715-7**
eISBN: 978-93-5447-713-3

10 9 8 7 6 5 4 3 2 1

To Ashishda,
in continuing gratitude.

To Rajeev,
two fellow travellers in a single dream.

Contents

PART THREE: The Inner Compass

Prologue

It has been over twenty-six years since *Faith & Fire: A Way Within* was published. Though my stay in a Himalayan ashram remains pivotal to my life, sometimes the eye of distance helps see the landscape afresh. When I lived there, I perceived life in a particular way. When I wrote about it, I was trying to catch within the net of words the essence of that experience. Even so, something remained unstated. With the passage of years, I hear the same words differently now, as if they were from another person. Towards that end, I have added and subtracted material from the original book and attempted to bring it more in line with the unstated; about the search that I had embarked upon. I have also added two chapters about my journey after we left Mirtola. In that sense it has become a different book, and hence the new title with its link to the old.

On re-reading it, I asked myself—'What can be the relevance of such a search today?' About living a life of contemplation and service in the afforested Himalayas. What relevance can there be of a quest for a deeper, more authentic self, the discovery of which can take years and years of unrelenting practice, which involves facing personal limitations, of questioning hopes and fears, and uncovering the prison of one's beliefs. And the only constant is the struggle to understand that one's anger, resentments and ambitions are nothing but the citadels of one's selfhood that must be let go of as a prerequisite to this endeavour.

Currently, the overarching ethos is to succeed, to 'get on in life'. To be practical in a practical culture, geared to a life of getting and spending, where ideals are considered sources of delusion. Moreover, young people who are traditionally more receptive to ideals are busy in the pursuit of values that promote personal autonomy, bodily fitness and technological fluency. This has its advantages—there is greater self-agency, a freedom from the collective. They are able to express creativity in hitherto undreamt directions and do not allow their energy and vitality to be shackled by the past. Borders—geographical or cultural—present no barriers. Yet, this has led to the dilution, even extinction, of any authentic ideals—no principles or standards, only the idealizing of successful people.

What then is the role, in the present context, of the traditional guru-shishya relationship? To add to the picture, the fact is that not all claimants to knowing this Self can be believed and trusted as there is no end of deception that goes on in the name of Truth. Are we then better off without such an intangible search?

Admittedly, economic and social progress is essential. But, doesn't it lose meaning when won at the cost of disowning the nature of the spirit that determines its course? In this march towards outward 'progress', if certain facets are overlooked, they will most likely create a vacuum in other directions. And, sooner or later, the ignored aspects will demand recognition.

Carl Jung, the Swiss psychologist, found that a third of his patients, in the second phase of life—that is to say, over thirty-five—were not in therapy for any known problem but from a sense of meaninglessness. They were suffering because they had lost that which the living religions of every age have given their followers, and none of them could be healed unless they regained the religious outlook in some form. Jung says, 'Life and spirit are two powers or necessities between which modern man is placed. Spirit gives meaning to his life, and the possibility of his greatest development. But life is essential to spirit, since its truth is nothing if it cannot live it.'

When I was younger, I too was perplexed if anything existed beyond my everyday concerns. *A Way Within: Seven Years in a Himalayan Ashram* is an exploration of what makes life meaningful; to grapple with the mystery of life; to be touched and guided by the wisdom of an extraordinary teacher. It is based on what I perceived and understood.

This account has an atypical setting. An ashram sanctified by three generations of Gurus. My guru, Sri Madhava Ashish (Ashishda), the last of the three, who while not being an Indian had the soul of a Vaishnav; who believed in the essential unity of life, and who had gathered around him a small community of disciples, some Indian, some not. Collectively, they contributed to their astonishingly integrated mountain home. It was a rare place in which every individual's search found expression in the way of life there. A man and his hermitage gave shape to my initial questionings, ardour to my longings. Somewhere along the way a perplexity was created by dissolving the boundaries that the mind erects. A de-husking of the personality was expected.

Writing the book gave me a chance to hold close every experience and to assimilate its meaning. And in the process, I discovered that my most meaningful moments were when I chanced upon a totally new way of perceiving myself and the world. I realised that the mental and physical exercises I underwent in the Ashram made me view everything from inside out instead of the other way around. It had engendered a state of inwardness because the centre of gravity had shifted. Trailing in its wake came an unexpected and inexplicable joy, which is not dependent on anything for its existence. The training allowed glimpses of a state free of all things known, thereby offering a truer and more primary perception of what is real.

After our return to the city, I was confronted with a disconcerting question by a dream. I was forty by then and had come full circle. Twenty-two years earlier, I had ventured out to discover my path. I had since then met a charismatic teacher, under whose vigilant tutelage I had lived for seven years. Another seven years had elapsed since our return to the city—time enough to absorb the intense experience of discipleship and to continue with the practices I had carried with me from the Ashram. But now, I was up against an even more fundamental question—how deep was my commitment to my inner search? It was no longer being shouldered by Ashishda, for he had passed on. I was faced with the responsibility of sustaining it without any inputs, save my own determination. What had been taken for granted when he was alive had to be revivified entirely by my own effort. It raised uncomfortable questions. How much did I really want it? How much was I prepared to surrender to it?

I oscillated between holding onto it, and letting my grip loosen. That I often fell short was apparent to me. This dream came against the backdrop of this unarticulated conflict:

I'm sitting for an examination, and the invigilator hands me the question paper. I realise this is no ordinary examination—it is a life exam. The first question is: 'What is your gravest doubt in life?'

I answer, 'My doubt is that nothing is permanent. Everything changes. Today's pleasure is tomorrow's sorrow; despair turns to hope, health to illness, love to indifference. In this constant flux what is permanent?'

I continue to write in this vein for some time, and then feel that I need to get on to the next question, since time is running out. Even though I have not completed my answer, curiosity compels me to turn the page over and look at what the next question is. In rather bold letters it asks: 'Who are you?'

I awoke feeling it would take time to understand the full import of this dream. Was it highlighting a question essential to my journey? It invoked the central teaching of the great South Indian sage Ramana Maharshi who believed the best way to realise the true nature of the Self was through an assiduous enquiry into 'Who am I?' If all is transitory and change a constant, then, can the quest for the essential Self be answered only by knowing who I am?

On the face of it, not knowing who one is seems ludicrous. In the days that followed I began to realise how difficult the exercise was. No matter how much I reflected on it, I was confronted with inadequate answers. If I addressed the question by my gender (woman), or my roles (wife, daughter, writer), or by abstract personal qualities (empathetic, introverted, impractical), no satisfactory answers emerged.

It seems that I am something more than my body, more than my desires and fears, more than the mind with all its thoughts and creativity and more than the chain of events I call my life. I may think that the sum of my personality traits, my thoughts and my emotions define the person I am, but in essence that is still not 'me', for when asleep they are not in evidence, yet I still am. Furthermore, my thoughts and emotions constantly change, my body undergoes changes, my personality traits change, so how can I search for an answer based on ever-changing attributes? There has to be a permanent 'someone' to whom these changes occur. Who is that 'someone', the unchanging 'I'?

Was the dream asking for a more direct approach to the 'I', the source of awareness? To go inwards to that which is deeper and beyond all that I define myself as? Was the dream pointing in the direction Ashishda always upheld? And which is enshrined in the small temple with the grey dome encircled by deodars rising above them as an emblem of an aspiration to meet the sky while being grounded in the foundation of everyday life. A life that seeks to marry the outer with the inner, so that each reflects and transforms the other. From ordinary activities like cooking, cleaning and gardening, and from everyday emotions like anger, irritation, fear and pleasure, a secret could be coaxed out, a self-observing awareness discovered. A practice rooted in the Ashram on how to live my life by standing apart and looking at myself.

It has been many years since Ashishda, our teacher left the body. Yet in the soft fall of the evening hour, when the aflame sun suddenly disappears behind the mountains, my teacher's words come back to me, 'It's a mystery. A mystery that lies at the depth of your being. So, restrain the outflows, build up the energy and turn towards the source of your being.'

The Ashram stands there as a representation of the Gurus whose dedication to this search imbues the place with the intangible sense of the sacred, a place where three extraordinary people found something real and though no longer in the body, they are still the guiding lights for anyone interested in the Path.

Nor is Mirtola limited to a geographical place. It has always been known by many names. It is a way of perceiving what is real and can be lived by anyone, anywhere and at any time.

And for that reason alone, this book may have relevance.

1

Off the Beaten Track

'We're leaving for good; we've decided to live at the Ashram,' I said.

My mother looked dazed.

'Rajeev and I have asked Ashishda's permission and he's agreed.'

'He's never encouraged permanent settlers, so how's that possible?'

'For some reason he's now allowing five couples to join him.'

'You're just twenty-six! You've only been married six years!' Her voice rose an octave, 'You haven't even started a family!'

'Isn't this rather sudden?' my father said, putting down his newspaper. 'After five years of hard work, Rajeev has finally got his business on the rails and now you are leaving it all?'

'We want to try and make a go of it, Dad.'

'Try and make a go of it?' my mother said.

'I've used the wrong expression. This is for good, Mom. Rajeev is pulling out of the business and handing it over to his brother; I'm quitting my job; we're leaving this house and selling most of our stuff,' I said, enunciating the words clearly, more for myself than for her.

'To go as a visitor to the Ashram is one thing, to live there another matter,' my father said gently.

'I'm sorry,' I said helplessly. 'If there was any way I could do this without hurting you both I would.'

My mother looked up, the dusk of the evening gathering under her eyes and in the hollows of her cheeks. I looked away, a coward when faced with her pain. I felt I was already surveying a past. The same beloved faces, the familiar drawing room with its bookcases, the rocking chair with the rug underneath it, reminding me of times when the end of the day meant returning to the comfort of all these.

Ashishda had said very little and yet everything as a prelude to what was, for us, a monumental decision. 'Simplify the entire paraphernalia of living. Come with only the bare essentials. The important thing is the inner attitude, for you can't reduce the outer luggage without inwardly being prepared to do so. Remember the Latin word for luggage is impedimenta,' he had advised, coalescing his upper-class English upbringing with thirty-five years spent as a sadhu in India.

'You are young, far too young to go,' my father said. 'Twelve hours of work every day, a remote wilderness miles from the nearest town, no radio, no television, no market place, no social life…just…an idea in your head. You don't know the reality of it.'

Reality. That's what I want to find, Dad. I want to confront it head-on. No philosophical wrangles, no second-hand versions, but a discovery reached through my own experience. This day-to-day reality we live in couldn't possibly be what life is all about. An incomplete poem, a knotted handkerchief as a reminder of a forgotten promise, age hardened by habit and marks on a page where the ink ran out. There must be more to it and I'm going to trust that feeling which says there is.

'Too young, too young to go,' whispered my mind. Too young to understand that sometimes, rather nonchalantly, fate sends an envelope flying in your direction. You open it and realise it has to do with you even though it bears no name. I could have made the plea that it wasn't meant for me, but since it had come into my orbit, I knew it was.

How had I arrived at this juncture? I functioned quite normally in my world, made up of family, friends, work and all such experiences. At a private level, I listened to a voice that laid claims on me, constantly asking questions, the answers for which eluded me. This vague questioning gradually found a focus through Ashishda, who shared with us his vision of life.

Big changes can only happen when the time is right, or when the season has changed and there is a new rhythm that demands obedience. Yet we were far from being like age-old trees that effortlessly shed their autumn leaves. In our tree the sap was still green, so that if we shook it perhaps not even a single leaf would fall on its own.

As we prepared for our move, an image of the life ahead began to take shape. In the lifestyle Ashishda had outlined, nothing was to be rejected. Every experience would be part of the effort to produce wholeness. He expected a harmonious blending of the inner and outer life. The body, the mind and the emotions had all to be harnessed to serve a single intent—to find yourself. Ashishda believed that an inner rootedness, leading to a higher awareness was best achieved through a life lived close to nature. With his lifestyle he had formed a bridge connecting soil to soul.

The Ashram aimed at self-sufficiency in food, which

meant we would learn how to plant, weed and harvest the crops. We would probably carry headloads of compost to fertilise the fields, milk cows, deliver calves, churn butter, bake our own brown bread, and make our own jams and pickles. We would even have to build our own tiny cottages. Besides a few local masons there were no carpenters, plumbers or electricians in that remote jungle.

It was going to be a 'hands-on' spirituality. Twelve hours of manual work each day would be offered in selfless service to the temple. This was intended to cut out the messy edges of gain and profit, and to give us the added dignity that comes from working for your own food. The internal resistance to this gruelling labour was to be tempered by introspection, while the complexities of our emotional nature would be clarified by dream analysis. Meditation would help to stop the internal chatter of thoughts so as to reach a 'still-point' within. The attempt was to give recognition—through the body, mind and emotions—to that higher awareness.

We already knew from our visits to the Ashram that it was in the evenings that everyone would come together with Ashishda, who would later help us see the inter-connectedness of various paths that led to the Truth. He would provide a context to our questioning by reading to us from a wide variety of books, including Plotinus, Meister Eckhart, Rumi, Ramana Maharshi, the Upanishads, Buddhist texts, Theosophy and the Zen masters. Ashishda always urged us to look for the universal content wherever it was highlighted.

'Why give up everything? What you're looking for can be found anywhere,' Aparna, my closest friend, said.

'I'm going to find out how to look.'

'But that's indoctrination. If you confine Truth to a particular sect or a guru, you've lost its true intent.'

'It's just a point of entry, Aparna, like in a wheel. You have to put your finger on one of its spokes and trace it to the hub—the centre. Otherwise, you can keep walking round and round on the rim forever.'

'You're not running away from something, are you?'

'It's hardly going to be a picnic.'

'Then why are you going?'

For over five years we had practised Ashishda's teachings through meditation, self-analysis and dream interpretation. Twice a year we trekked to the Ashram and tried to live our lives according to both his and our ideals. But now Rajeev and I felt we had to respond to a more urgent call and were uprooting ourselves of our own free-will to join Ashishda and meet the unfolding of a great challenge—wonderful, magical, all-consuming and terrifying.

For every person there is a somewhat predetermined path pointing to a particular direction that can lead to self-discovery. Some call it fate; others call it karma and Ashishda called it the opportunity for evolution. However baffling I found some of my experiences, I realised that they had compelled me to seek a deeper understanding of life. Each set of experiences left me with new questions and a growing desire to answer them.

Long before we took our decision, Rajeev had once asked Ashishda, 'Can we stay here permanently?'

'No,' he had said, 'This is not a place to run away to. It's a place where you finally come to face things.'

Two years later Rajeev had a dream, powerful in symbolism. Ashishda interpreted it as our 'call'. His face was flecked with feeling as he listened to the dream, in which a question was being asked of Rajeev again and again. An answer must be given, not tomorrow or the day after but now...here...in this room. I looked for it within Ashishda's still eyes; watchful, held alert by a moment amplified by crucial choices about to be made.

He offered no detailed interpretation of the dream, which was very unusual for him. He just stared at the cracks in the wooden floor. Don't say anything, Ashishda, I pleaded silently; please don't. He looked at me, with only the barest hint of a smile on his face. Confronted with the finality of a choice between one kind of life and another I felt myself creating a barrier of resistance. Ashishda seemed to read me and slowly shook his head as though to dispel my fears.

Rajeev looked at me, asking for a confirmation I was still not prepared to give. Silence stretched back and forth like the shuttle of a weaver's loom. Ashishda watched our faces with the look of foreknowledge that made me even more uncomfortable. He stretched his long legs and leaned back against the wall, closing his eyes, waiting. My heart kept beating faster as though trying to keep pace with what might come to pass.

'Can we stay here, Ashishda?' Rajeev asked hesitantly.

With a look of someone guarding ancient secrets, Ashishda had said, 'Yes, your time has come.'

Our time had come for what? To give up material things and comforts? To distil our emotions, and focus our mind on the inner enquiry? And finally, to surrender to a man, a guru, a belief. A belief which demanded total submission of oneself in faith. 'The ego has to go,' Ashishda had said, echoing what mystics the world over have written, from the anonymous authors of the Upanishads to the Neo-

Platonists, the Christian saints, the Sufi poets. 'It is the one obstruction to perceiving Reality. When there is nothing left of you, something real will be born.'

Nothing was to mark our intent: no bare feet, shaven heads or the conventional saffron robes of renunciation. Any transition we made would have to be done silently, inwardly.

Ahead of us was the journey of a lifetime, behind us memories. And with us now were Ashishda's words, 'Don't leave any back doors open. Burn every bridge as you walk across it, so that you give your all to the life you have chosen to live.'

Not even one backward glance at what was or might have been? All I had was the warmth of Rajeev's breath on my cheek as he stood behind me, looking at our parents standing on the porch. They didn't even raise their hands in farewell, as though this moment had no conventional responses to fall back upon. Just the grave tilt of a head, wordlessly conveying that what we won or lost ahead would be theirs to share with us.

The vapours from a January morning hit the windscreen of the jeep as we got in. I wanted so much to look past the blur, wishing the present would become transparent enough to show us the future.

'I can't say whether we've done the right thing or not. All I know is, we'll share each step of the way. The rest we'll have to take on trust,' Rajeev said as we covered the first mile of the journey.

Sitting in that jeep, could we have imagined that the anxieties we then anticipated would seem trivial one day? The difficulties that came our way emerged from situations we could never have dreamed of. In a life of seven years of solitude, I lost more than I can name and gained more than

I could contain. I kept no diary, no notes, only a record of my dreams. At one point in our years at the Ashram I reached such an abyss of despair that I abandoned all hope. All roads seemed dead ends. Then, quite unexpectedly, there was an affirmation. I was touched by something so profoundly beautiful that I dare not give it a name. It filled my being with an all-embracing experience of love that I have found difficult to duplicate.

It taught me, it guided me and sometimes it gave me glimpses of a state of being against which the limitations of my everyday reality stood out. It transformed my perceptions; for example, of the role of suffering in life. I do not pretend to understand the full scope of this mysterious force that graced my life. It commanded my attention as it increasingly directed the theatre of my dream life. Many of my dreams were more real than reality itself.

There were no easy answers given to me. What I pieced together of this mysterious force was subject to my own limitations. Yet for a while I felt the capacity to shed all that was 'me' in order to meet it whole-heartedly. This process of shedding myself was not easy. Later I wondered why I could not have made my surrender more willingly. For a long time, I fought the suffering, because I did not understand it. When I surrendered to it, I found I was actually free because I had dissolved into something far greater than myself.

When I looked for causes or explanations, I found none. As Rajeev said later, 'To understand this state of Grace one life is not enough.' All I know is that when we felt we had lost everything, help had come and whispered its final assurance. In those moments we felt that a gift had been given to us that would, in some small measure, be ours for the keeping.

It was after this experience that I could truly appreciate Ashishda's words: 'The true ashram is a state of mind, it doesn't belong to a particular geographical place. It stands for being united by love, for acceptance of suffering, not for escape into euphoria; for introspection not for blaming things on others, for service, not for personal progress. Finally, for intelligent enquiry, not for unquestioning belief; for dedication, constant watchfulness, courage, vigour, fire...'

If the most difficult part of this search is to unwaveringly hold onto the faith that we are all united by an immense, compassionate, mysterious and formless power, then the greatest joy is to receive a confirmation of its existence. My experience did not miraculously free me from the limitations of my own nature. Even now, I continue to struggle and stumble. What it did for me was to affirm, beyond doubt, that what I was seeking, existed. So overwhelming was this affirmation that it made every painful step of the struggle worthwhile. I knew I had discovered an unassailable ally whom I could always refer to, honour and rely on to be the navigator on my journey through this life and beyond.

PART ONE

Another Way

2

My Childhood Secret

I wasn't looking for a guru, yet Ashishda grew, as it were, out of the landscape of my childhood. I had seen photographs of him in my parents' room ever since I was ten or eleven. He was in his late forties then, very English, very good looking, with blonde-brown hair swept back from a wide forehead, and eyes that laughed right into the camera. I was twelve when I first met him; my parents were holidaying in Nainital and Ashishda was there on work. I was standing at one end of a glazed verandah overlooking the lake, when he emerged from the other end.

It took me a minute to recognise him because he had shaved off his beard. He walked over and looked down at me with eyes that held a hint of aloofness. It seemed appropriate that our first meeting began with his asking me, 'And, who are you?' for this was a question he was to pose in various ways throughout our association.

'I'm Shalli's daughter,' I replied, jamming my hands into the pockets of my windcheater.

'Ah,' he said, allowing the awkwardness of unfamiliarity to subside into an easy silence. He stood quietly, hands folded around his chest, his faded ankle-length ochre robe tied at the waist with a strip of hand-spun cotton cloth.

'And you? You are…Ashishda?' I said, more to say something than to confirm a fact.

He smiled. 'Yes, I'm Ashishda.'

I stared at him as he gazed out of the window at the lake, all green and weedy in its early morning robes. I barely reached his waist, yet standing beside him it wasn't the difference in our heights that I noticed. As I racked my brain to think of something to say, I realised he was very comfortable with silence. He did not ask the usual questions about school, my friends, my favourite subjects, whom I liked more, Mom or Dad, but just stood there; neither ignoring me nor acknowledging me with a burst of small talk. I felt that if he asked me something it would be out of interest, not because there was nothing else to talk about. He turned slightly and I smiled up at him.

'What a mischievous glint you have in your eyes,' he said, answering with a look of amusement. It was as though at that moment we had shared a telepathic joke and realised we had common tastes.

My mother would have been horrified at my irreverence at equating myself with Ashishda in any way. She had always talked of him with a kind of hushed awe, as the wise man who lived in the remote mountains in a small hermitage surrounded by forests. When I first asked her what Ashishda did, she said mystifyingly, 'He interprets dreams among other things.'

As a child, the mystery of Ashishda grew, as he seemed like a dream figure, sometimes real, and at other times veiled by the mountain mists. He was a figure I had encountered under the closed eyelids of sleep, but was loath to drag out and define by the light of day. Then one night I dreamt:

There were two tribes fighting—primitive tribes with feathers in their hair, short roughly textured tunics around their waists, sharp glinting spears in their hands; crouching behind two large boulders on either side of a wide-open area. I saw myself behind one of the tribal chieftains and as I looked at his face, I realised it was Ashishda's; clearly distinguishable through the war-paint and feathers, with eyes as clear as the first light of the sun.

I felt strangely protected in the aftermath of the dream. Maybe from that time on he became a kind of talisman who wove himself not overtly, but subliminally, through the ebb and flow of my rather strange and eventful childhood.

From a very young age, maybe four or five, I had felt that my mother and I were bound together by some dark secret that simultaneously held us together and tore us apart. My first memory of it was when I was once standing in the verandah of the sprawling army cantonment bungalow where we lived. My mother's friend lowered her voice and gesturing towards me with her eyes, asked, 'Does she know about it?'

Instinctively, sensing a threat, I turned around to look at my mother. Her usually smiling eyes clouded as she said, 'When she is old enough, I'll tell her.'

This secret that concerned me also seemed to exclude me; it was about me, yet I was not to be told about it. I have another very clear memory—lying under a tree, watching the birds chirping as they hopped from branch to branch. It was a hot May morning. Through my reverie I heard my mother call my name from the bungalow. Suddenly I couldn't remember her face, as though she had dissolved from memory. It filled me with a stomach-pitting shock. Why did other faces crowd in like a collage of half-forgotten people?

'I'm here, I'm here,' I ran in panic all the way to the house and wrapped myself around her waist.

'What happened, sweetheart?' she asked.

How could I tell her that I would continually train my eyes on her, afraid that a tiny lapse in attention would make her disappear? There was something here I did not understand, even though I unwittingly revealed my own secret, one day, to my five-year-old classmates.

We were sitting under a tree munching our sandwiches in school, telling one another where we had been born. Amidst shrieks and excited jumpings up-and-down we tried to share this momentous information all at once. Finally, when my turn came, I said, 'I was born in Calcutta, but my mother was in Delhi.' My words sounded like the clattering of a spoon on the floor of a silent room. None of the five-year-olds, including myself, wanted to show their ignorance by asking, 'How could that be?'

'She's funny,' said the girl next to me. 'She even calls her mother Aunty.'

Someone giggled. Then everyone started giggling and intoning 'Aunty...Aunty...' as though to create a distraction from the task of solving my peculiar riddle.

Yes, I was adopted and the 'mother' I referred to was my foster mother, who was in Delhi when I was born. I changed three homes before I finally settled with my adoptive parents, but that was something I did not know then. All I knew was that I didn't come to my parents the way most children came to theirs. I was routed another way. This was quite a secret to hold and forget simultaneously. It was not something I cared to remember most of the time, but I got reminded of it one way or the other. Like the time when my lanky bespectacled cousin said to me in Delhi, 'Do you know about yourself?' I nodded my head, more to avoid hearing what he had to say than assenting to any real knowledge. 'Well, if you don't, you should,' he said in a superior way.

On that same visit I overheard my cousin's father saying, 'She's not Shalli's daughter. Not her real daughter anyway...' He stopped short as I walked into the room. I still remember the guilty look on his face when he saw me and at that moment, I felt sucked into an ambience of deceit in which, unwittingly, I had become the protagonist.

These incidents left their mark on me during my childhood. However, when my mother came to my first school to enquire how I was doing, she was told by the headmistress, 'You've no need to worry about her. She's a true survivor.'

Also etched in my childhood memory are my father's army postings—a new one every three years. I exchanged one convent school for another, meeting the same blue-eyed Irish nuns in their black and white habits everywhere. Through all this I felt curiously at the edge of something, an intense feeling that I should know something. The guilt of a mistake I couldn't locate made me slide into a peculiar form of self-effacement whereby I refused to do well in any way—academically, in games, or even in making friends; not because I couldn't but because I felt I shouldn't. It was as though doing well would affirm my existence which I felt I didn't have the right to. Of course, the sensible part of me rebelled against this attitude, producing a tension that I sought urgently to resolve.

I could have talked to my mother, but instinctively I felt my difficulties would bring to surface her own problems as an adoptive mother. I couldn't handle mine, much less hers. This secret joined us by the common sorrow of wishing we were a natural mother and daughter.

Other points dotted my childhood, like markers on a page; question marks against difficult passages to remind me to come to grips with them later. I couldn't affix firm relationships to many of my relatives. My adoptive mother was my biological father's younger sister. As a result, someone who was Uncle became Daddy, Aunty became Mummy and my sisters became my cousins. Unlike most adopted children, I had the advantage of moving within the same larger family, being first adopted by one set of people then moving onto the next and then the next, feeling that everyone was fond of me but not enough to keep me for good. I ended up feeling there must have been something drastically wrong with me for them to keep handing me around.

I skirted the topic with my mother when I came to know, rather painfully through a cousin, that my natural father was still alive. I then repressed the entire memory of the incident surrounding this disclosure like someone stuffing old clothes into the back of a cupboard, hoping they'll never fall out on their own again. It is said that when you are trying to run away from something, you are most likely to trip up against it.

And trip I did.

I kept meeting my natural father now and again; the experience was utterly baffling. He was alive, yet I did not live with him. In spite of being an assertive man, he always looked at me with gentle eyes that sometimes seemed to plead with mine for understanding, almost saying, 'I'm sorry...'

In a strange way, I felt a mature sense of power emerging from me; a power that could release another bound to me by self-recrimination. Despite the separation, I felt an empathy with him. It was only later that Ashishda gently suggested that I look directly into my father's face to try and understand, in adult terms, what needed to be dropped, without the dark stains of repression.

The same Ashishda, in whose direction, it appears, the forces of my life, from adolescent years to adult ones, were already gathering momentum to meet.

What common ground could there have been between a tall Englishman who had left his aristocratic English roots, complete with nannies and public-school education, to come to India during the Second World War to repair Spitfires, and went on to take sanyas never to return to England, and an Indian girl firmly tied to the conventions of her middle-class upbringing? Nothing much. Except that Ashishda had swept aside his roots while I was looking for mine.

I had not inherited any religious beliefs from my family. Even my convent education, woven with religious doctrine where sin was intoned with a hiss, had left me cold. Perhaps this left a gap that Ashishda came to fill.

I wonder what about Ashishda caught my attention. Maybe it was that he worked in the here-and-now but was connected to something beyond it in a very real way. Whenever my mother returned from a five-day visit to Ashishda's ashram, she looked both exhilarated and exhausted. Of course, the journey was killing as she changed one bus for another till she reached that single mountain path which was swallowed up by the afforested Himalayan interior, where roads gave way to dirt tracks. Yet that was not all; for my mother tried to keep pace mentally and physically with Ashishda—gardening, cooking on a woodstove, scrubbing floors, cleaning drains, harvesting wheat. While she was at the Ashram it seemed to her that the most natural way to live was to work with your hands.

'What else does he say to you?' I asked my mother.

'That one's attitudes make up one's life. What one sees outside is really what one is like inside.'

I don't think I understood much of it then. However, I did gather that when Ashishda first came to India he had worked as an engineer at Calcutta (now Kolkata) airport. Disillusioned with war, he decided to travel around India. In a chance encounter he met his guru, Sri Krishna Prem (Gopalda), also British, a Cambridge educated philosopher who had come to India after the First World War to teach at Lucknow University.

My mother had a photograph of Gopalda's next to Ashishda's—clear blue eyes, shaven head, his fair skin aglow. He had adopted his Bengali guru's Vaishnav mode of life and had founded the Ashram with her, for many months begging for food like any ordinary mendicant.

I could picture Ashishda, who had come to visit and stayed on for good, in his robe; with his shaven head, vertical Vaishnav caste-mark on the forehead and wooden sandals, identical to Gopalda's; both men over six feet tall, walking with long strides against the convention of their times.

After twenty-five years in the Ashram, Gopalda began to simplify the very strict do's and don'ts of Vaishnav ritualism. He kept the essentials to ensure a personalised and direct enquiry that included dream interpretation, psychological self-understanding and the exploration of what was highest in humankind.

With characteristic English reserve they guarded their privacy for many years, having chosen a remote mountainside that daunted even the most ardent visitor. When the metalled road was extended to within two kilometres of their village, a small trickle of visitors started, curious about these two men—one with piercing eyes that seemed not to look at you but through you, and the other, much younger, who seemed to telepathically pick up a half-finished sentence from his companion. After Gopalda's death, Ashishda withdrew further into his privacy. Yet as the small but steady stream of people came asking for help, seeking answers to their inner queries, Ashishda extended himself, honouring the convictions and teachings of his late guru.

Before my mother left for a visit to the Ashram there was an unspoken build-up in the air. She became quieter, as though containing her breath, holding it in her stomach, only to release it in slow doses over the uncharted journey ahead. Often, I saw her sitting on her favourite chair, flipping through her dream book with its brown-paper cover. It was a book I had the greatest curiosity about. It lay on her bedside table, holding secrets about her that I wanted to know but dared not find out.

Once, when she was out of the house, I opened her diary, my heart thumping with guilt and anticipation. It had faint brown lines running across the page. The pen was lying where she had recorded her last dream. She had noted:

> *I am lying on the floor of the South Extension house. There is a white sheet over me and I'm dead. There is incense burning around me and mourners are sitting around in white. Suddenly I get up, fling the sheet aside and say, 'I'm not dead'.*

I shut the diary with a start. I felt alarmed at what she had written. My first irrational reaction was to feel upset that I was not in the dream when she was supposed to be dead. I did not like the images the dream conveyed and felt disturbed, both at prying and being confronted with its outcome.

'Why do you write your dreams down?' I asked her.

'They mean something.'

'What?'

'You remember once when we went to Shimla and climbed the top of the hill and you shouted your name? The echo of your voice kept coming back to you again and again. Dreams are like that. They are echoes of ourselves, our own voice coming back to us in a different language.'

The image stuck in my mind even though I hadn't fully understood her words. Whenever I watched my mother put two candles, an alarm clock, a torch and her dream book along with her clothes into a bag, I felt certain she was going to a land, like in her dream, where you could live and die at the same moment.

Being presented with such paradoxes since the time I was very young, I felt a curious psychic affinity with these journeys my mother made. She was going out to discover something for both of us, till I was old enough to do it for myself.

3

A Voice of My Own

By the time I was eighteen I began to feel I had to unravel something, and trace the threads that had wrapped themselves around me to their origin. Family life had overtones of a surreal Pirandello drama in which a group of characters, including me, found themselves in roles that had got interchanged. As I played my role, I was also looking over my shoulder wondering about the part I was originally meant to play. That is how I began an annual pilgrimage to Calcutta in my early adolescent years to visit my natural father who lived there with his second wife and my sisters.

I don't know what it was I was looking for in the two months I spent there each year, except perhaps, traces of myself in a household to which I could have belonged. It was a house bustling with activity; my sisters had more friends dropping in than I could keep count of, while my father was seldom visible between the pressures of his business during the day and his love for cards in the evenings. Often, he came home with a migraine and withdrew into his room. He was a figure I remembered more for his absences; he was always in the process of leaving, with briefcase in hand

and eyes that were kindly yet distracted.

I loved the energetic bustle in the house. My heart would beat a trifle faster when my sisters would casually introduce me to a friend, 'Meet our youngest sister,' as though they had recognised a piece from a jigsaw puzzle that was hard to put together.

My days in Calcutta had a dual quality about them. I felt comfortable, casually included, as though, there, I didn't have to explain who I was. Yet I knew I did not belong for there was no niche that was only mine to fill. What existed was not permanent.

When I returned to my parents, my mother would always ask, 'How was the holiday?' Her eyes alert, her tone studiously casual.

'It was fun, though I hardly saw Uncle.'

'What did you do?'

'Oh, the usual. I went to the pavement bookshops, listened to music and ate lots of Chinese food.'

Between us, straining to be heard, were the unspoken words: 'Did you want to come back to us?' Sometimes things left unsaid carry much more potency. I felt slightly choked, incapable of answering. How was I to explain to my mother that in Calcutta, I didn't belong but knew who I was. With her I felt I belonged, but did not know who I was. Sometimes family friends would ask me, 'So how is your father?'

When I began talking about my foster father, they would interrupt me. 'No, no, we mean your real father.'

Every time this happened, it was as though my present life was not being acknowledged while that which was not mine to keep, was being kept alive.

'Did you want a child of your own?' I had asked my mother.

'Very much, earlier on. After you came into our lives, not at all. You were everything I wanted.'

'But don't you wish I was your own child?'

'You are my own child. You know when I realised I couldn't have children I was quite heartbroken. I felt excluded from the magic circle of women discussing birth, labour and the initial days of holding a gurgling bundle of creation in their hands. Slowly I realised that most women don't love their children from day one. Such a love develops as you nurture and see something grow before you. It's no different from our relationship, for both are based on love.' She spoke with an intensity that united us.

Love there was; I only wondered why I had been put in a position where I could doubt it. This doubting had unexpected side-effects; one was a steady decline in academic results, to the extent that when I reached Senior Cambridge my mother was told by the nuns that they would have to demote me. My mother stood facing a semi-circle of nuns, like a newly planted sapling battling the winds. Something within me decided then to try and move out of the shadows.

I spent hours poring over books that I had earlier read without understanding. I studied by torchlight when the dormitory lights were switched off, stole down the red-carpeted staircase, hunched up against the cold to sit under the one landing light which burned through the night. When the final results came, I had done well. In the feeling of elation that followed, I felt I had returned something I had long owed my parents.

Maybe that's when I knew I had a long way to go. Some process had begun which I had to continue with. Each life has its truth, characteristically individual to itself. The discovery of that truth is the secret task we are all entrusted with. A secret that is ours to cage or to free but which struggles to find a voice of its own. Perhaps that was the voice I needed to hear.

On an impulse, without telling my parents, I dropped a letter to Ashishda asking if I could visit him.

4

A Sahib Sadhu

Midway through a journey, you sometimes wonder why you set off at all. That's how I felt after having travelled a full day and a night, reaching Nainital as dawn broke over the hills. The bus from there to the Ashram was like an open tin can that rattled more than it gained ground, collecting more and more villagers—some with goats—en route. Stunted pines gave way to taller ones, as the bus heaved its way uphill like an overweight jogger on a road that became narrower and narrower.

'Alone!' my mother had gasped when matador like I had flung the full cloak of my daring into her face. 'Why not with me? The journey is too long. You'll probably miss the bus or catch the wrong one.'

'I want to do this alone, Mom.'

'You want to prove something to yourself?'

'What's wrong with that?'

'At night, a single girl...' she trailed off, horrified.

'You yourself said it's safer to travel in the hills than in the plains. Anyway, Ashishda has written to you. You can't refuse now.'

I think I must have waited every day for his reply. When

it came there were two letters, one for my mother and one for me. Perversely, I had wanted to open her's first. His letter to me was brief:

'June 10th for three days is all right. I've written to your mother confirming your visit. In case you have problems when you get off at Panuanaula, ask for Bhavani Singh. He'll give you directions for the last climb up to the Ashram.'

I looked for a faint glimmer of something personal in his note but there were no giveaways in its impersonal tone. The courtesy he extended of gaining my mother's consent hardly suited the grown-up intent I had been flashing at her. Up until then I had felt invincible in my determination to go alone, but now I felt vulnerable. What kind of a man was Ashishda or, more to the point, what did I want him to be?

'What do you want to talk to him about?' my mother had asked.

I did not know then, much less now.

'He'll only respond if you ask him something,' she had said.

What do you want when you are eighteen? Maybe someone to tune into the urgency of your unsung song. To voice its tune, to refine its pitch, to give it form?

It was past one-thirty when the bus stopped and the driver said to me, 'This is where you get off.'

It was a sleepy village where big iron kettles hissed on spitting wood fires. In a small shop flies buzzed over gooey looking sweets. A roughly hewn bench stood outside a tea stall, occupied by weather-beaten villagers who stared curiously at me over the rims of their tea glasses.

I walked up to the owner and asked, 'Do you know where the Ashram is?'

'Ah!' he said smiling. 'That's where you are going.' He

waved his tea strainer in the direction of the road and said, 'After this bend you'll see a steep track on the left. Come off the main road and start climbing.'

As I turned around to leave, he called after me, 'Put the bag on your head. It will be easier to carry.'

I found the track easily, an unmetalled road with hairpin bends, wide enough for a jeep to squeeze through. My feet slipped on russet pine needles and I laughed when I saw a blue and white bird staring down at me, faintly puzzled at my ineptitude. Forty-five minutes later, out of breath, without having seen another soul, I was still climbing.

The last bend brought a building into view. It was a garage with a jeep parked in it, with rows and rows of hand tools neatly lining the wall. My eyes shifted uneasily to a black bull in an adjoining pen, snorting his disdain and stamping restlessly. To the right was a long cowshed and past the gate, terraced fields where wheat was ripening. I went up the narrow path to get my first view of the tiny Ashram.

I was charmed by my first impression. Poppies, geraniums, larkspur and daisies were dancing in between grey flagstones, splashing colour from their irregular flowerbeds. They swayed among the clover and snuggled under the peach tree in an unordered symphony. In contrast was the stark Ashram building, made from local grey stone with a faded red tin roof. The building seemed to be raised on stilts. Tiny windowpanes encircled the glazed verandah. Towering above the roof was a stone dome enclosing the temple shrine. In front of it a large brass bell hung against a sky-blue door. Rising even taller than the stone dome were ageless deodar trees, enclosing the place in their silent and unbroken vigil.

A hurtling mass of black canine fury came barking

round the corner, showing teeth as spiky as the collar around his neck.

'Stop it! Stop it, Kalu,' a man appeared behind him. This couldn't be Ashishda, this balding man with a twinkle in his eyes.

'I'm Don. We were expecting you. Ashishda should be down in a minute.' It was hardly a momentous meeting when Ashishda came down the wooden staircase and I made a sudden movement towards him to touch his feet. This set Kalu off in a paroxysm of barking, so that my well-rehearsed greeting was lost.

'So! Still in one piece? Did you have any problems on the way?' Ashishda asked, patting the dog.

'No, none at all,' I said in my best grown-up, matter-of-fact voice. He looked amused as he straightened his swept back hair which showed streaks of grey.

'Are you hungry?' Ashishda asked in a sing-song voice full of tenderness.

Actually, I was all but done in with hunger but I said nothing. I was instead totally transfixed by the expression of love in his eyes. Ashishda turned around and opened a cupboard below the staircase and took a dried-up roti from a stack. I was not sure what I was meant to do with this frisbee-like object. Eat it here, by itself; in my room...? I put my bag down, gingerly extended my hand that somehow got left halfway up, for Ashishda had put the roti straight into Kalu's mouth. The wretched dog began crunching it with saliva-drenched snaps, looking up into my face with open laughter in his eyes.

'Come, I'll show you your room. We maintain a quiet hour around sundown, which is followed by arati, the evening temple service. Supper is upstairs in the tea verandah after that.'

I followed Ashishda round the building as he took out a key tied to the cotton cloth around his waist. He opened a door, looked at me for a long second and asked gently, 'Will you be all right?'

I nodded my head and he walked away down the path.

The room was small and narrow, with a bed and a table. To one corner was a fireplace, opposite a single window overlooking the flower garden. It was like a monk's cell, bare of preferences. I walked back into the flower garden and sat down on the raised stone slabs under the shade of the oak trees. It was disconcerting to see no human being in sight, just this quiet, bee-buzzing afternoon, with a blue sky canopying the moment. It was the kind of quiet which fills your ears.

My eyes caught a movement. I saw a woman in white moving downhill. I watched her slow progression, but suddenly she disappeared. This place was having a strange effect on me. The marked absence of people was making me create phantoms. I concentrated on the spot where I had last seen her and a second later, she re-emerged, lower down the hill. I walked round the building, and met a short, grey-haired woman with a kindly, creased face.

'I'm Savitri.' She smiled and opened the door leading into the kitchen. 'Will you have something to eat?'

She lifted the gently hissing iron kettle from the wood fired stove and poked the grate to free the glowing coals from the ash. She stuck a piece of wood into the grate and blew on it with a copper tube. She was a comforting presence.

'Have you been here long?' I ventured.

'Over fifteen years now.'

'Don't you find it lonely?'

'It is at times. It's the kind of life that you can either hate or feel is unmatched.'

'Is that because of Ashishda?'

Savitri had gone to the back of the kitchen where a large barrel with a handle was mounted on a stand for making butter. A cast-iron stove with a chimney that seemed ready to puff up smoke like a steam locomotive squatted in a corner. She picked up two grass mats and spread them on the floor.

'Yes, Ashishda is a very important factor. I feel in the minority here though, being the only Indian. Dave is Australian; his parents live in that very English-looking cottage facing the temple.'

'Dave lives with them?'

She hesitated for a second, then said, 'No he lives with Ashishda who is like a father to him.'

'What made you stay here?'

She considered the question. 'It just made sense. From very ordinary things like cooking, cleaning and gardening, and from everyday emotions like anger, irritation fear and pleasure, I found that a secret could be coaxed out, a new awareness discovered. For me that awareness has made all the difference between just living and being alive.'

I watched her face as though the meaning of her words lay swathed in its wrinkled layers. 'Believe me, it's nothing fancy. No exalted faraway truth. Just a way of living in which your own life becomes more accessible to you.'

Evening approached, the sun dipped beyond the mountains, and darkness followed instantly. I was unprepared for the accompanying silence, quite distinct from the quiet of the day. In the day, there were sights and sounds to reassure one, different from this womb-like quiet of the evening. I ran my hand over the rough blanket Ashishda had given me, wondering what he had meant by a 'quiet hour' when nature had already dictated that choice. I felt I was lying in a tiny, peaceful nest in a remote untouched solitude. This was Ashishda's home.

Unbidden, a memory from schooldays came back of my standing outside the school parlour, hidden from view, as our tall Irish Mother Superior walked in with another nun. Mother Superior's brow was furrowed as she leaned over to the other nun and said, 'My spiritual life has dried up. I feel I'm stagnating. I don't know what to do, where to turn.'

I was shocked by her words. Until then I had believed that all nuns lived on a spiritual high, and here she was—the one who was supposed to be the most spiritual—expressing dismay after years of cloistered life.

And Ashishda? What of him?

Three clear peals sounded from the brass bell outside the temple. I left my room and followed Don, who was walking up the stone ramp, past the slate-roofed Samadhi, the cenotaph of the Ashram's founder, to the temple. In the anteroom, he picked up the wooden mallet to strike the gongs.

Beyond the anteroom was the inner sanctum where on a polished marble altar stood the Images of Krishna and Radha. My first impressions were of light and colour. The golden silk of Krishna's cloak contrasted sharply with his blue body. He was slightly tilted towards Radha who was dressed in a red brocade skirt and transparent veil. Her nose ring and bangles reflected the light caught from the oil lamps on the altar.

The service was short. No words were spoken for those three minutes as Ashishda, who was performing the arati, rang the hand-bell continuously, and Don struck the gongs in accompaniment. Ashishda, tall, head thrown back, offered in sequence the incense sticks; the pradeep, the oil lamp with its five points of light; a conch full of water; and the ochre cloth lying on a brass plate. The gongs reached a crescendo as the last offering was made with the chamar, a white-bristled whisk, that Ashishda moved deftly from left to right and back again over the deities in a final declaration of their omnipresence. Gradually, the tempo of the gongs slowed, and Ashishda put down the hand-bell. He stood for a moment watching the Images of Radha and Krishna as though immersed in silent communion with them. Never taking his eyes off them, Ashishda moved backwards from the inner sanctum, raised his hands over his forehead in salutation and knelt in homage. When I emerged from the temple into the darkness, the tiny oil lamp on the Samadhi seemed curiously like a hermit with a night lantern, shielded under the grey sloping cloak of stone. What was it about this evening hour that made things unreal seem real?

Supper was taken up the wooden staircase, in the glazed tea verandah. The dark wooden floor creaked as I walked over an uneven join in the floorboards. I made my way towards a corner where an open, L-shaped bookshelf hugged the stone walls. Cotton and woollen mats lay on the floor, with the only subdued light coming from a globe in a corner of the room. The place had a warm simplicity to it. Don brought in the last plates of food, each with two slices of brown bread, one layered with homemade apricot jam and the other with cheese.

Ashishda came in beaming, his blue-grey eyes alight with genial interest as he settled himself, cross-legged on one of the mats. The door opened again and a tall, blue-eyed, blonde man in his mid-thirties appeared.

'Ah, Dave! I was just beginning to wonder about you. Did it go off all right?'

'The usual problem of having to help her in the end. I

could see the legs when she was straining, but she couldn't push hard enough,' Dave said, his eyes darting around more than resting anywhere.

'Heifer?'

'Bull.'

'Oh!' Ashishda looked disappointed.

There was something shuttered about Dave's face, which masked the full scope of his otherwise fine features. He folded his lungi, a sarong-like cotton wrap, over his legs and began rolling a cigarette with his large deft hands.

'Don, why don't you clear all those papers in the corner? You edit one book and create the mess of three!' Ashishda said, pointing towards the corner where sheets of paper were strewn over three mats. Both men smiled at each other. Then Ashishda picked up his untouched plate and closed his eyes in a moment of prayer before eating.

As I bit into the rather dry, crusty bread, I realised I sat facing an English-Hindu mystic, and was flanked on one side by a Canadian editor and on the other by an Australian farmer. How I wished Savitri was here with her comforting Indianness.

Supper was a quiet affair and Dave left as soon as he had finished. There was a moment's pause before Don said, 'You always talk about facing fear in life and being free from it. I think fear has an odd fascination. Fear grips your whole being; it transforms you from a fragmented state to a focused point of "fearful awareness". Like a nation that gets united by the threat of war.'

'No, Don! That's evading the issue. Just as wars are sometimes created to distract people from the state of internal fragmentation in the nation, so our personal fears serve to keep us from the real issues of our life. Quite often we learn to live with a fear and allow it to prevent our growth in a certain direction. We might actually feel comforted by that fear and feel a reluctance to be freed from it. But real freedom can only be ours when we have faced that fear and overcome it.'

'You mean what we fear is freedom from fear?'

'Something like that.'

'It's possible. There is an odd sense of security in living with an old fear. You keep wondering what you may be trading it for.'

'You are trading it for certainty and the knowledge that most fears are an illusion.'

I felt like an outsider who had walked into a personal conversation of a previously discussed topic. It took me a little time to tune in, and when I did, I felt a twinge of discomfort. Was the fear about my past, my security blanket against change in the future? Surely, we do not live under fear voluntarily, I thought. It's just that we don't know how to get rid of fear. I couldn't put my thoughts into words, and realised soon enough that the conversation had run ahead of me.

'What happens if you simultaneously have a fear of, and fascination for a particular place—like I have for Rajasthan? I go back there year in and year out as though something in me belongs there,' Don said gravely.

'That's because you were tortured to death there once.'

My head jerked up to look at Ashishda. He had a brooding look on his face and his words sounded as though they came from elsewhere. Don looked stunned at the suggestion. Some strange point from his distant past had risen like a phantom to rub shoulders with the present and Ashishda seemed to be gazing at it.

'What do you mean?' Don whispered hoarsely.

'Just what I said.' With that Ashishda got up and left the room.

Don and I washed the dishes in silence for it was apparent that polite conversation was the last thing on his mind. Finally he said, 'I'm leaving tomorrow morning. Would you like to help Ashishda with separating the milk in the morning?'

I nodded my assent, past caring what I was agreeing to. Almost asleep on my feet, I felt reluctant to get acquainted with all of life's riddles in this one night.

'What time?'

'Five-thirty in the morning.'

The alarm shrilled and my eyelids opened to darkness outside. I reached for the light but there was no electricity. I sleepwalked my way to the tap outside the kitchen and splashed water on my face. The cool, early morning air returned me to consciousness. When I entered the kitchen, Ashishda had already lit the fire, and fingers of flame forked out of the mouth of the chula as he refilled the kettle.

'Would you like to knead the dough for the rotis? The tin is there.' He pointed to a row of canisters, sitting on a lower shelf.

'Take three measures of the small tin on top. Don't make the dough too soft.'

After these precise instructions, he picked up two saucepans and moved out of the kitchen to coat their undersides with mud.

The door opened and a villager appeared with two large cans containing more than twenty-five litres of milk. Ashishda emptied them into the large saucepans and put them on the fire. It was when dawn was breaking over the mountains that the conch sounded from the temple. It was a call of awakening. In a startling imitation, Kalu moaned its exact notes. Ashishda smiled at my surprise and said,

'He's not a one-dimensional dog. He is a four-legged yogi.'

Ashishda pushed in the logs which were casting a warm light into the room, lowered the wick of the kerosene lamp, checked the temperature of the milk and walked to the back of the kitchen to put the separator cups together. He moved like a nun with a silent glide and an economy of limb.

From the back of the kitchen Ashishda called, 'When I crank the handle of the separator, pour the warm milk into the bowl-funnel at the top.'

Back and forth I went between fire and funnel scurrying like a mouse chased by a broom. Standing on tip-toe, I poured milk into the bowl, barely managing to keep pace with the machine, which kept spouting a sensuous trickle of thick yellow cream on one side and skimmed milk into a large can on the other. For over forty minutes Ashishda cranked the separator handle without saying a word, till the last of the milk had been processed. I kept trying to anticipate what might happen next. It was disconcerting to see someone work with such a degree of absorption that it included others only if they knew where to fit in.

When I turned around, Ashishda was sweeping the floor.

I lunged forward, 'I'll do that, Ashishda.'

'You can swab the floor after this.'

Sometimes, it's the simple things in life that create the maximum complications. Like the agitation over an unlocatable swab. To be honest, I felt rather wary of Ashishda after his conversation with Don last night. So all my reactions near him seemed slightly heightened. One minute he seemed like a normal, down-to-earth man talking about farming and psychology; the next minute, in an equally matter-of-fact tone, he was talking about some tortured past life.

As soon as I found the swab, the temple bell rung. I

was left struggling to make up my mind about which was more important—the floor, the service, the swab...

'Finally, they are all the same,' Ashishda said. 'Whether you swab the floor or attend the service, the work is 'Theirs'. Attend the service; there'll be no one at the gongs.'

When I returned from the temple, three grass mats and shining bell-metal plates had been laid on the floor. In front of them were bowls of homemade butter, jam and pickle. Ashishda was rolling out the rotis and puffing them on a brazier heaped with coals, when Dave entered. Ashishda, flushed from the fire, smiled at him warmly. After feeding us breakfast, he made a stack of rotis for the 'four-legged yogi' of the Ashram and then settled down to his own meal. When he finished I said, 'Please go, I'll manage the washing up.'

There was mischief in his eyes as he said, 'Will you really?'

Without another word he washed his hands and just left the kitchen.

Actually I was quite disappointed he hadn't even once, out of politeness, insisted on helping. I looked at the back of the blackened saucepans, the innumerable separator cups and cans of milk. I rolled up my sleeves hoping someone higher up was crediting this to my freshly opened account of selfless deeds.

Forty-five minutes later, Ashishda came down with a bucket of laundered clothes, opened the kitchen door and smiled, 'Almost finished, my dear?'

I nodded my head in case I blurted out something else.

'Just one more thing, would you wash the entire floor after you put the dishes away?'

His room, I gathered was just above the kitchen, for I could hear his footsteps and the swish of a broom as he cleaned his room. As I began pouring water on the floor I felt better knowing I wasn't the only one cleaning floors.

I don't think I moved out of the kitchen all morning, for Savitri came in shortly afterwards. It was like watching a tennis match as she moved from the back of the kitchen to the front, pouring three saucepans of cream into the butter churn, swinging it around with a musical sloshing sound, stopping for a moment, sifting the flour for bread, lining the bread tins, and back again for a few more swings at the butter churn. Twenty minutes later she announced, 'The butter is out,' as a thump, thump sound was heard in the belly of the churn. She slipped most of the freshly made butter into a huge shining brass pan, and put it on the fire to make ghee.

'Don't you buy anything from the market?' I asked.

'The nearest market is one hour by jeep. Dave goes once in two months to get rice, lentils, sugar and tea. For the rest, we eat what we grow. The wheat harvest is on and, believe me, there's nothing like home-ground wheat flour.'

The subtlety of the flavour was lost on me as she mixed the frothing yeast into a mountain of flour and asked me to knead it. Meanwhile, she lit the cast-iron stove, which caught fire with a big 'whoosh'. Preparations for cooking lunch started as the dough for the bread began to rise like a rounded soufflé in the tins.

To put it mildly, the day had just begun. At a quarter-to-twelve, I was ejected from the kitchen, finished in more senses than one. Rounding the corner I met Ashishda, flushed, sweating, sickle in hand, returning unfazed from his morning exertions in the fields. What was going on around here, I wondered. Did people actually enjoy this slave labour, or were there other reasons for it that I couldn't fathom?

Later, as the sun dipped behind the hills, I felt both tired and relaxed; my body had enjoyed the exercise and it exulted in being able to handle it. The last rays of the sun glinted on the windowpanes, bathing the Ashram in a mellow gold. Beyond the vegetable garden the mountains seemed touched by the wand of timelessness, and in that fluid, mysterious, uncertain hour, everything danced before the nocturnal veil descended. While the day brought its own white truths, the night gave me the repose to reflect on them.

There was no electricity to guide my steps as I carried the supper upstairs. Ashishda and Dave were sitting quietly in the flickering shadows of an oil lamp. Darkness and silence seemed to intermingle with something unheard, unseen, untouched, yet very palpable in the room. Maybe the restraint in this life created an atmosphere in which the unexpressed was as potent as the expressed. It was like a feeling, an intent in the air, magnetised by powerful emotions—of seeking, waiting and believing. I sensed it in Ashishda's face as he watched the flame in the lamp with the concentration of someone who is used to focusing his energy on one point, believing there was nowhere else to look.

Soon after supper Dave disappeared. Ashishda stretched out his legs and asked, 'So what brings you here?'

It was a deep voice that reached me through the tunnel of a long, ancient memory—so what brings you to birth? What brings you into this body, into this country, into this family, to this joy and pain, to this round of experience? Yes, what brings you here?

'What does life mean, Ashishda?'

A half-formed smile crossed his face as though he had heard the question many times and yet did not know how he would answer.

'At one level it means everything and at another nothing.'

'Nothing?'

'Seek that which supports this life and yet is above it. Look within yourself for that which is truly free, essentially itself and totally indestructible.'

'Is there any such thing?'

'Yes, there is. Only, it cannot be given to another. You have to find it yourself. It's a lot of hard work, with minimum guarantees. Yet, in the end, it is worth every ounce of the effort you put into it.'

'Did such a life come naturally to you?'

'Not at all. Believe me, I was not born to this way of life. Maybe it all started with my leaving England to get away from my mother. Who knows,' he shrugged his shoulders, 'what led me here. I took the first chance to sign up for service in India during the war. After it was over I had some leave so I travelled around India, giving myself time to think of what I wanted to do with my life. During my travels I heard about an English sadhu living in these parts. That's how I came to meet Gopalda, my guru, and I never went back.'

'What made you stay?'

'I got interested in this search. It grew on me, till I realised there was nothing else I wanted to do with my life but this. When I took the robe at the age of twenty-six, I wrote to my father saying, "I don't know where this life I am choosing will lead to, but I will die satisfied knowing that at least I tried to find what is essential in life."'

Only half his face was visible in the lamplight, the other half was hidden by the latticed shadows of the night. He looked like a marble Buddha, partially veiled, full of secrets.

'But you did not come here to hear my life story, did you?' Ashishda countered, amusement lacing his voice.

'I'm still not sure why I came. Just that doubts arose which I couldn't define.'

'In general, doubts arise at your age because you are moving into adulthood and are unsure about leaving the security of the parental umbrella. It's a stage when you know you have to cut the umbilical cord, find your own identity and a path through life which is your own.'

'But I came here alone.'

'Yes, but to a place where your mother has been.' Ashishda laughed at my expression. 'You don't have to look so annoyed. There's nothing wrong in that. Only be aware that what you are trying to break away from is inside you, not out there,' he jabbed a finger towards an imaginary point.

I felt uncomfortable; he was nearing something I did not as yet wish him to approach. I changed the topic.

'But what do you teach?'

His eyes searched my face as he rubbed his chin thoughtfully.

'Never mind about all that.' His voice was gentle. 'I suspect your real problem is finding your identity as a human being. As yet you don't know who you are and what you can become. Go out, explore, put your energy into interests, people, activity. Chase your geese, so that if you are lucky, one or two may turn into swans.'

I had come with some vague conception of connecting with some exalted spiritual truths, but Ashishda was urging me to return to my life and to explore my potential. He was giving my natural reticence a push outwards, so that it may not collect in pools of inward fantasy.

'And then?'

'And then if your life experience so demands, your call will come.'

'For what?'

'To a way of living and thinking which requests admittance into a realm in which the answers to life's mystery can be found.'

'Do you understand this mystery?'

'Whether I say "yes" or "no" will make little difference to you. Each person has to carve his or her own way through the jungle of life. Footprints on the Path may tell you that others have gone before you. But that only reassures you up to a point. Ultimately it is your own two feet that have to walk this road and ascertain its truth.'

It sounded lonely, even bleak.

'But there is help,' Ashishda said softly.

Did this man read minds or just faces?

'If you really want to do it there will always be help. In some unknown, totally magical way someone will walk alongside you, holding the lamp high enough for you to take the next step.'

Next day after finishing the post-lunch washing-up, I was inwardly congratulating myself for having survived another day, when I heard Ashishda call out to me.

'Want to give me a hand with watering the garden?'

I wanted it as much as I wanted a hole in my head. It was an act of greatest deceit when I smiled brightly at him and said, 'That's a good idea. I'm just coming.'

The exercise consisted of dipping two watering cans into green, rather smelly water. This was the kitchen waste-water, collected in a tank dug in the ground and lined with a black plastic sheet. I trailed behind Ashishda trying to maintain both my dignity and balance, as he seemed easy and relaxed even when his watering can got completely clogged with vegetable peels. He just took off the spout, banged it on the ground, dislodged the obstruction and moved on. After twenty minutes of criss-crossing through beans, carrots and beetroot patches, my hands felt like limp spaghetti. As usual, Ashishda did not say a word till most of the tank was empty. Then he turned around, hair sticking to his skull with sweat, face flushed from the hot sun and eyes that looked as pleased as punch!

'That should be enough, don't you think?'

What a strange man. At night he talks of some mysterious unknown Path and in the day he zigzags through the vegetable garden as though this was a short cut to nirvana.

The place seemed a study in contrasts. At one level, it was primitive with its wood stoves, pit latrines, and cylindrical steel tubes which had to be fired from below with sticks and pine cones, to get hot bathing water. On the other hand, there was a jeep, a beautifully equipped workshop and cheddar cheese for supper! All the utensils were first taken outside the kitchen to be scrubbed with ash under a cold tap, and then brought back in, to be soaped in stainless steel sinks with modern detergents and hot water. There were no electrical gadgets in the kitchen except a second-hand instant water heater from which Ashishda took the hot water for his very English eleven o'clock coffee served in very Indian bell-metal glasses. This place was like Mohenjo-daro, which my school textbooks had described as an ancient city to which modern thought had been applied.

While washing my hands that smelt of waste-water, it occurred to me that Ashishda did not keep himself locked up in some lofty, spiritual ivory tower. He worked with his own hands and had carved a life for himself, out of nothing, in this inhospitable mountain terrain. He seemed to have applied his mind to very simple, daily chores, making them work without undue waste. Each task connected with the other so that a ladder was formed, grounded in the very basics of everyday life.

The feeling of having fallen through a rabbit hole was complete when on my last night, Ashishda said, 'If you like, record your dreams. They'll tell you what to tackle first.' As casually stated as 'Don't make the dough too soft, it doesn't make good rotis.'

'I don't remember my dreams.'

'You will, if you pay attention to them. They'll respond to your interest in them. Keep a notebook next to your bed and jot down whatever you remember, even if it is the tail-end of a dream. After that see how you feel about it.'

The lights of villages on the surrounding mountains seemed like glow-worms in the night, a vision preserved like a snapshot in my memory.

After wishing Ashishda goodbye the next morning, I started the walk downhill when I heard the temple bell ring in the quiet of the morning. I stood there remembering my favourite nun in school, Sister Catherine. Once, in our final days in school, she had taken out a ring from her habit and passed it around, asking each of us what we thought of it.

Our training had been such that discipline meant docile agreement. Our life had been an extension of the nunnery in which agreement was probably as exalted as chastity.

'It's lovely, Sister!' most of us exclaimed.

'Really?' she asked raising one eyebrow. 'And why is that so?'

'It shines a lot,' someone volunteered.

'Is that all you can see in it?' Sister Catherine asked.

An uncomfortable silence pervaded the room.

She picked up the ring and said, 'This is not even a

semi-precious stone; it is tinted glass. Learn two things from this: first, always strive to find what is real in life. And, if you are lucky enough to find that out, have the courage to say so.'

5

Adoption

I could not explain Ashishda to myself, so I let him float in my mind like a buoy that refuses to be chained to the anchor of stereotypes. He was certainly not a conventional Indian sadhu walking out of the pages of some Vedic text, nor was he a fame-and-funds fattened man passing off simplistic formulae as truth. He wasn't a scholar lost in dusty academia; his eyes held an innocent delight in life's simple truths; truths lived out more than read about. All in all, he was the most unusual man I had met in my life.

A year later I was sitting opposite him, once more, in his book-lined study. Looking at him, I couldn't help wondering if I was foisting a father-image on him. He seemed the archetypal fit, as he smoked his pipe and looked benignly out of the window in the direction of the weeping willow. I hoped I was seeing more in him than what slotted into my needs of a reliable father figure.

Something was struggling within me as I tried to keep a conversation going with Ashishda, but it was of no use. I stopped mid-sentence.

'What is it?' Ashishda asked quietly.

'Nothing,' I said, squeezing my eyes as though pushing

back an unformed thought. 'I'll use another word instead. As I was saying, I'll have to look at it another way.'

'*Adopt* another way of looking at it. Adopt,' he said softly.

Tightness gripped my throat as I looked down at the floor.

'Yes,' I said, without looking up.

'Would you like to talk about it?'

'What?' I stalled.

He kept silent.

'Maybe I'm not ready.'

'Then it must wait.'

He had put me on the spot by agreeing rather than denying.

'It's just that...' Tears welled up in my eyes. I was shocked at this offending evidence of pain. I looked helplessly at Ashishda, my face wet with the onrush of bottled feelings. He was looking at me gravely. No words, only the comfort of silence when it was most needed. I began to weep, tears flowing from an unending pool of indistinct memories. I confronted a dumb pain, so deeply embedded that it didn't even seem mine to own.

'What happened?'

It all came out in a flat whisper. My mother dying of stomach cancer a month after giving birth to me, her third daughter. The tumour was so large that my head kept hitting against it as I struggled to take birth. Later, they operated on her but found that the cancer had spread too far. After her death, my grief-stricken father shut himself up in a room and I was left to be cradled by one relative or another, with the single question looming large, 'Who is going to take care of such a young baby?'

For a few months, I lived with my mother's relatives;

then my father's elder brother and his wife, Pushpa, adopted me. I flew with them to Japan where my adoptive father was the military attaché. Volatile, eccentric, generous and pampered, he was a complete contrast to his quiet and reserved wife. I still remember waking up in a dark room in Japan to hear him shouting at her. Soon divorce proceedings began and my natural father had to bring me back to India.

What was to be done? Down, down the corridor of memory: at one end was Pushpa, back from Japan, undergoing divorce, teaching at a school in Dehradun; at the other end of the corridor was my natural father's sister, a house mistress in the same school. I walked out of Pushpa's room and was swept up in mid-air by my mother-to-be, who smiled as though surprised that I had taken so long to come to her.

Sometimes memories can be so flat, as though, having lived them out once, we have already squeezed them dry of content. These milestones in my childhood occurred so long ago—how am I to know what it all means to me now? Can I ever go back to what it felt like to be 'me' then? No, I cannot. All I have is the evidence, years later, of having once lived through something.

I felt my body had turned traitor, flinching under the tenderness of wounds it had kept so well concealed.

'You never talked about this?'

'No, I was ashamed.'

'Ashamed of something you had nothing to do with?'

I shrugged my shoulders. What I had to say had, for the moment, been said; I didn't want to be reached anymore.

What an untidy man he is, I thought irrelevantly, as I saw papers, a magnifying glass, stamps and pins all strewn around Ashishda's mat. He's not perfect, no one is, I decided disconsolately.

'It's a good thing you suffered when you were young. For those who have no early experience of it find the blows devastating when they come later,' Ashishda said.

One is never equipped for suffering, I wanted to say. Young, middle-aged or old.

'Yes, I suppose so,' I said agreeing, more to end the conversation than out of any conviction.

Why could I not feel anything? I felt as though I was consciously putting myself under anaesthesia, to numb my feelings against the whole operation of remembering. I was pushing myself back into forgetfulness. Ashishda hadn't seemed uncomfortable with the surfeit of emotions swirling in the room. He had neither brushed them aside nor hurried through them. The only way I could thank Ashishda was by telling him that I didn't expect him to provide any solutions. It was enough that he knew how to listen.

'I think I'll go to my room.'

In the fading November light, I felt the cold thread its fingers through the evening. Far away I heard the bleat of a goat, reluctantly being brought home for the night, as though the inevitability of homecoming is sometimes as disturbing as one's distance from it.

The next night Ashishda said, 'I've been thinking of what we spoke of last evening. I've come up with a few thoughts I'd like to share with you.

'Perhaps learning about adoption is traumatic because it threatens the child's security. Any child's security appears to be based on the assumption that the child belongs to its parents by right of birth. When an adopted child learns it wasn't born to its parents, it feels it has no rights. The child feels it belongs by agreement, by contract, and not by its status as a natural-born child. Contracts can be broken and destroyed because they depend on the concurrence of the contracting parties. On the other hand, the fact of being a natural-born child can never be altered or destroyed. No matter how bad the relationship may get at the personal level, the fact of parents being parents and their child being their child remains unchanged. The absence of such a fundamental and unalterable fixed point becomes a very threatening source of inner tension for an adopted child.'

'So, it feels as if nothing is permanent or fixed in life?'

'I think so. Maybe the adopted child, on learning of its adoption, feels that the adoptive parents are not unchanging facts of life. He or she sees the relationship as conditional. Therefore, there may be a greater need for parents to show how much they love the child, maybe more so than for a natural-born child. Adopted children feel that as long as they behave well and keep their side of the "bargain", the parents will keep theirs. On the other hand, the child may also behave badly, partly to discover how much the parents will tolerate before they renege on the agreement, and partly as a response to the normal pangs of growing up. But these adventures in disobedience are likely to be accompanied by greater guilt and anxiety for an adopted child than for a natural-born child.' Ashishda paused, but his gaze had not left my face for a second.

'It sounds pretty bad.'

'No, it isn't,' he said finally. 'Believe me, everyone has difficulties in life. If it is not this, it is something else. The idea is to be aware of what the difficulty is. Then something can be done about it.'

'How can I change the way I look at things that I'm not even aware of?'

'It seldom happens that a fixed emotional pattern can be changed overnight. The most important thing is to let yourself *feel* the unhappiness of that adopted child. Feel its loss, feel its fear, feel its grief. Pain by itself is not ugly. The lack of its acceptance is what is ugly.'

'I may not be able to do it.'

'You've gone through something very major in your life and survived it. Now you want to understand it. Talk to this child within yourself and help it come out. Be gentle with it, love it. Then finally, when you have accepted it, let it go. Let it go with the full knowledge that you are no longer that child.'

It's part of the human condition to mourn for a loved one who has died. We do it with family, with our friends, supporting each other in expressing the common loss. But how do you do it for yourself? Alone, in the quiet of the room, reflecting in the mirror of distance? How do you bring the dead back and give them a place among the living?

'Her time was up, she had to go', we say as a way of facing the inevitable death of a loved one. Maybe this child's time was up too—a child I had to let go of without having seen her face. I felt I was trying to recall something that had already slipped through the hourglass of time. All I had left was this prickly, gritty sensation between my fingers through which the sand had slipped.

6

Return to Silence

Is the past worth recalling or is it best dismissed? In raking up the dregs, will anger increase because an adult intelligence is now the judge? Was the child of the past more forgiving in her ignorance? Who did I have to forgive? Myself or others? My natural father for giving me away? Or my first adoptive father, his face red with anger as he brought his fist down on the glass dining table, cracking it? I had run out in fright and since he cared, he came after me to make amends. I always considered his comfort an extension of his aggression, and found both difficult to handle.

These memories returned but brought no feelings with them. Just the thought, 'Yes, it must have been bad.'

Then one night I dreamt:

We are travelling in a caravan. A car stops in front of us. Two people get out of it. One of them is Annie Besant. She lifts a small girl of about nine or ten, who appears to be dead, out of the car. Suddenly Annie Besant's face changes and begins to look frightening as it enlarges and sags, making her look ninety years old.

I noted the dream and sent it to Ashishda. He wrote back: 'I wonder if you know that Annie Besant "adopted"

Krishnamurti as her son, to finally groom him to become the successor to the Theosophical Society. The dream is probably centred on the theme of adoption, since it has picked up symbols connected with that topic.

'When dreams refer to particular numbers, try and look for what their association is for you. Did something happen at the age of nine or ten which felt like a kind of emotional death? Can you try and remember what it was at that time, which suddenly made everything look very frightening?'

I found that many childhood memories are buried under the rapid rush of new sensations that are experienced as one is growing up. What needed to be extricated were the splinters buried deep within. It demanded unrelenting persistence to pull them out. Slowly it all came back, like an old reel being rewound.

It was a family wedding. I was ten years old and enjoying every minute of it. I could play as long as I liked, eat whatever I liked, all strictures had been removed. Only benevolent, indulgent gazes of the elders followed us.

On the afternoon before the wedding, the groom, my cousin, put his arm around me as we strolled into one of the rooms. A fat maid who had always been part of the household walked in to collect some red cellophane to wrap the sweets with. The groom pointed to her and said, 'You know she looked after you when your mother died. Do you know the people you live with are not your real parents? Your real father is alive but he gave you away. These people took you in because you had nowhere else to go.'

For years, I had suspected that I had not been born to my mother. Now, for the first time I was being made to face it. I was stunned and just looked at him disbelievingly. One minute I was standing with him and the next minute I had shot outside looking for my mother. I dragged her into the room and asked her, 'Are you not my real mother?'

Her face registered horror as she looked accusingly at the groom. Then she burst into tears and confirmed my worst doubts. 'I wanted to tell you all these years, but not like this, not like *this* my dearest.' Her tears pleaded for understanding.

My world fell apart. My mother looked greatly distressed and I kept thinking, 'Maybe she's upset because she doesn't really love me and I've only just caught her out.'

These remembrances came upon me like a low fever. Then they swept over me with a dominance that cannot be easily described. So many emotions came to the fore in the days that followed; for a while I thought I would not be able to stand their charge.

Perhaps I had put up a defence against my world and my mother as a reaction to what I perceived as an injustice. I began by rejecting my adoptive mother's love. I felt betrayed by her. It was a peculiar mix of blaming her for taking me away from my father, and blaming him for not keeping me. She had looked distraught and I interpreted that as evidence of her guilt. After that, I just folded my hands across my chest in self-defence, while she held me close, refusing to acknowledge the distance I was creating. It's strange that we are most defensive when we least need to protect ourselves. She was there with all the reassurances I needed, but the time had not come for me to accept them. Everything I had known and was familiar with was being replaced by an abstract fog.

That was when I had turned to my natural father. I created a link with him in my mind, searched for him like a subterranean river that believes it will join the main waters one day. That's when my visits to Calcutta started and my mother stood bewildered, absorbing the punishment for an act she hadn't committed.

How was I to explain to her that it was a compulsion, which I had to pursue? I was no longer a child who could take for granted her sense of belonging to a set of adults. I was suddenly an individual, reassessing all relationships in an effort to find a structure I could identify with. As I distanced myself, all the people in my world became mere concepts I had to grapple with. Amidst this emotional confusion, I also grieved for my dead mother whom I had never known. Strangely enough, at another level, I started trusting my relationship with my adoptive mother more than I had ever done before.

Perhaps my adoptive mother sensed I needed the idea of a real father, however mixed up my feelings were. But the father I was seeking was her brother after all, and how could she harbour competitive feelings towards a man who had given his own child to her? Did she subconsciously feel her brother had more rights over me than she had, or was that just the natural attitude of a younger sister giving way to the male sibling?

Sometimes letting your own grief flow out clears a space for you to see others more distinctly. I began to perceive my adoptive mother's difficulties:

What did you feel when people asked you, 'Can you *really* love this child as your own?'

Did you learn to rest wholly in the strength of your feelings for me, without the props of biological motherhood?

Did I think our relationship was a bargain, a contract? Yes and no. Yes, because I felt I came to you through others' decisions and not your own. As a teenager, I had to find out by testing you, and the more I tested you, the more I found that you actually believed you had willed my coming to you. Like a desire that believes unshakably in its moment of fulfilment. 'I knew all along,' you said with a happy conviction, 'that we would be together. I just had to wait our time.' Slowly your faith became mine too. That was our bond, the feeling that what we shared outstripped these restrictions.

As my adolescence passed, besides the anxiety that you might disappear like the others, I gradually began to see something else. It was as though, behind the flux and foam of the waves, there was always the implacable secret solidity of the ocean floor. I sensed it most when outwardly I had the least reason to believe in it. Somehow you allowed me to rest in the security you gave me and together we found a place where sandstorms didn't blow grit in our eyes. We explored our roles afresh, re-establishing our relationship to something larger than the earlier one.

That's what the child in me learnt: that life is full of suffering but it also has that strange alchemical quality which can mysteriously turn lead into gold.

Where was this child whom Ashishda talked of? I couldn't call out to her because there was no name to which she answered. So, I imagined her as the child whose photographs I had seen in the family album. I picked her up and put her on my lap to talk to her. As I rumpled her unruly mop of hair and held her close, her small body seemed to relax in this new-found contact. She was a silent child and I had to coax her to speak.

One day, quite unexpectedly, she said, 'I haven't spoken earlier because I felt I had no right to. Only natural-born children have rights, not adopted ones. All this while, I felt I had no right to be angry or upset.'

'That is nonsense, isn't it?' I asked gently. 'You may finally want to let go of your hurts, but there is no question of your right to feel them.'

Indecision flitted across her little face. I reached out, clasped her tiny hand in mine and began the walk home.

Maybe adopted children feel they have no rights to anything. No rights to their adopted parents, their biological ones, their brothers and sisters and finally even to their own feelings. They separate these from themselves as a punishment for not being natural-born. They then react against their own self-denial by feeling uprooted.

When I was nineteen, I remember standing on the terrace of our house feeling amazed at this discovery. It was as though someone had given me back my right to feel. For some time, I experimented with this right, but realised that I had to guard myself against the self-indulgence it could promote. My task was to ascertain which of the feelings that were surfacing were relevant to my life now.

Watching the child within me, I noticed how often she would start when she heard loud voices raised in argument or sensed tension in the atmosphere. This child felt she was to blame for whatever happened, as though she held herself responsible for other people's states of mind. But then she surprised me with her unpredictability. She would burst in on me with unfettered enthusiasm, as though nothing could stop or bind her.

I also learnt many things from her. She was a child who was not afraid of the dark and the quiet of her own company.

I have a childhood memory of waking in the dark in the back seat of a car. One moment I was asleep, and the next moment I was awake, staring into the most beautiful night sky through the car window. The stars were polished to perfection, studded in the blue velvet of the night. The dark trees faintly stirring in the breeze seemed to brush the moon's face with their leafy fingertips. Snuggled under my mother's shawl, I felt a sense of belonging, an odd empathy with everything around me. That small child in me still goes back to find that silence, when in the noonday brightness of life, I cannot understand many of life's dualities. I had to bring that child out of the shadows and give it confidence to live within me.

7

The Double Vessel Sound

This delving into my childhood memories to unthaw them from the deep freeze of suppression, held a mysterious wonder for me. I felt like a child who plants a seed and runs each morning to see whether it has sprouted. Something was alive and kicking, searching for its own way out, desiring its own soil to grow. It had to find its own momentum. That momentum gained ground when I met Rajeev again as an adult.

Rajeev's mother, Uma, was my mother's closest friend and from the time we were children, there hadn't been a holiday the two families hadn't spent together. But something had changed in the five years since I had last seen him. The boyish face I was familiar with all through my childhood was now that of a man's, with curly hair, a French beard and large teasing eyes.

We surveyed each other, attempting to slot the other and not really succeeding. Was he a childhood friend? Was this a brotherly hug or were we both aware of other undercurrents? Suddenly, I couldn't keep pace with all that we were so easily sharing—past memories, similar backgrounds and now, even Ashishda. Rajeev had been visiting him for three years and had taken initiation from him.

Often when people fall in love they say, 'We feel we've known each other for ages.' In our case this was a fact.

Sometimes an internal process falls into place when, in another person's attitude, you see the rightness of what you have been groping towards. Rajeev engulfed my parents and me with his special kind of acceptance that was unconditional but definitely not uncritical. His abounding energy conversed well with my new-found emotional freedom.

He asked me, 'Didn't you want to go to a Delhi college?'

'Yes, but Mom and Dad wanted me here in Chandigarh.'

'And you accepted that just because they said so?'

'Well, what was I supposed to do?' I replied irritably.

'Put up a fight, of course!'

That was the first thing I noticed about him. He did not tread gingerly on difficult terrain, but treated us like a normal family where bursts of rebellion and breaking a few rules were as important as keeping some. My fits of defiance seemed as natural to Rajeev as breathing. I found a comforting sense of normalcy in his attitude towards each of us, which made us feel no different from any other family with its ups and downs. To my parents, he said, pointing towards me, 'It's her job to disagree with you and yours to try and persuade her out of her disagreements.'

Unwittingly, he encouraged us to cross the reserves of our natures, to feel free to communicate, as much with disagreement as with agreement. He treated my parents as the only ones I had had, and teased them about my upbringing. 'You didn't bring her up, you dragged her up,' he would say, giving them the mantle of natural parents. By teasing them, he voiced my mother's deepest fears as an adoptive parent, and inadvertently showed her where they were exaggerated.

It was a time of change in which I felt an old cloak slipping off my shoulders and a new one waiting to be worn. Easily, naturally, we fell into step. One minute I was weaving the pattern of my life with a single thread and the next, with equal ease, with a double. An invisible fragrance exudes from the love born between two people. What had got created between us was neither wholly of our doing nor ours to claim. It existed because of its own laws—a gift which we had to honour by some commitment. The social one was made when we got married; the inner one was private and wholly ours to formulate and follow.

'People don't really believe love lasts; they think it's a hangover from an adolescent dream,' I said to Rajeev.

'All dreams have a possibility of becoming real,' he said.

'Yes, but how? What is that point in a relationship, which both people can honour without either feeling trampled upon?'

'It has to be a point beyond,' Ashishda said when we visited him soon after our marriage. 'You submit to love, not to each other's personalities. You submit to the strength of your own feelings for the other person. Look for the promise of perfection—the ability to love, the ability to change, the vision of a fulfilment that lies beyond self-gratification. That is the impersonal point you submit to.'

'What happens in the nitty-gritty of life, Ashishda—the hurts, the anger, the usual disagreements?' I asked.

'The one rule is,' he said raising his finger, 'never sleep over a fight. Work at it and learn to let go of that constricting feeling before the day is out. For that is the ego talking, not your love for one another.'

'Speaking practically...' Rajeev began only to be cut short by Ashishda.

'I'm not suggesting something impractical. Remember your marriage must count for more than anything else in your life. It's part of your search. You're doing this together. What is coming naturally to you both now may have to be worked on consciously later. Cut off negative feelings; petty grievances are a poor substitute for personal honesty. Don't only blame the other but examine your own attitude that is contributing to half the problem. That is the self-discipline you will have to learn,' Ashishda said. He then, while getting up from the floor, raised himself on his hands and walked unsteadily to attend to a visitor who had rung the temple bell.

Later in the kitchen I asked Savitri, 'Is something the matter with Ashishda's feet?'

'A few years ago when Gopalda was still alive, Ashishda was repairing the temple roof and fell off it. He crushed both his ankles and was in traction for over six months. Do you know what Gopalda asked him after his fall?'

'What?'

'Whether he'd had any warning of this in a dream.'

'Had he?'

'The night before, he'd dreamt that he was sitting on a very high wall reading from a book about fate.'

'What does that mean?'

Savitri sighed, dipping her chapped hands into the coal bin. 'Maybe his falling off the roof was fated. But then, what is fate but the sum total of our attitudes in life? Events in our life tell the story of patterns which need to be looked at. Maybe Ashishda had some internal conflict at that time which he couldn't resolve, and it took that form. Anyway, who am I to say what he felt,' she concluded the discussion.

So Ashishda was human too. He was subject to the laws of cause and effect, yet he had made more sense of them than most. For once, Ashishda did not appear to be a faraway figure giving advice and inspiration, but a man who had arrived at wisdom after toiling hard. Was he now free of all the dualities of life, which plague human beings, or does the struggle never end?

The next morning, I took Ashishda's coffee to his study. He wasn't there. I stood uncertainly till I realised he was in the adjoining small room to which he retired at night. It had an air of privacy so I cleared my throat to let him know of my presence.

'Ashishda, coffee.'

'Bring it here, my dear.'

I walked into a small mud-plastered room in which the only piece of furniture was an old chest of drawers. He was sitting cross-legged on the age-darkened wooden floor, facing the fireplace over which, on a mantelpiece, Gopalda's photograph rested. Hanging above it was the portrait of Yashoda Ma, the founder of the Ashram, a woman with gaunt cheeks sitting in meditation. A harmonium and a rolled-up mattress lay in the corner of the room that had been occupied by three generations of gurus. The air of stillness made it seem as though their prayers had soaked into the walls.

After putting the coffee down, I stood there, unwilling to leave. 'Ashishda, may I take initiation from you?'

Ashishda stopped writing and looked straight at Gopalda's picture as though asking him a question. Then he nodded his head and said, 'Yes, my dear. It takes two to walk the Path of Love. But before it, I must talk to both of you. I'll call you later.'

I left his room a bit dazed, not knowing exactly what I had asked for, and what I was getting into.

'What is it that I'm committing myself to?' I asked Rajeev.

'I can tell you but its true impact is in experiencing it.'

A slow rumble of feelings was building up inside me as though some old, well-preserved secret was unwrapping itself, having been protected all these years against my own ignorance. It had held its peace, awaited its moment, and was emerging now as a longing, as strange in its beauty as in its sense of loss. I felt alive, questing, in search of meaning in everything.

A tired, silent Dave returning from the fields in the evening reminded me that life has a time for tilling and a time when the secret of the seed must be preserved in the dark soil. Had my time come to see its first sprout in this place with its haunting, blue-purple evening shadows and its daytime labour?

Just who was this Dave—sitting opposite us at supper, hardly speaking?

When Rajeev had first come to the Ashram he had contradicted Dave on some small engineering issue and Ashishda had swiftly interjected, 'Don't contradict him, try and emulate what he is trying to do.'

Dave was a silent man who seemed to have withdrawn from almost all ordinary social contact. The way he sat, the way he moved from one room to the other was deceptively quiet for a man who seemed coiled and tense within. Frequently, Ashishda looked at him, smiled encouragingly, but he rarely got a response. None of this seemed to bother Ashishda one bit.

'What is it with Dave?' I asked Rajeev.

'A very difficult childhood, probably. He's a touchy chap, but quite intuitive. He'll pick up your thoughts at times—he'll pass you the salt during a meal just when you are about to ask for it.' Rajeev responded.

It was Dave who called out to us next day. 'Ashishda wants to see you both.'

We went up to Ashishda's study and after a moment's pause, looking at Rajeev, he said, 'Madhu has asked for initiation. I hope you both realise it's a serious commitment. It is an attempt to dedicate your life to the highest in yourself. I prefer two people to walk this Path together, for unless you learn to submit to the love you share for each other, how can you submit to a faceless, impersonal Divinity. In some sense you have to honour the commitment of a personal love before you can appreciate a universal one.'

'What is this submission, Ashishda? If he has a particular interest do I have to tag along or vice versa?' I asked.

'Oh no!' Ashishda laughed. 'That's not submission. That's bullying! I'm not talking about that. Countless factors make up a relationship: one's own predisposition, personal background and cultural bias. With one hand, we hold onto these rather ingrained patterns, and with the other we hold our spouse's hand. When you have children, they'll do the same. This forms an endless chain which locks people into grooves. I feel love demands that you leave both hands free to hold each other with. The overflow of that love will go onto your children. If both of you can break this chain, then, not only will the ripples be felt down the line, but you will become like twin stars revolving around a common centre of gravity—love.'

'What kind of patterns are these which prevent love from flowing?'

'The kind which makes either of you say: but that's not what my father or mother did. My father never came home late, how can you. Or my mother never cooked like this, I can't eat this. These are relatively simplistic patterns compared to the ones we imbibe without even being aware of them. They've got to do with how you viewed your own parents and their marriage. The effects of that can either make you subconsciously perpetuate their mistakes or take on a consciously opposite stance without being aware of its deeper pulls.'

'Just becoming aware of these patterns doesn't make them go away.' I said.

'No, it doesn't. But try and let go of anything that blocks the foundation of the relationship. Learn to let go, drop yourself. Meditation is that free point within from where you'll get the courage to do that.

'It is a question of seeing that the ordinary personality is at the mercy of events. It is automatic, mechanical and compulsive. You have to find a centre of awareness in meditation that is apart from this. A centre that watches your thoughts, your joys and sorrows, but is not affected by them.

'In meditation, go quiet, stop thinking. If thoughts don't stop, let them be. Don't identify by getting carried away with them. Just watch them. Then one day by this constant watching, you may find that when the "you", as you normally associate yourself to be, is not there, something real has been born.'

Ashishda fixed the day of initiation for the day after. He said it should be a day of withdrawal. I should keep to myself, eat very little and still my mind, holding the intent of my commitment before me.

On the morning of initiation, I sat outside the cottage while Rajeev squatted on the stone steps reading. I watched the white dragonflies with their net-like wings hover over the lily leaves in the small pond outside the cottage. Meditation, I rolled the word over my tongue, trying to get used to its flavour. 'Watch your thoughts,' Ashishda had said. I felt a strange apprehension. How was I to watch? What or who was I to watch?

I became aware of various sounds impinging on the early-morning silence. The kitchen door opening and shutting, Savitri's voice instructing two visitors on how to light the recalcitrant hamam to heat their bathwater and, a few minutes later, the clang of a bucket, probably Ashishda bringing down his laundered clothes. These simple everyday sounds drew my thoughts back like iron filings to a magnet, to the initiation ceremony. There was a quiet expectancy in the air. Savitri smiled in the morning as though she shared a treasured thought with me. Ashishda, who rarely came for the morning service, this morning stood close by.

After the midday service, Dave came up to me and said, 'You are not alone today. For Ashishda too, it is a day of fasting, silence and meditation. For different reasons, the day is important for him too.'

I nodded gratefully, unsure of what to say. So, it was a day of commitment for Ashishda too, I thought. A soul was coming under his care and he was well aware of the responsibility. According to the old tradition, after a great man dies, he is asked by the powers above, 'No doubt you made it to the other shore. But tell us how many others could you bring to the same rung as you?'

The afternoon hours slipped by; I wanted to ask Ashishda about the evening preparation so I walked up to his room and knocked. There was no answer, so I lifted the latch and saw him sitting cross-legged on his mat with eyes closed, head slightly bent. Slowly he opened his eyes, which seemed unfocused; then he lifted his eyebrows enquiringly. I asked him what I had come to ask, he replied briefly and I left.

A bath, fresh clothes, a plate full of flowers in the centre of which I placed a small, silver bowl of freshly ground sandalwood paste. With these offerings in hand, I attended the evening service where Rajeev played the drums to the beat of the brass gongs. The large temple bell rang as though in celebration, or was it a plea, a request for admittance. The tempo of the music rose in the final moments of the service, seeking a release; then Dave put down the hand-bell, the gongs became softer, the drum a faint rumble in the air. After the service only Ashishda, Dave, Rajeev and I remained. Ashishda shut the blue temple door and then walked into the inner sanctum that was softly lit by oil lamps. He motioned me to enter.

I'm not going to describe the ceremony for no words can do it justice. All I know is it touched me profoundly with its simple honesty. It was an event which seeps deeper into me the longer I live with it.

Later I touched Ashishda's feet and he raised me by the shoulders and said, 'May He give you courage to seek and with His grace to finally find.'

I rested my head on his chest as he enfolded Rajeev and me close to his heart.

The following day, I had my first real look at the apricots hanging from the trees around the temple. They were picked and brought in large wicker baskets to the kitchen to be turned into jam. We cut and cored the fruit, added an equal quantity of sugar and set it on a strong fire, stirring continuously. The fruity smell of the jam cooking, the changing hues from peachy pink to orange gold have remained as a memory of a simple joyous activity.

The next morning when I was helping label and wax the jam bottles, Ashishda came into the kitchen and stood watching us. When I finished my work and was about to leave he said, 'Come here.'

I went up to him. He took a bottle of apricot jam and put it in my hands saying, 'This is for your breakfast at home.' The gift seemed at many levels much bigger than what he placed in my hands.

At the end of our trip he embraced us saying, 'Look after each other.' As we slung our bags over our shoulders to make our way downhill, he said very softly, 'Come soon.'

8

Quietening the Mind

We began settling in soon after our return from the Ashram. Rajeev was totally involved in setting up a factory along with his brother while I looked around for my first job. That was easier said than done. The response I invariably received was, 'But you have no experience.' Face plastered with a smile, I would say, 'Unless I get a chance how will I gain the experience?' Of course, such profundities were lost on my prospective employers. When I was interviewed next, only to hear the same words repeated, I took a deep breath and replied, 'I'll work free for two or three months. If you like my work you can pay me after that.'

That's how I got myself into the employed-but-unpaid category in an office as small and as hot as a solar cooker. It comprised two people and I became the third. There was the almond-eyed Aparna who was my age and Mr Swaminathan, who was seventy plus.

When I told them the terms of my employment, Aparna exclaimed, 'You mean he is not paying you!'

'No. Actually I volunteered.'

'You what?'

'Well...I...'

'You mean you actually volunteered for the Gulag?' and then immediately burst out laughing.

I plodded through old files to familiarise myself with environmental issues, answered letters, spoke in a cultivated, correct voice on the phone, and listened to my boss drone on about how the 'information retrieval system', the name for the humble-looking filing cabinet in the corner, should be updated. Gradually I realised how shatteringly prosaic working life could be. The only bright spots were when Aparna showed me the second-hand books she had bought from the pavement vendor, or the occasion when her first article was published in a magazine and Mr Swaminathan bicycled to the nearest Chinese vendor and we celebrated with three greasy plates of noodles.

Winter had come to Delhi with the dahlias and gladioli marking its pinnacle. Six months had passed since our last visit to the Ashram. I was twenty and Rajeev twenty-six. Like any other young couple we went through the trivial ups and downs that accompany the adjustment needed in the early years of marriage. However, over the years, we discovered we had been blessed with a strong bond that never betrayed us.

'Love means leaving both hands free to hold each other with, not one hand tied behind one's back with the threads of conditioning and inflexibility,' Ashishda had said when talking about the barriers that could arise within a relationship.

The conditioning we had to overcome was basic and concerned the deeply entrenched values we had unconsciously imbibed from our parents and peers. I soon discovered how tiny points of tension could impede the flow of a day. This made me realise the need to pay greater attention to my own reactions to situations. The ability to occasionally watch myself during the day had also developed from my faltering attempts at meditation.

'Watch, observe, don't identify with your thoughts,' Ashishda had advised.

If during meditation I expected quick results, I was in for a surprise. My image of attaining an uninterrupted, unconcerned calm by sitting in a yogic lotus posture to meditate was rudely shattered. In reality there was not a moment's peace. The most ridiculous thoughts became the centre of my consciousness, repeating themselves incessantly. As though this wasn't enough, one thought caught the tail of the next like monkeys in a procession. On top of this, I couldn't sit cross-legged for more than two minutes at a stretch. My legs grew numb, and I fidgeted so much that Rajeev would mutter through closed eyes and clenched teeth, 'Stop shaking the damn bed.'

'Obviously I'm doing something wrong,' I said to Rajeev later.

'I guess we're in the same boat then. These days my mind has turned into an assembly line of factory machines.'

After two months, I wrote to Ashishda:

'I had no clue that I had so many thoughts and such unstoppable ones at that.'

He wrote back:

'This feeling is quite natural. Don't panic. Just check into one thing. Observe your thoughts to find those that repeat themselves. If you can locate a recurrent theme or pattern, then later, after meditation, you should try and understand the root cause of those thoughts. They are drawing attention to themselves in order to be freed. Analysis helps you understand these thoughts and meditation to drop them altogether.'

I shut my eyes and tried, again and again. Slowly I found a clue. My thoughts arose from the uncertainty of being 'me'. Will I be able to get a better job; will I form a stable relationship; do I know what I want to do; can I become a good cook...? These thoughts were like yeast, fermenting in the warm pool of my wants, fears and expectations. And it was disconcerting to know that there was no reconciling point of focus in their wanderlust—they were mechanical, and seemed to follow a circular movement. Then one night, while I was meditating, I saw an image of my dead mother lying on a hospital bed covered with a white sheet, her black hair spread in sharp contrast on the white pillow. Startled, my eyes flew open. Until now she had only been a name. I felt very uneasy.

This pain was to be looked at afresh when we had an unexpected visit from Dave. We found him standing at our doorstep looking very different, dressed in shirt and trousers, which he never wore at the Ashram. His blue eyes were a shade less aloof as he smiled shyly and said, 'I got lost finding the way otherwise I would have got here earlier.'

A shared aim, and a need to understand ourselves made the trust between us grow quite easily. Slowly a story emerged as Dave talked of his childhood—a troubled eight-year-old whose apathetic conduct led to his being taken out of school.

'You take your education for granted,' he said to us, 'but I had nothing to start with as I grew up. If I went to a shop to buy things, I couldn't add correctly. When I met people, I felt self-conscious about not being able to read or write properly, or speak fluently. I never played games, and I didn't make friends, for there was no group I could belong to. '

'What about your parents; what did they feel about all this?' I asked.

'I don't think they understood any of my problems.

They were constantly trying to nag and push me to become something I couldn't. My father drove me to work harder and harder on his orchards. Yet, I knew I was always a disappointment to him. Once when I was running a fever, he got me out of bed to work, hating my infirmity.'

'Your mother must have been a softening factor?' Rajeev asked.

'I don't know,' he said, his voice trailing off. 'She seemed strangely resentful of having to bring up four children, look after a home and a husband.'

Dave grew up believing he had been put together all wrong; a strong anger built up inside him which he felt hard put to contain. Then, at the age of seventeen, Dave's parents sold their orchard and moved to the Ashram.

'Ashishda seemed to know and understand my problem instinctively, without my expressing it. He gave me unconditional love and accepted me as I was. Whatever I might do, I knew he would not reject me. Slowly I began working in the Ashram and Ashishda taught me farming. We also set up a small workshop and he trained me in basic engineering skills: sawing, filing, threading, repairing farm machinery. All the while he reassured me I could do it.'

'What did you feel about your parents?' I asked.

'As the years went by, I wanted to have less and less to do with them, even though they were only ten steps away from me.' His tone was laced with anger. 'Anyway, Ashishda became my father and that's all there was to it. I have one regret, though.'

'What?' I asked.

'When my father lay dying, I couldn't get myself to go and see him. Ashishda insisted that I visit him during that time but every time I thought about it, I was filled with anger. I just couldn't do it. I couldn't forgive him. If I had, it might have done me a world of good,' he said, and began pacing the room.

Strange man. In the Ashram he didn't say a word and here he was talking about himself as though the fount of words wouldn't stop. Was this his way of explaining his behaviour at the Ashram?

He talked, and thoughts of my dead mother kept coming to my mind. All I had seen of my mother were photographs—her face alive, eyes bright, a faint smile colouring her lips. But her features were hazy, like her memory. Looking at her photographs, all I had wanted to do was to locate myself in her.

I had been strangely reluctant to think about her death; but here was a contrast too sharp for me to ignore. Dave had refused to see his father on his deathbed, while I wished I had been there to see my mother go. If I felt guilty about her death, I also felt guilty thinking about her. I suppose I felt too much interest in her would hurt my adoptive mother so I never brought it up with her. Or was it the guilt of having survived while my mother died?

Listening to Dave, I began to comprehend why I wished I had been there to see my mother go. My mother's last act was to give birth to me, willing me to enter a world where I could survive. I would have wanted to hold her hand while she was in pain, dying, and say to her, 'Thank you for helping me survive. I'll try to do something with this gift you gave me, even though you won't be there to share it with me.'

Dave stopped pacing the room. He turned around and said, 'There was an incident which has stuck with me. It was during one of those heavy, monsoon downpours, and Ashishda was driving the jeep up the dirt track to the Ashram. The jeep skidded and went into the rainwater drain and Ashishda was pretty upset because he felt he could have been more careful. Usually, I do most of the driving and would have known which patches to watch out for. Anyway, we managed to get it out but not before we were completely drenched and mud plastered. I instinctively got into the driver's seat and waited for Ashishda to climb in next to me, but, grim-faced he kept standing in the rain, and said, "Either I drive or I walk up that hill." It was his way of telling me that if you stumble or make a mistake, you just climb back and start all over again. But I couldn't do it with my father.'

Dave seemed to be telling us that he regretted never having gone back to confront the greatest pain of his life—his relationship with his parents. His view of them and his childhood circumstances may well have determined the way he viewed all relationships and, possibly, even life in later years.

I grieved for Dave, who could neither study nor form healthy relationships. Was he perpetuating, through his behaviour, his mother's perception of him as an unwanted child?

Perhaps our early experiences set invisible patterns that remain so until they are consciously recognised and broken. In my own case, my early difficulties at birth and thereafter made me perceive the beginning of every new experience, whether in work or in relationships, as demanding. Unfortunately, without realising it, we lose the ability to separate the pattern from what life may be offering us in terms of new opportunities and beginnings. But the question was how could an old pattern be erased?

Could the desire to meditate be a subconscious need to erase an old pattern in order to affirm and reaffirm a new pathway? I was trying to free myself at a deeper level, sensing that the path of analysis had its limitations. Of course, at times I did neither; it required too much effort and I kept asking myself, 'What for?' Perhaps I held back knowing that through meditation and introspection I might come too close, for my own comfort, to certain internal truths. Fearing I may not be able to handle what I discovered within, I beat a hasty retreat.

Then, I had a dream:

I'm telling the gardener that just watering the lawn is not enough. There are weeds which have to be pulled out too. I ardently advise him not to take care of only a part of the garden, but the whole of it.

Ashishda wrote back saying, 'The garden and lawn can represent the whole person, including the unconscious parts. You are the gardener. Taking care of the whole lawn and not just part of it implies that it is not enough to develop only particular qualities or abilities, leaving the rest underdeveloped. The whole of you must be in harmony.

'Weeds in the dream could be mechanical thoughts, laziness, vague depressions etc., which have to be uprooted, through meditation or otherwise.'

As usual something in Ashishda's letter set me thinking. It was difficult enough to get a regular practice of meditation going, but to treat this as a full-time effort was a daunting task. Ashishda had done it, but I doubted if I could. I wondered how the inner and outer life would come together, and what they had to be in harmony with.

'With that centre within which is free and beyond the mind.' Ashishda explained in our next visit to him. 'You have to make meditation a part of your life so that its calm certainty spills over into other areas of your life.

'When you are learning to swim, a lot of energy is

expended. But once learnt, you realise that very little effort is required to keep afloat. It's the same when you are trying to gain control over the mind. You wonder how it can ever be a peaceful state. Once you learn to swim you can float in a calm, peaceful pool where waves of emotion don't assault you.'

Once more, without any clear signposts, I started all over again.

9

You Have to Be Ripe for It

Quite unexpectedly, I chanced upon this 'still point', but not in meditation. This overthrew all my preconceived notions. It was oddly enough triggered by intensely mundane tensions. Two summers and two springs had passed since my initiation. Two years in which I had changed my job, and now worked to raise funds for physically challenged children.

We were organising a musical concert. Besides brochures, tickets, and advertisements, our main effort was to pull in as much support as possible for the cause. We were rushed off our feet. Unfortunately, on the morning of the show, Rajeev developed a high malarial fever so that I was rushing between home and the auditorium most of the day. Late at night, after the show ended, I felt my boss's coldness, as palpably as opening a deep-freezer door.

The next morning, I was summoned to her office. She pointed out certain problems that had arisen during the show. To me, they seemed minor and did not warrant the dressing-down that followed. I was lectured on the importance of responsibility, the privilege of holding a job such as mine, and how my predecessor knew the difference between home and work.

My anger was rising but I kept a studied silence in case I lost my temper and my job, which I valued. In time she went for my jugular. 'I don't know what your future in this organization will be, but if you are serious about your work you'll find I'm a very fair-minded person.'

Indeed, I wanted to say, the show went off well, but you're nit-picking because I was not chained to your side.

I felt terribly churned up inside, and the day passed in a haze, the arguments and counter-arguments that I had not managed to present to her invading and scissoring my mind to shreds.

I still remember the exact moment. I had just finished writing a letter and had given it to the typist. Clarity overtook me as though I had suddenly been cleansed of every sharp-edged resentment. It was a moment of utter stillness without any pulls in any direction. It had a quality different from anything I had ever known. I felt a heightened awareness. Its tranquil stillness reminded me of T.S. Eliot's words in 'Burnt Norton' in *Four Quartets*:

> At the still point of the turning world. Neither flesh nor
>   fleshless;
> Neither from nor towards; at the still point, there the dance
>   is,
> But neither arrest nor movement. And do not call it fixity,
> Where past and future are gathered. Neither movement from
>   nor towards,
> Neither ascent nor decline. Except for the point, the still
>   point.

Unfortunately, as unexpectedly as it had come, it went and left me wondering why I chose to live any other way but in its fold, for it made a mockery of the ambiguities we allow ourselves to be embroiled in. That night, before going to sleep, I thought that if this 'still point' existed, then, maybe, this much-talked-about Path did lead somewhere.

Does one ever know the starting point of any event? Is it possible to trace the exact moment from which a new direction emerged? Was this incident that one small factor on which I was to build a new life later? It was a pause, clear of the past or the present, with a reservoir of endless possibilities to refine both. What I chose to make of it would be dependent on me alone. I did not want this experience to be a momentary flash, easily forgotten, but a guiding beacon for a new direction.

Returning home in a scooter-rickshaw from the office one day, at the traffic lights, I glanced at the man in the next vehicle, just an arm's length away. He sat in his faded blue Fiat, his broad forehead glistening with beads of sweat. His eyes stared emptily at the road ahead. His facial expression registered alarmingly on my consciousness—as though he was driving because everyone else was driving, the surge of traffic just carrying him, chugging along 'streets that follow like a tedious argument of insidious intent.'

I was suddenly hit by the purposelessness of much of our activity.

On reaching home, I opened the door and felt a sense of relief in its quiet. I sat curled up in a chair, noting the whir of the fan-like cycles of thought which reached no conclusion. I heard the loud voice of the woman next door as she called her child's name followed by a stream of indistinguishable words.

The doorbell interrupted my thoughts. Rajeev came home and over a cup of tea we talked of those ordinary, everyday things which make greater sense when shared: how the generator in the factory had broken down, the unavailable sales tax forms, and the work on the forging hammer's piston. Then Rajeev trailed off in mid-sentence and looked out of the window, 'Another day gone. I feel sandwiched between time gone by and time about to go by. Will I ever be able to account for either?'

Sometimes, a single shared thought connects two people more than conversations. In his voicing this thought, I felt a sense of relief. He too, at the end of a trying day, mirrored the hollowness that I was feeling.

'I feel this just isn't enough,' he continued. 'Spending my whole day running around like a headless chicken, earning a profit that is bound to be someone else's loss. Then in the evenings, I'm supposed to miraculously drop it all and think about the highest in humankind. There has to be some link between what one is doing the whole day and what one professes to be interested in otherwise.'

'What is the choice?'

'A simple life. A quiet life. A more reflective life instead of this mindless rush towards dead ends.'

Unsaid, left floating in the air was the thought...a life like Ashishda's. A faraway place surrounded by trees, where the quiet, clear air soothed the wavy outlines of thought into an even, rhythmic breathing. A place where work and contemplation joined hands to share the secrets of both worlds. Where within the confines of time and space, Ashishda explored the possibilities of freedom. Something of the taste of wholesome, home-baked brown bread and garden-fresh peas, a walk up a root-fastened mountain path seemed to rise clear and unsullied over the noise of the ceaseless traffic and the apathy of an etherised day.

I raised my eyes to the window, the curtain flapped gently in the breeze and my thoughts broke, the dream, giving way to wakefulness. My mind reasserted itself to argue, 'Do you know what a life like that means? You've only seen it from afar in all its greenery and harmony. Have you seen it in the dead of winter or in the harsh stripping away of autumnal leaf-fall—which is as much a part of its cycle as its illumined summer?'

No, I had not seen all its aspects: subliminally, maybe, but never with a dissecting eye. I had always imagined it as a whole and never seen it in the separation of its parts. As yet I could not even conceive living that way of life but I knew Rajeev had often considered it.

I watched the three new permanent residents closer, when we next visited the Ashram for Janmashtami, the festival celebrating the birth of Krishna. I was asking myself if, like them, I could live here?

Mahesh was in his late fifties, a retired senior government official, who was not only disconcertingly similarly attired as Ashishda in an ankle-length grey robe but had also adopted his pipe-smoking posture.

What had made Kersy and his wife give up their extravagant and luxurious lifestyle to settle within the confines of monastic austerities? Kersy seemed stripped of his former persona as he came up the hill, dressed in a soot-stained loose shirt, carrying two large milk cans. As he rounded the corner, a growling Ashishda greeted him outside the kitchen, 'Why is the milk not boiled?'

Kersy stuttered, 'I thought Usha was going to do it here.'

'Don't blame someone else,' Ashishda didn't mince his words. 'I told you to correctly weigh the milk and boil it. This is the third day this has happened. Sometimes I feel you're going backwards instead of forward.'

Kersy's face was flushed as he rushed into an explanation.

'I don't want to hear excuses, go in and get on with your work. Sometimes I feel the man in the street is more self-possessed than those who claim to be working on themselves,' Ashishda fumed.

Breakfast was as warm an affair as a night in the Arctic. Ashishda's unsmiling face had brought the room temperature down and he kept interspersing the silence with frowns. As we cleared up, Kersy and I kept banging into each other like the Laurel and Hardy duo. I kept trying to get out of the way while Kersy kept trying to grab more and more work to do. In other circumstances, it would have been funny, but watching Kersy dejectedly hunched over the kitchen sink made me wonder—it may not be easy being a guru but it's hardly fun being a disciple either. It was one thing seeing a soft, glowing Ashishda and another matter seeing him spit sparks with every word.

Mahesh, on the other hand, looked like a gliding figure without substance since he had lost so much weight. Silent, speaking only when spoken to, he seemed preoccupied all the time. Moreover, just why was Dave so rude when he asked Mahesh to pluck the leaves from the tea-bushes?

I sensed these were not just tensions and undercurrents of people living together and rubbing each other the wrong way, but a struggle within each individual trying to submit with full trust to Ashishda. Submission meant commanding an absolute obedience from the ego and Ashishda was now the judge of that. If you tried to defend yourself or give an explanation, as Kersy had, the unspoken answer was 'When you think you're right, you're definitely wrong.'

A self-surrender was demanded in which, by losing yourself you found your true Self. The ego had to be sacrificed—or prised open to reveal the pearl of wisdom within. I remember what I had read in Paul Reps' *Zen Flesh, Zen Bones:*

These old Zen teachers complimented their students by criticism, blows even. When they praised, it usually meant belittling. This was the custom. They had deep concern for their pupils but showed it in presence, not words. They were strong fellows, shockers. They gave questions for which the only answer was one's whole being.

Was it possible to trust a human being so completely that you mortgage your reasoning to them? Just suppose the attempt failed and all one was left with was a beleaguered and crumbling ego, without any inner certainty to break its fall. Who was going to pick up the pieces then? Blows and shocks are all very well, but can any human being, including the guru, be so utterly stainless in motive as to administer this treatment without their own bias interfering in the process?

'Ashishda may not be perfect but he knows much, much more than us. Isn't that enough to trust in and obey?' Rajeev asked.

Ashishda's own training had been a test by fire. It had started with a letting go of his English identity. Shoes, trousers and meat were replaced by wooden sandals, shaven head and lentils. 'No one learns by soft words,' his Guru had said. 'You have to be shaken clear of your habitual way of thinking to be able to perceive something more. Can you pay the price, or can't you?'

Ashishda had recounted the time when he had filled the wrong oil in the temple lamp. Realising his mistake, he froze with fear. He knew there would be hell to pay, for earlier he had been hauled up for much less. Without uttering a word, he put the lamp at his guru's feet and stood there, all six feet of him, head bent and tears pouring down his cheeks. He still could not get himself to say what he had done.

'Those days were hell!' Ashishda had reminisced. 'I used to wake up with dread, not knowing which side the ire would come from, and go to sleep in fear. But if that suffering brought me to the point I now know to be true, I'll choose it again and again, life after life.' There was a throbbing intensity in his voice; from the black coal of that suffering he had polished his own diamond.

A self-surrender was demanded in which, by losing yourself, you found your true Self. It was all there, only I had not seen the connection. Submit to love in the marriage...submit to the highest in yourself. Surrender in order to find. I had read about this method of training in books and had been thankful I wasn't at the receiving end of it. Why then did a premonitory chill run down my back?

Living here, I saw, would be far from easy. It had its own price tag. I realised even if we exchanged one life for another, nothing really changed. For the lessons to be learnt remained the same, irrespective of the change of location. Yet, like all human beings, I wanted the best of both worlds, the autonomy of my present life as well as the inspirational life of the Ashram.

Inspiration, there was, during that visit, in the sheer uncontained outflow of feelings to celebrate the birth of Krishna and the love he shared with his consort, Radha. Self-surrender could perhaps take place only on the crest of pure feelings. The tiny Ashram filled with people as this symbolic birth was celebrated with verve and devotion.

Didi from Nainital, bent and bespectacled, cleaned the lotus seeds for the offerings while Girish, deep-throated and gangly, polished the temple brass and oiled the wood on the Samadhi. Don, who I had met on my first visit to the Ashram, had recently married Parveen—the two of them almost inseparably linked to the happy air of festivity around them. John and his Parsee wife, Persis had just arrived from Bombay (now Mumbai) where they ran a design magazine. Little did I know that these two couples would be part of the small community that would settle here later, together with soft-spoken Mike and his Indian wife Promila, who said, 'The bus broke down so we hitched a ride in a truck up to the road.'

Mike put his arm around Promila's shoulders and said, 'It felt just like our university days in England, didn't it?'

The next morning the women thronged the kitchen. Cupboards were opened and their dark secrets aired in the sun, while the broom swished on the kitchen ceiling, dislodging a filigree of soot onto the floor. A fresh coat of mud plaster was applied to the walls and the stove. A thorough spring-cleaning was on except it was not spring but monsoon time. It was August and the African Giant maize, twice as high as the tallest man in the community was ready for the sickle.

Janmashtami day arrived with the sun kissing away the previous night's rain on the trees. The kitchen chimney belched smoke as fifteen kilos of flour was roasted in homemade clarified butter on the fire. Persis and Parveen shelled almonds while Didi grated the coconut. Rajeev looked flushed by the fire as he, Girish and Ashishda stirred the flour rapidly over the fire to brown it evenly. After a day of fasting, at the midnight hour the entire village was fed the prasad.

This was another Ashishda altogether: no longer wielding his rapier-sharp intellect, nor breathing fire at some hapless disciple, but all compassionate and flowing. He sat on the temple floor polishing Radha's and Krishna's anklets making the ornaments sparkle. He bathed the Images, anointed their feet with sandalwood oil and made Radha almost twirl around in her new, red brocade skirt as she caught her reflection in the white of the marble altar. Krishna, after his rose-petalled bath, was dark and enigmatic in Ashishda's fair hands. Love softened Ashishda's eyes as though these were not idols but people dear to his heart.

Love was shining not only in Ashishda's eyes, for Dave's gaze seemed to follow every movement of Chitra, Savitri's granddaughter. It was a different Dave who actually smiled and even managed to tease without it sounding like a growl. Chitra, half Dave's age and still not out of school, didn't seem the least averse to having Dave riveted to her side, despite Savitri's warning glances.

Emotions became subtler as the afternoon approached. Whilst threading a basket of flowers into garlands for the altar, Didi recounted in low tones what had happened to her the previous Janmashtami.

'I was sitting right here,' she pointed to the inner temple, 'making the wicks for the evening service, when my left ear started burning. I rubbed it absent-mindedly. But it wouldn't stop. I rubbed it again. Then, quite casually, I looked up. To my amazement I saw that Radha's left earring was missing. It was almost as though she was nudging me to see that it was gone. I quickly got up and searched the altar. The earring was lying nestled in the petal of a dahlia. You can say what you like, but it was uncanny. There is some mystery here you can't explain away,' she said to herself.

Indeed, there was a sense of both mystery and anticipation. Someone was coming. A special visitor, an honoured guest the sound of whose flute would spiral through the air, no longer estranged from human beings by the distance of Infinity. To celebrate the occasion, the harmonium was brought out and everyone sang to Krishna, the lover, the friend; and Krishna, the ever-present longing within the heart of human beings.

At midnight, the clouds lifted and a few stars looked down as celestial witnesses. The inner curtains of the temple were drawn back as the conch blew deep into the night. Dave performed the service surrounded by copper and brass dishes full of the offerings. Ashishda stood behind him, a silent, meaningful presence.

Riding the crest of festive feeling Rajeev, much to my utter dismay, asked Ashishda, 'Can we stay here for good?'

Ashishda turned to him, assessing the seriousness of the intent behind the question. Into Rajeev's expectant eyes he smiled and said, 'No, I'm afraid not. You don't know what living here means. You have to be ripe for it. Go back, face your life and meet its challenges. That's where your work is.'

10

You Don't Have to Draw Water
from Only One Well

We continued to explore our life with the tools Ashishda had introduced us to. We kept a dream diary and, with constant feedback from Ashishda on them, we began to appreciate the nuances of introspection. We tried to maintain a time for meditation and attempted to let its flavour spill into the day. The more thought we gave to these practices, the more questions we had.

On our next visit to the Ashram, Rajeev said to Ashishda, 'Books on meditation recommend that one should concentrate on the breath. They suggest visualizing the in-breath as white, and healing, reaching every area of the body, and the out-breath as dark and stale, taking the impurities out of the body.'

'Yes, I know,' Ashishda said. 'By concentrating on the breathing, you may get your attention away from thoughts but then it will now be focused on breathing. So, all you've done is traded your thoughts for your preoccupation with the breath.'

'What about the posture?' Rajeev asked. 'I read that

if, during meditation, the head is slouching, you cannot be receptive to the cosmic energy, while if your head is held too high, you are refusing to surrender to it.'

Ashishda leaned forward and emphasized, 'If the attempt is to get past the body and mind then why be so concerned with breathing or body posture. I, myself, have experimented with various meditational exercises including a very strict adherence to particular body postures. Then, one day, I saw a picture of the reclining Buddha, with one hand under his head, stretched out full length with eyes closed in inward contemplation. It suddenly struck me that he was meditating.

'What is important is the in-turned state which takes you beyond body-consciousness. Choose a comfortable posture for yourself. Before starting your meditation, try and relax the body and then seek this state beyond the mind and body.

'Look at the freedom it gives you not to be bound by any posture. You can meditate when your bus is taking you to work; when you have to wait indefinitely for someone, or when you've returned from work and are sitting on a chair trying to unwind. Every opportunity can be used to withdraw and keep the in-turned awareness alive. It will then flow easily and naturally into everything you do, enhancing even your evening meditational hour.'

If in Ashishda's teachings the inner and outer life flowed from one to the other, it was in his way of life that the teachings came alive. He had a unique level of inner clarity, an outward sign of which was his expansive concern for everything around him. The extent of his involvement with his entire environment became amply clear to me when I spoke to Jagdish, a professor of forest management in an American university, who was also visiting the Ashram.

'Ashishda has given so much thought to every little detail, seen the chain of connections and created a truly viable, regenerative estate. This is the most densely forested part in this vicinity. Much of the Ashram forest is oak and not pine as is the norm around here.'

Pointing towards an oak tree on the side of the path Jagdish added, 'Take this oak tree; only its upper branches have been chopped. The wood is used for cooking food and heating the rooms in the winter. Charcoal is retrieved from the wood fires and serves as additional fuel. Even the bark from the branches is not wasted as it is burnt in the sheet-metal hamam for hot bathing water. Everywhere else I've been, trees are being cut down without a thought, while here on this estate not a single tree is being felled. Ashishda has an efficient eco-friendly system working here.'

Jagdish paused and then continued, 'Here the green leaves are stripped off the felled branches to be used as fodder for the cows and the fallen dry leaves as cattle bedding. Mixed with cow dung, they produce farmyard manure, markedly reducing the need for chemical fertilisers. Farmyard manure reduces the growth of weeds and cuts down on the use of pesticides, making the food more wholesome. Eliminating the use of chemical fertilisers brings down the consumption of water for irrigation. Don't forget, there is a shortage of water in this area.

'I'm sorry; I sound like a professor giving a lecture.' Jagdish smiled apologetically.

'Not at all. I hadn't seen these connections in the terms you just described. Please go on.'

'Besides his concern for the larger environment, Ashishda has also applied himself nearer home. He has not only designed his own smokeless chula for the kitchen but has given it another dimension. By putting a sheet metal recuperator around its flue and connecting it to the water supply, he has ensured a permanent supply of hot water to the kitchen.'

We continued walking past the dairy building to the threshing floor and looked down at the terraced fields. Jagdish said, 'Look at the grading of these fields. To prevent the topsoil from being washed below, the fields have been cambered backwards, away from the edge. They've also been graded appropriately to allow water to flow out from one of the sides.'

Pointing towards the edge of the fields he said, 'A small embankment has been formed all along the edge, wide enough for a man to walk along, and it has been strengthened by planting grass on top, which also contributes to the daily fodder for the cows.'

My admiration for Ashishda grew. He wasn't only a guru concerned with metaphysics, but a human being concerned with the wholeness of life. 'Are you telling me that Ashishda is responsible for all this?'

Jagdish laughed. 'Please don't think Ashishda has invented everything. He has however addressed himself to local difficulties in a focused manner, sought solutions by talking to many experts, and translated ideas into a working reality. This was not the only blueprint available to him. Yet, he picked on ideas that ensured a healthy option for this land.'

Ashishda was a man of varied talents. Often in the late afternoons I saw him attending to a villager in need of medical help. He would bathe and dress a wound on the mason's heel, administer a homoeopathic drug to someone else and, at times, even extract an infected tooth.

In all that he undertook, there was a lively curiosity and

an intelligent enquiry and even the smallest detail didn't escape his notice. Seeing the criss-cross of cattle tracks on the side of a hill, and knowing that cattle walk up steep gradients in a zig-zag manner was not enough. It prompted him, out of curiosity, to measure the gradient of the zig-zag path. He later told Rajeev that they were all one-in-eight.

The beauty of Ashishda's life lay in its interconnectedness to everything. He had once said, 'A true mystic is not a mere visionary with special clairvoyant powers. He is a person who "sees" and experiences the essential unity of all things, and tries to live in a constant awareness of that unity. He is connected to his own inner centre and therefore can connect to everything around him.'

Every day the few residents worked the soil, fed themselves off their labour and silently watered the internal garden of their faith. Like the fields, the mind was embanked, cambered inwards, so that a focus developed, which prevented one being washed away by the first flood of events. In the evenings Ashishda shared the magic of his sweeping knowledge with all those present. His own passion and reading were riveting; his wondrous excitement for all creation held his audience spellbound. And running through all this was his deep commitment to a Path, which he rejoiced in every step of the way.

His life, his affirmations of the Great Beyond were magnetising for us. His conviction about the reality of that state was like a glowing lamp around which we sat and dared to believe. We only had his eyes to go by, as they were softened by love, or set aflame by passion when he talked about the vision of Unity. Even more compelling were those moments when his eyes took on a look of yearning-love as he talked about our true inner guides, the Perfected Men and Women, the crest-jewels of creation.

Ashishda, now and again, hinted about the guidance and help that comes through these Great Beings who have passed on, but have never stopped their teaching—that love and compassion is the highest state of being. Late one evening when Rajeev and I were alone with him, I had asked, 'Ashishda, who receives this guidance?'

'Those who seek, or those who may need an affirmation that there is something beyond what they are struggling for, or for anyone whom "They" choose to reveal themselves to. I prefer the personal "Him", "Them" or "They" over the impersonal "It" because...All I can say is that if you ask a personalised question, you'll get a personal answer. What is required is sincerity. But to have the privilege of such an inner encounter, either in dream or vision, you must first clean the windowpane of your psyche to enable the light to pour in.

'I like to compare our dream life to a windowpane,' he pointed to the glass-pane near him. 'The glass is reflecting the light from the room, but also allowing the light from the outside to come in.

'Similarly, some of your dreams, the psychological ones, mirror your personal desires, aspirations, hopes and fears. But besides these there are other kinds of dreams—Jung called them "Big Dreams"—that come from the Great Beyond and contain significant teaching and transpersonal truths. If the windowpane is not clean, very little of this will shine through, and most of your dreams will pertain to and reflect only your inner turmoil. Our attempt must be to cleanse the mind so that we can be reached by this transpersonal light.'

'And how is that done?' I asked.

'If you record and analyse your dreams; if you step back from your fears and desires, and still the chattering of the mind; if you spend time in meditation, quietly associating with the essential stillness of the uninvolved Self; then you are cleaning your windowpane—preparing yourself for such guidance as you may need, or are fit to receive.'

His last words before we left the room were quietly spoken, 'When you seek the light within your heart, you are most open to "Their" teaching. These Great Beings can be reached by anyone who truly loves them.'

I was very moved by Ashishda's words. He was making everything come alive and his whole life was my reason to believe that nothing else counted but this. All I had to do was to begin the walk.

It was Ashishda who told us about Nisargadatta Maharaj, who lived in Bombay. His talks with people who came to meet him were published in two volumes called *I Am That*. Ashishda had paused thoughtfully and said, 'Many people write about the Truth, but very few have experienced it. I've read the books and I feel they come from genuine experience. If ever you get the opportunity, go and meet him.'

Ashishda sounded as though he was encouraging us to meet another guru. We were confused, for in our story there had been space for only one. Ashishda seemed to pick our thoughts, 'Don't limit yourself; this Light is not confined to one particular person; see it, meet it, look for it wherever it is shining.'

A few months later, we went to Bombay and located Nisargadatta Maharaj's residence. His room was up a narrow wooden staircase. Fifteen or twenty people were quietly sitting cross-legged on the floor. On the mantelpiece was a photograph of his guru. Incense sticks were burning in front of it. Ten minutes later, up the stairs, came a short man in a dhoti and kurta. His black eyes were alight like burning coals. He was in his eighties. We had been told he was suffering from cancer of the throat. However, his did not seem a dying body; there was so much palpable intensity in him. His eyes roamed the room, not calm, not benign, but fiery.

'So, anything to ask?' Nisargadatta Maharaj enquired. He was direct in his answers, refusing to be side-tracked from his all-encompassing perception of reality. All questions on human desires, fears, and suffering, were answered with one statement—'find your true nature which is apart from thoughts and conceptions.'

'All self-identifications,' he said, 'were utterly misleading for in it we take ourselves to be something we are not. By changing the focus of attention, away from all these things, to the state of "I AMNESS", we revert to our true nature.'

Nisargadatta Maharaj spoke about three levels of reality—the 'person', the 'witness', and the 'Absolute'. The person refers to the individual personality with its desires, thoughts and experience which we tend not to look beyond, taking that to be the only reality. 'In witnessing, the sense of being this or that, is not. Unidentified being remains.' In reality there is only one state; when distorted by self-identification, it is called a 'person', when coloured with the sense of being, it is the 'witness', when colourless and limitless it is called the 'Absolute'.

Maharaj constantly urged his audience to disengage from the person and rest in the witness. When asked what remains if we don't identify with the person, he replied, 'It's like asking what remains of a room when all the furniture is removed? A most serviceable room still remains, and when even the walls are pulled down, space remains. And, beyond space is the here-and-now of the Absolute.'

A man asked him, 'You can be compared to a big power-generating station while I to a mere forty-watt bulb. What should I do to become like you?'

His reply was succinct, 'Blow your bulb!'

Much more teaching was involved in his statement than what I could comprehend then. It seems the initial effort is to go from the person to the witness, and most of the practices involve cutting our identification with our body and mind to reach the stillness of the witness. The second leg of the journey, from the witness to the Absolute was too rarefied for me even to conceive. What I could grasp was that at each stage one has to let go of something. First the sense of 'me' or 'I' has to be dropped. Was this what Maharaj meant by blowing the bulb? When the identification with the 'I' is dropped, then one can rest fully in the witnessing consciousness. It is at this point that the next stage presents itself. Even the awareness of the witnessing consciousness goes. Then what remains? The ultimate Unknowable?

In comparison, to the witnessing reality, he felt, the rest of our life was a dream from which we must awake to be freed. He said that liberation is not of the person, but from the person.

Ashishda, in his own way, was saying the same thing to us—look for the knowledge in the only place that it exists, namely in that which is the 'Knower'. I wondered whether Ashishda's knower was the same as Maharaj's witness? Ashishda's effort with us was to clean the windowpane of our psyche so that we focused not on the reflections of our personality but on the Light that shines from the Beyond. His effort was to make us identify with the 'watcher' and to operate from that state alone.

The next day, we were shopping in Colaba, mingling with the throngs of people spilling out of movie halls and cafes, listening to the market place of life hum. I'm not sure who said it first, Rajeev or I: 'What are we doing here?'

In a flash we hailed a taxi and soon climbed up that wooden staircase to listen to Maharaj.

For five days, every morning and evening, we saw Maharaj uphold his experience of Reality by his words and presence. He burnt away the inessentials by unfalteringly living and speaking from that Reality. Those who met him went back with a sense of what the ultimate state could mean. There was so much urgency in his words as though the state he talked about was well within our reach, and realisable within a lifetime.

Nothing seemed to exist beyond the confines of that small room. Everything that needed to be known was present there. And, Maharaj sat there offering it to anyone who was willing to take it.

I was disarmed by the reality of an old man fighting against the scorching pain of a cancerous excrescence in his throat, affirming with his last breath, the conviction that had illumined his life. That which illumined Nisargadatta Maharaj's life only heightened my awareness of what Ashishda stood for and was guiding us towards. I felt myself being pushed in a new direction by the transparent simplicity of these two remarkable teachers. Seek it with all your being, something in me urged, for what else is worth doing? What barriers could I erect against such overwhelming evidence of the Truth?

During that period I recorded a dream:

We are in a plane with no seats. A friend and a few others are there. At a predetermined moment we are all expected to jump out without parachutes. My friend says that it's impossible to take such a high-risk jump without appropriate training. While she is speaking, I look out of the plane and see far away in the distance, the outlines of people who have already jumped. I realise that they are not falling but seem to have touched invisible ground mid-air. Each of them has a look of great happiness.

I point them out to my friend and say, 'Look at them. They made the jump although they were untrained. We've got to do it, otherwise this plane will be our home forever.' The hatch at the bottom of the plane opens and we prepare to jump.

My trepidations of making a dangerous jump were being voiced by my friend. Yet the people who had done it, seemed to have received an indefinable something. What was this jump which needed to be made?

11

The Hatch Opens

I woke up early one morning to see Rajeev sitting in meditation. His days had been a hectic rush of starting and stabilising the factory. The new venture had gripped him with its challenges, but suddenly something triggered disenchantment in him. I was surprised because his competence had found expression and been rewarded with an early stability. Yet the Rajeev who came home one evening to say—'this is not essential; I have to do something about my belief in a greater purpose to life than making a comfortable niche for oneself'—was someone determined to look beyond.

In the days that followed, I saw him change and change again. Awake every morning by four o'clock, he stubbornly intensified his meditation and began to steal an additional hour in the evening for contemplation and reading. I watched him with a growing sense of excitement. He was creating something whose potential I could only sense. For the moment, the intensity was his alone. I merely basked in its glow.

One month later Rajeev had a dream:

I see a numinous figure sitting in the drawing room of our ancestral house. Even though he looks Rajasthani, I know his true identity to be other-worldly. I'm awed when I'm told his name. He is sitting in the middle of the room on a divan with people forming a semi-circle around him. He asks his ten-year-old daughter to sing a song. She hesitates and then begins singing a Rajasthani folk song to the beat of two sticks held in her hands. As she strikes them together she comes towards me and asks me a question. I don't understand her and in place of a reply, give her a polite smile. She appears puzzled but continues to sing and moves to my neighbours.

In her song she asks each person a question, builds up the tempo with the sticks, and then restates the question. The tempo reaches a crescendo and the question is asked once again. The tempo eases to a steady beat as she waits for an answer. If none is forthcoming, she moves on.

I still don't understand her question. She dances and addresses my neighbour—Nahar Singh (a favourite school teacher). She increases the pace of her song as she asks the question a second and then a third time. Suddenly I feel that I know what the question and its answer are. She is asking him: Who he is? So the answer should be, 'I'm Nahar Singh, your brother.' However Nahar Singh does not respond.

She then comes back to me and formulates her question for me. I try hard to understand. The tempo is building up again in the usual manner. By the time she asks the question a third time, I still don't know the answer. I panic. She is marking time—pausing, waiting, demanding...I now notice that she has a few sentences pinned on her dress. One reads, 'Bow your head.' I do so. She moves away satisfied.

The tempo in the dream left no time to think, only to act. The girl restated the question for Rajeev three times, a number that mythically suggests an ultimatum. Rajeev had to provide an answer in a now-or-never situation. In the dream, he appears to consent to something he has no knowledge of.

Two months later when we went to the Ashram, Rajeev recounted the dream. Ashishda listened to it with more than usual interest and then for a while became still as a stone.

'Bow your head to the inner life and make it dance,' he said inaudibly.

'What does that mean?' Rajeev asked.

'It means the time has come for a change.'

'What kind of change?'

'The death of the old and the birth of something new.'

Rajeev and I exchanged glances.

'The old and the new?' Rajeev tried again.

'What happened ten years ago?' Ashishda asked abruptly. He was referring to the age of the girl in the dream, seeing it as a symbolic milestone.

'I came to the Ashram for the first time.'

'It all fits. The child is ten and she is pausing, waiting, demanding something of you. And that ten-year-old is the daughter of a great being in your dream. So, the message is coming from there,' he said gazing out of the window.

Nothing was spoken, even the room seemed to hold its breath.

'What are you going to do about it? Not only you, all of us have to bow our heads to this command,' Ashishda said strangely.

'Does this mean that I have to change my life altogether, or...' Rajeev trailed off.

'Yes, a change in your life.' Ashishda lent back and withdrew.

It had been two years since Rajeev had asked Ashishda if we could stay in the Ashram. He had refused us then.

'Earlier you didn't think much of our idea to move out of the city,' Rajeev said feeling his ground.

'That was then. This is now,' Ashishda said, watching him.

Rajeev turned to me his eyes sharp with excitement. This time he felt he had not misread Ashishda's message.

'Can we live at the Ashram?' Rajeev asked.

Very quietly Ashishda said, 'Yes, you can. Your time has come.'

PART TWO

Building a New Life

12

The Unknown Calls

The fog was thick that January morning when, eight months later, we climbed into our jeep and finally set off for the Ashram. We crawled out of the city, our headlights on full beam. The road ahead was barely visible and the road behind was being swallowed up in darkness. The back of the jeep rattled with the sound of supplies and tools—saws, hammers, wood-planes, pipe wrenches and screwdrivers, mattresses, pots and pans and a kerosene stove—our practical appendages.

We thought we had equipped ourselves fairly well to build our own cottage. We still had to bring in construction materials, since apart from locally quarried stone, the rest would have to be carted from long distances.

'You don't have a clue how to build a house with your own hands,' Rajeev's father had warned him. 'It'll take you forever before you settle down.'

Besides being a practical necessity, building our own cottage was to be a symbolic gesture in the changed life situation. We were the last couple to make our way to the Ashram. The others had already arrived and begun their building work.

Rajeev had armed himself with a battery of do-it-yourself books ranging from plumbing to electrification. We also carried with us the well-known medical handbook, *Where There Are No Doctors*. On the domestic front, I had been worrying about the lack of 'modern conveniences'—of having to bake bread and cook meals on an erratic kerosene stove for the rest of my life.

The tail-end of that thought trapped me. Up at four-thirty in the morning, when even the stars seem to huddle together for warmth; to go out and heat the bath-water not with the flick of a switch but with twigs and bark. Then to spend my days scrubbing, cleaning, washing; or planting, weeding and harvesting the crop in the fields or the kitchen garden.

Had such dramatic changes in their lifestyles induced Mahesh and Kersy to leave after only three years at the Ashram? Or was it the rumoured friction with Dave? Tight-lipped about his departure, Mahesh had only said, 'Ashishda said the key issue in this whole business is stickability. I've failed in that.' Kersy, on the other hand, left one winter on account of his health never to come back to stay permanently at the Ashram again.

The fog thinned and the rising sun spilt over like an egg yolk. The reassurance of family relationships receded as Rajeev picked up speed in the open stretches. When we would meet them again, and how, was not in our hands any more. From now onwards the unfamiliar terrain into which we were venturing to plant our roots would dictate our lives, and perhaps preclude us from connecting with them in the old way. My mother had voiced my thoughts when she had said to me, 'It's not that you're going on a posting or leaving to study abroad. You're joining a monastery. I wonder if the rules of that life will include us.'

Going to live at Ashishda's Ashram brought us face to face with a strange dichotomy. We had lived our lives in big cities, enjoying a freedom virtually unknown to our earlier generations. They had lived by a strict code defined by their elders, while we had greater opportunity to assert ourselves as individuals, less encumbered by parental control and authority. Many young people could now decide what they wanted from their lives, as also how to achieve it. Now suddenly we were going to an ashram, where the laws of submission to the guru applied, where sadhana meant hard work with little regard for yourself, where you did not pursue self-interest and autonomy but practised surrender and service.

It was a tiny ashram where we couldn't lose ourselves in a throng of organised disciples. On the contrary each one of us would be closely observed by Ashishda, the heat of his scrutiny might, at times, be hard to sustain. The effort we made would be judged not by our standards, but by Ashishda's.

Part of the ethos of a guru-disciple relationship, in the Indian religious tradition, was that you did not leave the guru either till death parted you, or you found that which you had set out to seek. Anything short of that was termed failure. Probably, that is what Mahesh had felt when he left the Ashram. This had always worried me. There seemed such finality to this relationship, as though the disciple's psyche is bound to be permanently imprinted with its outcome.

Yet there was a sense of finality in other things too. Like the time when we stood in our drawing room with most of our belongings up for sale. Strangers came, assessing things I felt they had no right to examine. When one man asked the price of our dining table; or a woman felt, with prying fingers, our table-lamp, I felt exposed, vulnerable, as though my life was up for auction.

Six hours later we covered the last stretch in the plains and got our first glimpse of the pine-covered hills. The cold air lanced us as Rajeev put the jeep into a lower gear, the engine roaring in the surrounding quiet. The smaller pines rustled uneasily at the intrusive noise.

New signposts of change were emerging in the hills. When we stopped for tea at a village shop, we learnt from the owner that the specially designed fuel-efficient smokeless chulas, introduced by voluntary organisations, had met with resistance. The women, fearing the change, had protested saying that the new chulas would burn too much wood. This was clearly an attitudinal barrier. I could empathise with their emotional reaction to a change imposed from the outside on the most fundamental thing in their life: the chula. Perhaps over time, I hoped, their resistance would give way to greater acceptance of change.

A change was taking place in the Ashram too. Earlier, Dave's sole companion had been Ashishda. Now he was married to Chitra. Ashishda, well entrenched in his solitude, looked bemused at the excited chatter of eighteen-year-old Chitra. Dave and Chitra were putting finishing touches to the small cottage they had built for their life together. For Ashishda, so much domesticity was new, as was the task of organising the new arrivals into an effective group.

It was only four o'clock in the afternoon when the clouds darkened overhead and night seemed imminent.

'It may snow,' Rajeev said. 'What rotten timing!'

He switched on the headlights as the gentle spray of mist teased the road ahead. Fog, when we started from

Delhi, and mist, when we arrived at the Ashram, as though neither the beginning of the inner journey nor its finishing point is clearly visible. And in between is a stretch when the travelling is more significant than the arriving, for goals tend to recede when we seem to be nearing them.

Six o'clock and the darkness was complete as we swung into Panuanaula. Rajeev put the jeep into low gear-ratio and began the climb to the Ashram. I had travelled this road many times, but that night as the jeep swung around curve after curve, I felt I was entering an unexplored terrain. The forest looked inky blue. A fox darted out and crossed our path. I remembered the Tibetan yogi Milarepa's words:

Amidst the lonely solitude of caves,
There is a mart wherein thou canst exchange,
This whirlpool of life for bliss eternal.

The first few snowflakes began to fall and the dark clouds turned silvery-grey as we reached the garage.

'We'll unload later,' Rajeev said. 'We don't know where we are staying, so let's go and see Ashishda first.'

A warm yellow light spilt onto the flagstones from Ashishda's study. We climbed the steps and entered.

'Ah, so you've arrived,' Ashishda beamed. 'That's good, because the snow is going to settle in for the night. Come and warm yourselves by the woodstove. I can hardly see your faces through your scarves.'

'We haven't unloaded as yet,' Rajeev said.

'Yes, yes! Now where do we put you up? How about the Akhara, temporarily?'

My heart sank to the ground. The Akhara was an open shed, with no doors and windows. A wooden plank on the ground served as the bed. Ashishda often let wandering mendicants shelter for a night or two there. They had to build a fire even on summer nights and this was the dead of winter!

Ashishda's deep chuckle made my head jerk up. 'That wasn't very nice of me. Of course, I'm not putting you up there. Take the key to Pandekhola and settle in there for the time being. We'll play it by ear after that.'

Pandekhola was the old workshop just below the vegetable patch which Ramesh and Urmila planned to live in after Ramesh retired from service. As we walked down to Pandekhola, the snow steadily painted the landscape white, the tall deodars looking elegant in their winter furs. We opened the cottage door to find the cold air wriggling in through generous gaps in the woodwork. Next to the glazed verandah was a small room with a woodstove. Rajeev immediately set to work on it. I ran to get a few logs that were stacked outside. Unfortunately, there was no kindling and the logs were damp. In lieu of the fire, the tension mounted, as match after match sizzled to a stop on the logs.

'Kerosene, we need kerosene,' Rajeev said mutedly.

'The jerrycan is in the jeep,' I said.

'Oh hell! I don't have the energy to go and fetch it. Let's see if there is any in the house.'

There was no electricity. We lit candles and roamed the house like ghosts checking into their new lodgings.

'Why don't we get the jerrycan instead of wasting time?' I asked irritably.

'Oh, why don't you just pipe down.' Rajeev snapped. 'Here, here it is,' he said as he raised the candle to an oil lamp sitting on the mantelpiece. 'This old thing should have some in its belly.'

It was sheer music to hear a sloshing sound when we shook it. A generous dose of kerosene on the logs and soon we had a fire going.

Early next morning I woke up and relit the fire. I wiped one small frosty windowpane and caught sight of a bird, no taller than my thumb and with a proud red chest, hopping about on spindly legs. The only trace she left behind, before she flew into the white silence, were web-like footprints on untouched snow. Outside everything seemed to be in repose. There were no paths that led anywhere. Below the snow, nature slumbered, brooding over the experience of all the seasons. Even in its white-bearded winter wisdom it did not know what course life would take when spring came. All it knew was that it held life's seed as a caretaker of things yet to unfold.

13

Ariadne's Thread

The sun came out after a full night of snow. We trudged to the jeep and began unstrapping the luggage from the carrier. A gate clanked behind us, and suddenly we were engulfed by a hearty hug from Don.

'We're so glad you've got here. I kept an ear out for you yesterday but obviously missed the sound of the jeep.' He helped us unload, and as we walked back, pointed into the distance saying, 'That's John's site. He's still quarrying stone for the house, and hasn't yet got going on the building.'

The site overlooked the lower cowshed fields closer to Pandekhola.

'How's your building going?' Rajeev asked Don.

'I actually belong to the suburban part of the Ashram,' Don smiled. 'I'm renovating the old post office building on top of the ridge. It's taking more work than a new one! At the moment I'm planing the wood for the windows, which is sheer murder. The pine in these parts is so knotty and the damn stuff keeps oozing resin. In the West you get pre-planed, seasoned wood that you can knock into position. Here you have to start straight with the tree, ripping off its leaves first! Anyway, I'm learning less by trial and more by error,' his eyes twinkled in spite of the straight face he kept.

'How's Parveen?' I asked.

'She's finding the cold a bit much after Bombay. On top of it our kerosene stove went on the blink, so we ate biscuits for lunch yesterday. In desperation I took the stove to Ashishda who repaired it, but I don't think it's going to last another meal. Either it's a dud piece or the kerosene is adulterated,' he said, dumping the luggage outside our door with a thud. 'I hope you checked your stove before bringing it here.'

I smiled, relaxing in the knowledge that others shared these minor worries as well.

'Here comes Mike,' Don announced, beaming.

Soft grey eyes greeted us as Mike clasped our hands. 'Welcome aboard.' On that note we all entered Pandekhola.

Flinging off the hood of his windcheater Mike said, 'Good, you've got the hang of the woodstove. I've spent half my month's ration of kerosene on keeping us warm. Ashishda looks down on anyone who starts a fire with kerosene, but I'm leaving that occult initiation until after the winter!'

'How're you settling in, Mike?' Rajeev asked.

Don answered for him, 'Oh, Mike is doing just fine. He arrived with a steel trunk, the size of an aeroplane, which took six men to carry. We all collapsed on the way, so another team was commissioned to recover the casualties.'

Mike laughed. 'Don't listen to this fellow. He's just green with envy because I did a smart thing. In this infamous steel trunk were some window and door-frames that I got made by a carpenter in the plains so I would be under lesser pressure when the walls of the house go up. Don, of course, kicks himself every day for not thinking of it.'

'How much of the house have you finished?' Rajeev asked him.

'Dave got hold of two local masons to raise the walls to roof level. I'm working on the windows and of course the water tank.'

'Is the black sheet lining of the tank in place?' Rajeev asked.

'No, we are still digging the ground. The soil is pretty hard and winter has slowed us down further.

'You still don't know where you're going to build?' Don asked Rajeev.

'Ashishda hasn't told us yet.'

'Well, I hope it's near our side. The post office is very much in the wilds of the Ashram land. It would be nice to have another couple nearby. Mike and Promila have a level walk from the temple, through the jungle, to their site. Then the view opens up to more trees!' Don said with an amused twitch to his mouth.

'Why don't you two have lunch or dinner with us while you settle in,' Mike said, checking his watch. 'I've got to go now to the cowshed. In case you didn't know, I'm the local James Herriot.'

'I'd better return to the salt mines too,' Don said, getting up. 'Do you know this is my third attempt to stay here? These days I'm doling out free advice on how to make it in the first try! That includes how to saw through unrisen bread, how to live with cracked windowpanes in Bhagiya's Cottage and, most important, how to assess your guru's mood from the way he begins his first sentence, when he sees you!'

We were still smiling when the door shut behind them and we turned to survey our packages dotted across the room. There was ease and a flow as though we had stepped right back into the fold of a family. It left me warmed and comfortable and set, what I thought, would be the tenor of things to come.

A little later I heard another jeep coming up the hill—probably John bringing up a load of stone. This place was hardly quiet anymore with four jeeps constantly on the prowl, hauling stone up or going down to the village sawmill to get wood cut. 'Four trips a day to the quarry and you're all but done in,' Mike had said.

In the early days of the Ashram, the village men brought up the stone piece by piece on their backs, their efforts consecrated in the temple building. Savitri's cottage was one of the old buildings with uneven, mismatched floor planks that let in the cold. It had thick baulks of timber for rafters on which split wood was laid, evened out by a mud-coat to seat the stone slabs of the roof. Dave's cottage was the first in the new generation of buildings coming up. The floorboards were tongue-and-grooved to prevent drafts, and tin sheets had replaced the old stone-slab roofs. Picturesque as the old slate roofs were, they bred a variety of wildlife within them, from scorpions to spiders and any number of whirring beetles—the sorts that make entomologists dizzy with delight. Luckily, we were spared this joy, at least to start with—Pandekhola had a tin roof—but later we would have more than our share of creepy-crawly company above our heads. Dave's cottage had large plate-glass windows that offered a sweeping view of the hills, as well as allowed for passive solar heating. The combination of stone, wood and glass blended harmoniously with the local landscape.

We were not walking into an institution already running to a set plan. The small community, of which we were now members, was still at a formative stage and nothing had been 'worked out'. Along with us, the winds of transition were also passing through the corridors of Ashishda's life. From the life of a recluse, he had opened his doors wide enough to let a few enter. He was accustomed to only two or three disciples staying with him. They had eaten together on the kitchen floor and had been accommodated in the temple rooms. The resources from the temple garden, the fruit trees, and the few cows in the dairy had provided enough for their needs. All that had to change now, as obviously these resources would not extend to meet everyone's needs. Since the temple building could not house all the new arrivals, tiny one-room cottages were being built to accommodate the newcomers.

Ashishda had said, 'One room should be enough, about fourteen by twelve feet, in which you roll out your mattress at night and roll it up during the day. No furniture or any beds, please,' he had added firmly.

The cottages were to be double-storied, with the ground floor divided between a small kitchen and bathroom, the living room on top. To conserve water, each cottage was to have a pit latrine outside the house. Because of this shortage, and the pressure created by the arrival of eight extra people, Ashishda had designed an ingenious water harvesting system. Large swimming pool-sized holes were to be dug and lined with a thick plastic sheet to collect rainwater from each cottage roof via gutters. This water would be used for bathing and washing-up. Drinking water was to be carried up in jerrycans from the temple tap.

All this fresh construction meant quarrying stone, an increased demand for wood, not only for doors and windows, but also as firewood for cooking and keeping the residents warm during winter. To conserve firewood Ashishda had ruminated, 'Maybe we could build a large wood-fired oven which we could light an hour before, and like in English villages a bell would sound when the oven was hot, and all the women could bring their risen dough for baking.' Such musings indicated that Ashishda's ideas on how the Ashram resources could be extended were still forming.

Even a simple thing like garbage disposal now had to be 'worked out'. All biodegradable matter would be put into a pit outside our cottages. Mixed with leaves this would form the compost for our gardens. Combustible material such as plastic and paper went into the hamam while broken glass and bits of tin went into a large five-foot deep pit a little away from the main buildings.

In working out the practical details of everyday life, Ashishda, I felt, was guided by and determined to keep the original purpose of forming this community intact. He was, consequently, designing the outer lifestyle to be simple and functional, so that the inner enquiry could be intensified. What that meant I had yet to find out.

A cheerful, large-eyed Chitra opened the door and said, 'Have lunch in the temple for the next two or three days. You can begin cooking on your own once you settle in.'

'Thanks.' I said.

'I have to rush because I've got to clean the wheat before it's sent for grinding this afternoon.'

Everyone seemed hard put to finish their sentences, marching off to do something or the other that was racing ahead of them. This was a far cry from the contemplative life I had told my friends about. No one was meditating all day, focusing on the Eternal, instead everyone was only trying to keep pace with the external!

Rajeev burst into the room, and rummaging through his tool box said, 'Can you believe it, the diesel is frozen in the tank of the jeep after last night's snow! I've spent an hour with Dave trying to warm her.' Without waiting for a reply he marched off, spanners in hand.

I sat down on an unopened carton and began to laugh.

The pace was totally unfamiliar to me but I liked it. Perhaps it was because the sun was out and I felt I was in the right place, at the right age. An age where you willingly learn how to clean wheat for the first time, grind it and knead the leavened dough, hovering over its dormant form, waiting for it to rise. It was fascinating to watch Savitri bake bread in a tin box on coals, no microwave ovens or food processors in sight, just human hands creating something in empathy with nature's ways.

A certain harmony emerged in the utter absence of noises from televisions, radios and car stereos, and settled like snowflakes on a new landscape. I sensed the possibility of another kind of freedom here. The freedom to discover, within the confines of a few acres of land, and an accompanying simple lifestyle, the ability to look at old things in new ways.

I was to become aware of many things through my life at the Ashram. When, finally, that bottle of jam was cooked, waxed and sealed, it wouldn't have been bought from a shop with its glut of choices. I would have been involved from start to finish, though not sequentially so—right from digging the hole in the ground, collecting cow dung for manure, planting the seed, waiting for its first blossoms, worrying about the hail and birds damaging the first fruit, to seeing it simmer in the cooking pot—a process in many ways intertwined with my own growth. I knew it wouldn't be easy because I had not grown up in such an environment.

The feeling that a new attitude was needed was confirmed when I met Persis wearing a baggy sweater and mud-stained pants later that afternoon. 'Gosh...sorry, I couldn't get to see you earlier, but our temporary workshed roof collapsed with the snow. John and I spent the better half of the morning fixing it. I didn't get time to cook lunch so by the time we got round to eating, it was pretty late.' Quite out of breath, she kept pushing her spectacles up on her nose.

As I observed this rushing around, I realised that a welcome was given by everyone and help extended for the first two days or so. Then self-reliance was expected. Community life did not mean that someone else took care of you like some surrogate parent. Of your own volition you had come here to do something, and you better get on with it, with a minimum of fuss. There was an invisible beat to the tempo of work, and everyone, willy-nilly, was trying to keep time.

We were the only Indian couple at the Ashram. All the others consisted of an Indian married to a foreigner. My naive impressions of a community were in the nature of an extended joint family where everyone ate together, shared common resources and found their identity through the collective. Soon enough I realised this community was entirely different. You ate on your own, not depending on the temple garden or trees for their produce, but enjoying a sense of exhilaration when your own little plot produced a few beans or tomatoes. Since no vegetables were on sale locally, we did without them till someone happened to go into town on work. Ashishda discouraged a trip to town more than once a month, for he saw this as a crutch of instant city-based conveniences, contrary to the purpose of the life we had now chosen.

Each couple at the Ashram supported themselves with the interest that came from their savings. Since life was simple it was possible to do so. A fixed monthly contribution— roughly matching our monthly expenditure was given to the Ashram for the upkeep of the temple estate. Besides this, the temple sold milk, butter and ghee (clarified butter) to the residents according to their requirements. This financial arrangement freed the Ashram from having to raise funds in any other way, and gave us all an opportunity to pursue our essential goals within its precincts. This arrangement was also consonant with Ashishda's views about a community. If you live in a place you must contribute to the services provided: roads, drinking water and firewood. What we did with our income beyond that was our affair. Since we had all withdrawn from our professions, our savings had to last us as long as we lived there; they also had to pay for our small cottages, which were built with the clear understanding that, if anyone left, they would continue to be a part of the Ashram's assets.

These rules did not apply to Dave and Chitra. Dave had grown up in the Ashram without ever having worked outside its premises. He had always eaten in the temple with Ashishda. When he married Chitra she took over the temple kitchen and cooked for them and all the other visitors who came to see Ashishda for guidance. Dave was given a modest monthly income by the Ashram for the work he put into the farm and had complete access, free of any charge, to all temple facilities. It was from these resources that he had built the cottage in which he and Chitra were now living.

Traditional Indian influences were strong in many ways. The temple was the centre to which you gave yourself in service without hope of any reward or personal gain. At one level we had to maintain our separate identity by total self-reliance, and at another, give ourselves to Ashram work, whenever required, without thought for oneself. Service first, your needs come second. In as many ways as possible we were to strive towards a total loss of self in the flow of this new life.

This unstated understanding was confirmed when a week after our arrival Ashishda called the community together for a talk after supper. He was sitting in the small room adjoining his study, resting his back against a rolled-up mattress and warming his feet by the fireplace. Promila moved closer to Mike to make place for Chitra; Dave sat close to Ashishda while John and Persis squeezed in between the chest of drawers and the bookshelf. Finally, Don opened the door with a cheery 'Hello', echoed by Parveen, who followed him in, bundled up in layers of warm clothes.

Quiet descended as everyone watched the huge log burning in the grate. Ashishda looked around and then started: 'The purpose of forming this community is not for an early retirement from life into peaceful and beautiful surroundings. It is to give each of you an opportunity to pursue an inner enquiry undistractedly. If you wish to search earnestly for an answer, then the conditions here will serve that aim wholeheartedly.

'For me working with more than two or three people is a new experience. I have not worked out a plan nor do I know the outcome of this community venture. Yet there are a few basic things that should set the tone of this endeavour.' He paused and stared into the fire.

'You may well ask: What is this search all about?

'It is the journey to seek the source of your being. What you're seeking is a state of pure Awareness—unchanging, unattached, calm and silent. It is an undifferentiated state of unity where no categories exist: of you and I, me or mine. For it is the mind that creates separations, and when that is transcended you reach a state beyond habits, beyond struggle, beyond grief and pain. This Awareness is a trans-egotistic centre. That is why it usually has to be found first in a meditational practice which aims at stopping all perception, thought and sensations. When the operations of the mind are stilled then what is left is Awareness.

'The troubles of the personal life and the troubles of the world are to be seen as the spur which urges one to find that Awareness in reality, not merely to believe it. Indeed, it is often in times of greatest trouble, when the personality is shaking that one finds the real presence of that Awareness in waking life. It often happens that people become aware, while they are suffering, that there is something calm and steady within them which watches the suffering without being disturbed by it, no matter how disturbed the personality may be.

'To experience that state means practising a way of living which carves a path that will lead you to this Awareness. What has to be trained is the whole of you—mind, heart and body so that all three seek the goal in perfect alignment. The lifestyle here is an attempt to do so.'

In the days that followed I was to discover how difficult it was to pin my thinking on such an abstract concept. We not only had to focus on this unknown awareness but to live by it in thought and actions. How were we to do it without knowing what that state of awareness was? It was like being taken to a dark room and expected to identify all the objects in it.

Ashishda seemed aware of how intangible this path could be in the beginning. 'At first you'll have to trust that this Awareness exists. The very attempt to sense it all the time may become an invocation. For your steadfastness may turn your faith into the certainty of experience.

'To know that state you must meditate, because that awareness is eclipsed from us by the countless thoughts which churn in our minds. In meditation you must initially learn to control your mind—to gather within all the energies that have been lost during the day in activity, anxiety, fears and desires. Learn to drop all that imprisons you, and find a silent space within, which is free and clear. Let your thoughts settle down, like muddy water in a glass, allowing the pure waters of Awareness to rise to the surface. Don't use force with your thoughts by trying to subjugate them. Just watch them stream past you without identifying with any of them. Observe them, watch their gyrations, their persistent attempt to attract your attention without passing judgement or getting swept away by them. Practise this repeatedly and you will see how the inner silence grows.

'Remember thoughts do not stop. But your identification with them can. If you pay attention they gain power. If you feed anger by going over it again and again, the end result is more anger. Instead, if you view your thoughts with the detachment of watching a play being enacted on stage, you'll see them for what they are—obstructions to your effort to pass beyond the mind.'

I knew he was outlining the central and most difficult part of the teaching. How often had he insisted that we must acquire the ability to control our thoughts at will, so that we would quickly rest in that inner silence.

Ashishda pulled his legs back and stretched across to push a log into the fireplace. All eyes were fixed on him as his words were being mapped with soft rhythmical breathing.

'There may be certain thoughts which will persist. Recent resentments, long buried angers, unnamed fears may rise and become amplified when you meditate. Be patient with these thoughts. Try not to react to them. Hear them out as you would a friend who is complaining about someone else. The sheer act of observing them will make them settle down. For always remember you are not your thoughts.

Identify, as far as possible, with that watching awareness which sees all, but singularises nothing. This restraint will also throw a new light on your old thoughts and habits.'

Ashishda paused and stared into the fire. It was leaping, dancing in a ballet of orange and red, only to vanish into the oblivion of the chimney. Like a hundred thoughts that mesmerise one in the fireplace of the mind, fed by the logs of hopes and fears to vanish, having warmed us only a single winter. How intangible this search for the elixir of life seemed, and what we cling onto with our plans so ephemeral. Between these two, we humans struggle to make a life for ourselves. How are we really meant to live it?

Ashishda glanced up and his eyes had a light that had nothing to do with the fireplace. 'This Awareness you're seeking is not meant to be an isolated event confined to your morning and evening meditations. It has to become a way of life. The Awareness you sensed during meditation has to be translated into the work you do, into the thoughts you think, into the feelings you experience. Always try to locate that Awareness which silently observes the fluctuations of the day.

'When someone's tone of voice riles you, or you are tired and resentful about work, or envy attacks you, try in those moments to centre yourself. Each difficult emotion or thought can be used as a jolt to recall you back to yourself. This very watchfulness will help you during meditation. The more centred the day is, the easier it will be for you to drop your thoughts in meditation. Also, the more centred you are during meditation, the more collected your day will be. Try constantly to remember you are not your thoughts—neither the so-called good nor the bad ones.

'This also implies working on your motives—a psychological understanding of them. This will help you deal with those repetitive thoughts that can't be dislodged easily. Someone may have triggered these thoughts, but remember, the wound lies within you. The salt may be theirs but the sore is your own.

'You will never get to the bottom of a stubborn and difficult thought if you continue to find the reason for its existence outside of yourself. Any interaction implies that two people are involved. Find out what it is that you have contributed to the situation. Free yourself from your own identification with it and you may help set the other person free too. It's ironic how often our most incisive criticisms about someone else, usually mirror many of our own characteristics. We can't see our own faults but we are remarkably perceptive when seeing it in others. Take back that projection, see the identification for what it is, and then let it go.'

A Tibetan mystic had once said that he was not really impressed by a display of miracles like turning fire into water. The real miracle was liberating oneself from one negative emotion.

'Negative emotions are like leaks in a vessel. They never let the container of your being fill up with enough energy to make this search possible,' Ashishda continued. 'They are always self-asserting, self-demanding, self-pitying in essence. They may be about another person but always with self-reference: he/she is inconsiderate, lazy (I have to do the work), unkind (I am hurt), inattentive (I get no attention). They only affirm me and my importance, and they harden and strengthen self-identification. This is the barrier we have to pass when we want to find the root of the awareness which observes all the thinking.

'I've tried to find a balance between the outer and inner life here, so that each reflects the other. For that reason the temple with the Images has been, from the time of my discipleship, the focus of this place. At one level they are just images and their worship is merely a ritual; at another they are the tangible symbols of the intangible. I know how difficult it is to live by an abstract concept. It will take you time and practise to identify that Inner Watcher; in the meanwhile, the Images in the temple can become the concrete representation of that awareness in your outer life. If you can dedicate your work, your sleep, your thoughts and feelings to Radha and Krishna in the temple, then that symbolic offering will one day take you to that Pure Awareness you seek within. So, offer your day's labour and your night's rest to "Them" and all that "They" represent. Whatever you do, do for "Them".

'As far as the day goes, you'll each be given a workload connected with the temple gardens, the cowshed, the dairy, or the farm. Besides your normal duties we will require all hands on deck at times of planting, harvesting, collecting leaves for the cowshed and for carrying head-loads of compost to manure the fields. Even though we have half a dozen men from nearby villages to help out, I would like each of you to work alongside them. Here we cannot rely on the conveniences of a market place and so we aim for self-sufficiency in food.'

Unease hit me. I knew from my readings that physical work played a role in all monastic communities. But was so much physical work necessary? Don shifted his weight on the mat while Parveen stared at some point on the floor. We had all led sedentary lives in the city and here we would have to keep pace with farm workers who had developed their capacities to till and harvest, cut and carry right from childhood.

'Be in tune with your body,' Ashishda said. 'Be aware

of its natural rhythm without fussing over it unduly. It will take your body time to adjust to this pace of work, but it will help loosen you up. In time, as you master the work, your bodies will adjust and find their own natural rhythm. The blocks, the resistances, both mental and emotional, will give way to a natural self-confidence to deal with any kind of work.

'However, the greatest benefit is that continued manual work can get the body really tired. This can help a great deal in meditation. Usually when you meditate, either the legs cramp or something else hurts or itches. When fatigued these are easily dropped. The quality of your meditation will then have a dramatically different flavour.'

The fire spat in the grate and sent out sparks. For a moment I actually felt my vision shift. I did not see only the hard work ahead. Beyond tired limbs and chapped hands, I saw the birth of something as soft as lambswool and as magical as the winter sky. Freedom means many things to many people. To me it meant breaking the barriers that enclose me in myself.

'Work and contemplation go hand in hand,' Ashishda's voice was low. 'I've never practised group meditation, not because I feel it's wrong but because it hasn't been my way. So continue your meditation privately, twice a day at least. In addition make small markers during the day that will help you centre. When you are working, offer your labour to "Them". Just before every meal spend a moment remembering "Them". If there is no electricity in the morning and you're cranking the milk separator for forty-five minutes, don't let your mind wander. Quietly repeat your mantra in your mind. Its repetition should become such a habit that it can be kept going at the back of the mind all the time. It is of no consequence that it becomes mechanical. It acts as a constant reminder, something the mind can hold onto, instead of chattering uselessly on daily worries and concerns.

'When the first seed is planted in the soil, when the first bushel is harvested, when the evening lamp is lit, each of these can become reminding points of a day woven together in "Their" name. For that reason attend all three services as far as possible. If you're busy at work and far from the temple, then on hearing the gongs, stop. Be still for those few minutes, inwardly witness the service wherever you are.

'In my earlier days here if I stopped work ten minutes before the midday service and quietened my mind, I found the rest of the day was more centred than if I rushed to the service, out of breath with work. But you'll have to see how it works for you.'

The mood in the room had shifted from the robust outward thrust of physical work to the tempering quiet of half-closed eyelids brooding over glowing embers. Ashishda's voice seemed like a prayer which had risen spontaneously. A prayer, which by its evocation, released some unknown power that throbbed to a collective heartbeat in the room.

When I glanced around, what I saw was a group of people who were here because each felt that Ashishda could give their aspirations an added impetus. The unspoken plea of each person seemed to be—teach me, train me, discipline me, scold me, put me through the paces, but get me there.

'It is not only the day which you should offer to "Them" but also the night,' Ashishda continued. 'The night is a time when a hundred mysteries unfold. Knock on night's window and you won't see the pitch darkness of oblivion but the illumined windowpanes of light. If you want to get there you have to send a request for admittance, you have to wait, you have to believe.

'Prepare for this nocturnal dance by slipping into sleep with some degree of "wakefulness". Don't fling yourself into bed and pass out. Collect your thoughts and hold your awareness before drifting into sleep. Then one day when your body is asleep something within will remain "awake". You'll be aware of it more than any other experience of your life.'

It seemed that a conscious alignment had to take place in one's everyday life so that at the right moment, when the body was asleep or fatigued, a different perception may be apprehended. Almost like falling asleep in body but coming alive in soul.

'Some very basic practices need to be followed if you want to be a witness to the night-time journey of the soul. For this reason, let your mattress be thin and the blankets not too heavy in the cold weather. That's why we have one main meal at midday followed by a light supper in the evening. These small observances prevent the body from getting too comfortable. They make your sleep light, helping you towards "wakefulness".

'On the question of sleep I suggest no afternoon naps. If you are very tired just lie on the wooden floor for ten or fifteen minutes. No pillows, no covering. That should be enough to refresh you.'

Ashishda closed his eyes and seemed to withdraw. My eyes urgently sought out Rajeev's, asking, 'Is all this humanly possible?' His answering glance said, 'Alone no, but together, maybe.'

The old clock on the mantelpiece swung its pendulum in its glass enclosure. We all seemed like tiny flints embedded deep in the womb of the night. The frosted night, the dark room and the fire throwing shaded patterns on the uneven mud walls—all seemed carved out of some isolated cave in time.

Ashishda opened his eyes, 'I know what I'm asking of you is not easy. In this life there are no holidays, no entertainment. The shoring up of energies without any distractions to let off steam can make your mind wander, fantasize and rebel against it all. It is then that your real work starts. You'll have to bring those thoughts back to base camp, by first understanding them, and then stilling them. If you can transform the anger, the fears, and the doubts into something that spurs you on to seek, you'll come upon an unsuspected vantage point where the view is breathtakingly clear. If these energies are not transformed they can degenerate into destructive tensions and uncontrolled compulsive behaviour. Always keep in mind that you are a community working towards a common aim. One person's persistent negativity can weaken the link that binds this group together.

'I'm not underplaying the struggles this life entails. For those very reasons you may feel pulled back to the known security of your former life. If you want to resist that, I suggest you don't go down to the plains unless work demands, or it's absolutely necessary. Consolidate your life here so that the pulls of the old don't distract you prematurely.

'Accept the suffering these struggles will produce in your nature. Hold these tensions and transform them, instead of finding easy releases by blaming others.

'I'm taking it for granted that you're all watching your dreams. We'll continue to discuss them individually. If one is to get full value out of dreams, one has to accept that what is good and right in one will look after itself. The effort is to see what is wrong and put it right. One has to see it first, and one cannot see it unless we are ready to accept criticism. Dreams often show us things we are totally unaware of. They are our tools of introspection. As time goes by, I hope your dreams will guide you and change from being mere psychological signposts to becoming the windows of vision.'

Sitting there, I felt Ashishda had put music to a song whose words I had never known, but the echoes of which often woke me up in the dead of night. Impatient with its lack of substance I would fall asleep again. Now he had shaped an entire life for us to follow. With his teachings, like Ariadne's thread that guided Theseus, we too could find a way out of the maze.

14

The Nights Keep a Vigil Over My Deepest Longings

This was Ashishda's first comprehensive teaching. It was inspiring and many things fell into place. Not only had he outlined our tasks and responsibilities, but shown their connection to our higher aspirations. What Ashishda had said seemed so simple, so attainable. True words of inspiration are like that. However, they never tell you how far the goal is, only reassure you of its existence. They don't tell you of the miles, the months and years of questing that lie ahead, but help to light the way.

Ashishda's attempt was to focus on an awareness that was normally concealed from us. To build a muscle one has to use it. To develop a skill one has to practise it. To become 'aware' one had to practise 'self-awareness', he had urged.

I could respect a view which stated that the whole person—mind, body and emotions—had to be aligned to walk the way. For Rajeev, Ashishda's talk meant the confirmation of all he had hoped this life would mean.

'Why didn't we come here earlier?' he wondered.

The next morning I met Don near the cowshed, collecting his bottles of milk.

'That was quite a talk last night,' I remarked.

'You bet. I told Parveen that this was going to be for good now. I'm making this my last and final attempt. They'll carry me out dead from here after this.'

In direct contrast to Ashishda's talk, life was a comic come-down. The shrill call of the alarm shocked me awake every morning while it was still dark outside. Sleep lightly, Ashishda had said. I had to drag myself out of sleep and direct my body, through sleep-soaked eyes, in the general direction of the hamam outside! Water had to be heated in time for Rajeev to bathe before the conch blew at a quarter-to-six, when he had to swab the temple floor and wash the service utensils. To wake Rajeev up was like trying to shake a log that had suddenly developed roots. I would, then, roll up a still warm mattress to sit and meditate. This usually ended in a catnap, sitting up instead of lying down. A jolt, as my head banged against the wall, and suddenly I was alive to the crackle of the fire in the hamam and the darkness easing off outside. Rajeev had by now managed to graduate to a sitting position with his head drooping to chest level. A gentle wheezing sound, suspiciously like a snore, would emanate from him. I would rudely clang the hot water bucket on the bathroom floor and startle him. I knew when Rajeev would be fully awake—three-fourths after his bath, and the rest when his bare feet touched the frost on the ramp leading to the temple.

'Follow the rhythm of your body.' There was no such thing, I decided, as I opened the door to the pit latrine and saw, in the beam of my torchlight, a spider crawling towards me from the dark walls. I banged the door shut wondering how poets could talk with such lilting wonder of the spidery web of illusion that is life; the spider was a creature least conducive to my peace of mind.

The blowing of the conch was always a calming note. With it, the day was declared open for all to come forth. Almost on cue, five minutes before the service, John and Persis, Promila and Mike, and Don and Parveen would appear and sit silently on the stone slabs, or stand near the sundial. When I passed the kitchen, from the clang of a pan in the sink, I knew Chitra was inside. Then Dave would come down the ramp to lay flowers on the Samadhi, before performing the arati, and everyone would rise to attend the service.

Afterwards we exchanged smiles, sometimes a quiet word or a hushed conversation took place about some practical detail of the day. No one lingered, for Ashishda had told us, 'Try and be aware how often one hangs around chatting aimlessly. If you're not working you should be reading or meditating. Often aimless talk ends up in gossip and complaints.'

So, we all bifurcated to our points of the day that were supposed to flow into a central theme. It was hard to remember that centre point, as the day became a fast-paced rush of hands and feet in which the only things running ahead of my limbs were my thoughts.

'Why don't you learn how to churn the butter for the temple?' Dave asked me.

Outwardly I smiled agreeably, but inwardly I groaned and made some rapid calculations. Butter, an hour's operation, would have to be fitted into the morning between cooking our meal and picking vegetables for the temple lunch. Not to mention the bread, left rising in the sun, mid-stream of a full three-hour process. Every task had to be fitted in, for immediately after lunch the women were expected to work in the vegetable garden. Rajeev was now someone I saw only at meal times, or briefly at eleven, when I took coffee for him after he arrived with a load of stone at our site.

While the division of labour, apparently followed a rather traditional logic, it was, however, only superficially so, for both men and women also shared numerous tasks in the kitchen, and during the construction of the cottages and farm work.

Ashishda had led us to our site and we had followed, wondering which spot had been earmarked for us. We walked past Dave and Chitra's cottage up the hill in the direction of the Post Office. Ashishda opened an iron gate and pointing to a fallow field below, said, 'That's where I think you should build.' Fourteen or fifteen fields above was the post office which Don was renovating; standing on the jeep path I could hear the 'shik-shik' of his plane slivering off golden curls of wood.

My first impressions of the site were disappointing. Below was the sweep of the forest ending with the view of the red-roofed garage. I had imagined that our house would be perched strategically above treetop level to give us a sweeping view of the mountain ranges. Here, trees enclosed us on all sides.

Ashishda looked at me and said, 'Try and look at it imaginatively. It has great potential and will grow on you.'

And it did, with every trip I made daily at eleven o'clock armed with a flask of coffee. I looked at the growing heap of grey stones lying at the site and in them I saw the building blocks of more than just a house.

It was strange how each of us was attuned to whose jeep was chugging up the hill, and on which stone trip. Then the coffee would be on the boil as the engine grunted to a stop outside the garage, before turning to whichever path led to the person's site. I heard Rajeev reach the garage and then take the track uphill to our site. He would be alone, or with another villager to help him. The rest would be at the quarry pick-axing the stone for the next trip.

I reached the site as our jeep came to a halt on a field above the site.

'The track was very slippery today,' Rajeev said, opening the back flap of the trailer.

'Despite the sun being out?' I flung out the smaller stones while Rajeev heaved down the bigger ones.

'The tyres were slipping on the debris. Even though I had the hand-brake on and my foot on the brake-pedal, I was still skidding!'

I had been on one such trip with him to the quarry five kilometres away. A very rudimentary track had been improvised for the jeep. It was nerve-racking when the loaded jeep started its descent downhill on the steep gradient; if you looked behind you felt the trailer was bucking, goading the jeep downhill.

From a skidding jeep to a slipping butter churn, with no attempt at self-remembrance or developing my witnessing consciousness! How could one calmly focus one's mind when the midday service was twenty minutes away and the butter had turned into a watery mess instead of a thick heavy mass? In desperation I added a little cold water, and then a little hot, hoping one of the two would work. Neither did the trick and with every turn of the handle the liquid began to ooze from the rubber-ringed top of the churn. Four litres of cream had suddenly turned into eight litres of moisturizing lotion. As the gong struck twelve for the midday service I felt like willingly turning into a pumpkin. At least then I would not have to deal with an irate husband demanding lunch, impatiently checking his watch, as he had to drive the men down for the one o'clock trip to the quarry.

Don went up to Ashishda and asked, 'I'll need someone to help me chop some firewood.'

'Don't ask me. Ask Dave. He'll decide,' came Ashishda's prompt reply. Dave was the piper who played the tune for this march past of our daily life.

Unschooled Dave and intellectual Don met on grounds of mutual incompatibility while renovating the old post office building. Dave was supervising the masons in raising a wall. Don wanted it done another way. Dave said curtly, 'It can't be done.'

'Why not?' Don asked.

The argument splintered in numerous directions with Don finally saying, 'With you Dave, it is always your way or the highway.'

'If that's how you think I'm not going to help you anymore,' Dave marched away, flushed with anger. Unfortunately, true to his word, he never did.

Later Ashishda said to Don, 'You're here to listen, not to argue. If Dave feels the wall has to be at that place, then that's where it should be.'

We took Ashishda's word for it and listened to what Dave had to say. Rajeev was having much more to do with Dave than before, but his basic fondness for Dave helped Rajeev take his outbursts better. Quite often, after the day's work, Dave would ask Rajeev to do some work or the other in the garage. I had to quell my disappointment at this encroachment on our precious time together.

My favourite time was five o'clock when the last stone trip was over. I looked up from weeding the vegetable patch at the now mellow sun that had warmed my back all afternoon. Persis smiled at me, reading my thoughts. Promila was pulling out cabbages. With Dave's consent we had all been getting our vegetables from the garden, ever since we began working in it. Parveen, who had been cutting grass at the edge of the vegetable garden, put down her sickle and flexed her shoulders looking across the distant hills. Following her gaze, the lines of Christina Rossetti's poem flitted through my mind:

> Does the road wind up-hill all the way?
> Yes, to the very end.
> Will the day's journey take the whole long day?
> From morn to night, my friend.

In that hour as the day receded, I heard the dogs being rounded up and put into the cowshed for the night. The six farm men would appear in a single file on their way home to their villages. Dave often came in last, stopping for a moment to survey the day's work in the garden before going up to Ashishda's room. Almost on cue Chitra would come out of the kitchen, go round the corner to collect wood to start the fire for the evening supper.

These were small markers in a day that ended with my looking out for Rajeev who would be trudging up the path with slow steps. The day's work was visible in the drag of his feet as we walked into Pandekhola together. A hush descended over the temple as the red sunset sky turned dark to meet the night. Now all was quiet, only the jungle noises serenaded the approach of the hour of rest. Eyes closed very naturally at that time of day, to bring together the day's spent energy in remembrance of what it had been devoted to.

The evening arati bell sounded so different from the morning one. It seemed softer, almost fading away into the first faint gleam of the stars and the fragrance of the narcissi in dim yellow-white conference above the Samadhi. Touching one's head on the threshold of the temple door seemed like a ceremony forgotten during the rush of the day, which I had to re-learn every evening. In the circular light of the pradeep I felt my senses heighten and clarify—as though the churning cream of the day was only now, at this moment, transforming, taking shape.

If the dusk-time prayer was one heightened moment, the other was when, after supper, we all met in Ashishda's room for the evening 'session'.

'Dave not coming?' Ashishda turned to Chitra.

'I don't think so.'

'Probably welding those trusses got him. He must be tired.'

So were the rest of us, I thought, looking around the room. Don, sitting cross-legged, slouched over to one side while John seemed present only in body.

That evening's session included a photograph for us to look at. The book was passed around. When it reached John, he stared ahead wide-eyed, not even a flicker of registration on his face.

'John,' Mike said softly, 'have a look.'

There was no response.

Don looked up with a chuckle and said, 'I've heard of people falling asleep on their feet, but never with their eyes open. John's just done that. I don't blame him. Sometimes I'm so tired that I don't even have the energy to meditate.'

Ashishda smiled gently, 'It will become easier, I promise. Just remember, when you're fresh and full of energy meditating can be a strain, since shutting out your thoughts can be more difficult at that time. But if you put in the effort to meditate when you're tired, you could slip into a quiet state effortlessly.'

'I guess I'm not used to physical work,' Don said.

'We have to grow our own food,' Ashishda said appealingly, sensing the subliminal complaint. 'I know it's tough, but the whole thing requires effort and persistence. You're changing a life orientation and that's seldom painless.' Ashishda grew silent as he watched Don rest his head against the stone wall. 'By struggling you are building an intensity that will take you directly to the centre within. What you're doing now with effort will come naturally once the initial momentum has been set.'

'What will the intensity do?' Don asked.

'It will light the sacred fire.' Ashishda said softly. 'All these disciplines are a means to an end. None of them, by themselves carry you to the goal. But they help you focus all the scattered energy to a single-pointed enquiry. After that it all depends on Grace.'

'How do I know that we're going about it the right way?' Parveen asked.

'Your dreams will tell you that. Don't underestimate the dreaming intelligence. It will give you all the guidelines required to negotiate the fast currents and eddies.'

House-building, farm-work, gardening, cooking and cleaning for the temple, all mingled in the months ahead. We got used to our lives being a blend of personal work and manual work dedicated to a non-personal aim. Our cottage walls slowly reached roof level, enabling the roof-sheets to be bolted on. But our home-in-the-making stopped at that stage; Dave assigned Rajeev to work full time on the farm. John, Mike and Don moved into their houses and, to mark the event John had a house-warming. That evening Don climbed up John's improvised staircase, and without warning went down on all fours to inspect the floor.

'How about a hello, Don?' Ashishda said in amusement.

Utterly oblivious, Don frowned, and prodded the perfectly made tongue-and-groove joints in John's floor. 'What am I to do if my wood is so rotten! My floor is like a series of speed breakers on which, to add insult to injury, I trip every day.'

We all laughed as Don's attention was locked up completely, at that moment, in a recalcitrant tongue-and-groove joint.

It was a special evening! We feasted on newly baked bread, redolent with the fragrance of freshly harvested wheat, jacketed potatoes and lettuce leaves. By the time coffee was served, John had brought out his guitar and, when Ashishda didn't object, began strumming it. He looked enquiringly at Persis who interjected with whispered staccato instructions like, 'C minor' or 'F sharp', for, being a pianist, she had the ability to hear a tune and immediately convert it into its musical notes.

This rather Western ambience created by the food and music of the evening did not seem unnatural, since more than half the population was from the West. Somehow, they could bring their cultural patterns into the Ashram lifestyle, and also accept living and working in a dominantly Indian way, with all its monastic simplicity. The Vaishnav do's and don'ts were the predominant cultural note, evident in our strict vegetarian food that excluded even onions and garlic.

Another tune was not far behind as spring came with its daffodils in buttery colours, making the place look like a delightful country garden. One day, below Pandekhola, I encountered a black snake thicker than a hosepipe curled in the sun. My legs began to tremble and I rushed up to Ashishda's room and said in a hoarse whisper, 'There is a python outside Pandekhola.'

'Python?' Ashishda said, frowning. 'There are no pythons in this area.'

'Well then this one has just migrated.'

'What is it like? Black, thick as a hosepipe and coiled up in the sun?'

'Yes.'

'Oh, he's come out of his hole, has he?'

'You know him personally!'

'Of course!' Ashishda smiled as though an old friend was visiting him. 'He's our local rat snake, utterly non-poisonous. We have a very good relationship. He eats all the rats and we never bother him.'

'You mean he's going to lie on that path all the time?'

'He's just sunning himself after the winter. He'll soon join the rat race,' Ashishda said, amused by the look on my face.

A python-sized snake coiled outside your doorstep was probably the perfect Freudian dream but it was my personal nightmare. Once, in the middle of an evening session, Ashishda stopped mid-sentence to listen to the jungle noises outside. 'Can you hear that? That rasping cough, like someone rubbing sandpaper on wood? That's a leopard's cough. He's probably below the Pandekhola jungle.'

A comforting thought indeed to sleep with at night! A leopard just below Pandekhola and a snake to keep it company. I was convinced Ashishda had deliberately passed on this information, for there was no other way he could get us to sleep lightly!

The sights and sounds of this new life gradually filled us and helped awaken new instincts that had to replace old habits. From being used to walking on flat gradients we now had to raise our feet just a little more, so as not to stub our toes against a stone, or trip and stumble over a concealed root as we traversed up and down the inclines. Sharpening our instincts included developing a pair of eyes to see in the dark, and learning to distinguish the jungle call of the barking deer warning its mates of a leopard in the vicinity. As if to confirm such tidings, the dogs would be frantic the next day as they sniffed at and retreated from an area below the cowshed. Their barking suggested that for them the presence of the leopard lived on and the clearly imprinted pug marks left no doubt a leopard had visited the fields.

One didn't develop these instincts only for predators and jungle animals, but also for the cows that we had to learn to milk. I had the distinct impression that these large-eyed lumbering animals were far from dumb.

'The first thing to do is to tie their hind legs,' Mike instructed, when I went for the first milking session. As I fumbled with the rope around the cow's sturdy brown legs, she kicked with uncanny precision in the direction of my shins. Most of the time I was jumping from side to side in an effort to get the right angle to tie her legs and save mine. Finally, I squatted on my haunches amidst cow dung buzzing with flies, and squeezed her teats. This, she thought, was just too much to bear and kicked out wildly. I squeezed harder, keeping my head pressed to her brown, cow dung-smeared belly. I had read somewhere that physical proximity to the animal was essential for human-animal communion. Obviously, the cow hadn't read the same book, for she shook her head and stepped backwards, effectively loosening the rope from around her legs. Her wet flanks brushed my cheeks and her whip-like tail lashed across my head before resting lazily on top of it. Undeterred by the minor fact of losing my composure, I shifted the bucket and tried to milk her again. The cow waited as she chewed the grass meditatively. Then she launched her final offensive. She lifted her tail and began to urinate with gusto. I was totally unprepared for the yellow jet that sprayed all over the bucket and around us. I sagged. She had undoubtedly emerged victorious in this round by proving she could produce more urine than I could squeeze out milk. When I got home that evening Rajeev said, 'You're smelling awful! Have you been milking cows or bathing with them!'

The next month was a battle of mind over cows as milking was done three times a day. Often, I returned flattened like a squeezed-out toothpaste tube, feeling less than human with the bovine company I was keeping lately.

'Collect yourself, centre yourself' seemed remote words in this haze of pushing myself from one job to the next with no other thought but to cope. I hope this is leading somewhere, I told myself as we climbed the stairs for the evening session. Was it a coincidence or just a collective thought in the air that made Ashishda recount an incident from his years of discipleship?

'It was a time when I was rushed off my feet going from one job to the next,' he began. 'My guru was ill, very ill. Till late at night I used to press his feet and often while doing so, I'd fall asleep. The erratic pressure I was exerting on his legs would wake him up and he would chide me. On one such night I fell asleep again with my hands on his feet. At that moment though my body was asleep, something real was fully awake and conscious. Spontaneously I found myself in a state of Pure Awareness.'

Before going to sleep that night I felt reassured that our personalities—the battleground of so much conflict—can be shed like a skin to meet another state infinitely more fulfilling. These few moments before sleep were very precious to me. They imparted a sense of privacy away from the heat of a demanding day. Aware that my life was no longer my own, I felt this hour belonged to me alone. Lying in bed, my heart seemed to keep time with the deep throb of the silence outside and my thoughts had the freedom of the star-spangled sky that I could see from our window. Each star seemed like a question mark set against human mortality and purpose. Is there a meaning to my struggles? How long will it take me to ascertain the truth for myself? And what if, in the meanwhile, my courage fails?

Often, I would simply succumb to the secure solace of sleep, while the night kept a vigil over my deepest longings.

15

The Pike in the Pond

Gradually the talk about nuts and bolts, clamps and windowpanes died down, for everyone, except Rajeev and I, had shifted to their houses. As a mark of their having settled down, the rose bush Don and Parveen had planted outside the Post Office produced a single yellow rose in welcome.

The tin roof of our house had progressed, though the house still had no floors, doors or windows. We wished we could move in, but Rajeev had no time between the added responsibilities on the farm and the frequent trips to buy cattle concentrate or building materials for the temple. On the whole, the incessant roar of jeeps, up and down the hill, had lessened and the air was clear of the constant banging of hammers.

Spring came with its peach blossoms in candyfloss pink outside Pandekhola. Plum trees lined the route to the threshing floor, their white blossoms settling on the ground reminiscent of winter's snow, and the hillsides blushed red as the rhododendron lit up with the sun's ardent glow.

To keep pace with this warming urgency in the air, we were all summoned to join in the first swing of farm work.

Dave announced that 'leafing' would begin the following day. We were all to gather at one o'clock above Savitri's house.

On the face of it, the task seemed ridiculous. We were to sweep not our front courtyards, but the entire hillside! When Dave arrived he collected a few thick, dry twigs put them together and said, 'Make a broom like this with which you'll sweep the leaves downhill. We don't use rakes because they scrape off the top soil.'

Up we climbed to the top of the hill, John more sure-footed than the rest. We stood twenty-feet apart, peering down uncertainly at the impossible task ahead. Bushes, trees, creepers and boulders were the immovables around which we had to coax the fallen brown leaves.

'Just keep sweeping downhill,' Dave instructed from below. 'Once you reach the bridle path, we'll collect the piles into nets and load them onto the trailer of the jeep.'

The jeep would then be driven to the garage and the leaves unloaded behind it into an enormous pile. These were to be used for cow bedding, round the year. Mixed with cow dung they would provide manure for the fields and the gardens. Just as we began sweeping Ashishda came uphill and took his place on the far side near Mike.

The first few days saw our brows furrowed in concentration, for all we could manage was to hold the twigs together without letting them fall apart as soon as they made contact with the ground. Ashishda was the only one who, with slow rhythmic movements, was creating a growing pile that went cascading downhill like a waterfall with its own momentum.

'I don't think I'm writing to my mother this fortnight,' Don announced, as we walked down for tea at three o'clock.

'Why?'

'I'm going to shorten her life span considerably by saying I spend my days making cow mattresses!'

His face looked so funny with its floppy white cap and lopsided smile, that playfully I picked up a handful of leaves and threw them at him.

'Don't,' he protested, 'you're just trying to take a leaf out of my book!'

After tea we took armfuls of leaves and stuffed them into the nets. 'Pack them tighter,' Dave instructed. Persis threw the leaves into the net while I held its mouth open and stamped them down with my foot. Rajeev was trying to outdo himself by carrying a huge netted mass of leaves on his head towards the jeep. The net was so heavy that it sagged in front of his eyes and he walked straight into a low branch.

'Occupational hazards,' Mike muttered behind him as he tried to retrieve a staggering Rajeev from the branch and the elliptical orbit of leaves.

Nine middle-class city dwellers struggled their way through a job that every hill girl does as a matter of routine. For us it seemed as unending as Psyche's task of sorting out millions of mustard seeds by dusk. As in the old myths, was there a magical formula that solved the riddle? Yes, possibly, there was—it lay in getting one's body to relax, in steadying one's breathing, in training one's mind in joining hands to free the task instead of fettering it.

I looked up to watch Ashishda, his body bent, one arm behind his back, ease in his movements. There was no hurry, nor a slackening of pace, as though he had nowhere to go, nothing to think of but this place with its patterned sunlight filtering through the trees; nowhere to be but here, as his long white arms swung backwards and forwards like the pendulum of a clock which kept time to the dark beat of the mulch-covered earth.

Looking at Rajeev's face, concentrated in attention, as he reversed the loaded jeep and trailer into the dirt path, I realised it was 'attention' that was of essence. Not to grip the task with tension nor to slacken it by resistance, but to find an equicentre which could distinguish between the body's tiredness and one's own reaction to that state.

I noticed how much physical tiredness reflected the emotional content of the day. Some days my mind kept thinking, 'Am I going to be doing this for the rest of my life—sweeping hillsides like a crazed janitor? What is the point of this work? Is the common farm hand nearer divinity because he does manual work? How long can I sustain this pace in which the day never seems to end?

On days when these thoughts persisted I found myself unmitigatedly tired. It was not the work that was the problem; it was my perception of it. The mind assigns its own categories, and sweeping hillsides was at the bottom of the bin. When I could see that the work I was doing would produce our food, my hands automatically relaxed and I worked rhythmically. It was as though the body could only ease itself into work if the mind let it.

When I could deal with the mind's resistances, I found the tiredness different. No doubt it was there, but it did not have the leadenness I had experienced at other times. Often there was even a sense of lightness in which the body seemed refuelled instead of feeling run down. It was a double process in which, at one level, I was expending energy and, at another level, building it up. This was especially true since there were no distractions, no easy releases, and this fed into an impersonal vibrancy. I tried to define for myself what this pushing against resistances meant to me. Don't sit down, just keep moving. Don't give into the body's need to stop the task especially when the mind calls a halt much before the body is fatigued. A task like leafing could provoke a variety of reactions which we had to cope with. In trying not to give into any of these thoughts, I became aware of something getting honed within me. By resisting these mental and physical pulls I was acknowledging their limitations on my life, and in doing so I was focusing my energy on a point beyond them, where the claims of the body and mind did not exist. In many ways this was still an imaginary point for me, but in trying to keep my attention on it, something hitherto submerged was stirring.

No doubt it was, to a large extent, our faith in Ashishda's word which broke the huge internal resistance within us—not the work itself, nor the meditation. Faith carried us from one day to the next, teaching us to build on our own resources. Circumstances like these can have a peculiar effect on the psyche. At times you may feel your internal resistances are being broken down too fast to handle, at other times you change with ease in order to cope with the outward situation. Learning to change, I found, meant undoing a tight knot formed by an old habit. As you attempt this, a clenched fist seems to come hammering down within. It is then that you are confronted by an uncomfortable choice: to slip back into the comfort and inertia of an old personality, or to summon every resource to create something new.

This was a voyage into uncharted territories that was not being steered by fully mastered skills. This became clear when two weeks into leafing, we moved to Ratwani, the steepest and dampest hill we had combed so far, thick with trees and thorn thickets. We were a silent group concentrating hard on keeping our foothold, at the same time vigilant to what we could hold onto in case we slid. One minute Persis was next to me and the next she was tobogganing downhill. She couldn't stop the momentum of her slide till half way down the hill, when she grabbed a sapling. Her feet were dangling over the edge of a steep drop to a dried water bed. Two of us reached her as fast as we could.

Dave, standing at the bottom of the hill, shouted precise and clear instructions to Persis on what she should do. Persis managed to grip a hollow tree-trunk with her feet, clinging onto it in fright. We got to her, one of us picking up her fallen spectacles and the other tying a hanky around her torn fingernail and bruised ankle. She gave a wobbly smile, and soon afterwards got up and collected new twigs to start 'leafing' again.

Such experiences taught us the importance of holding on. Falling down is inevitable, but picking yourself up as quickly as possible was important. Don't linger by dwelling on the injured part in self-pity. If attention is needed, give it, but only long enough to get you going again. An exemplary lesson in the unimportance of the 'I'.

After a month of 'leafing' we moved to cutting the ripe golden barley in the fields. Squatting on our haunches, we moved ahead in crab-like fashion learning en-route how not to uproot the stalk nor saw at it with the sickle, but to cut it in one clean stroke. With such a stroke we preserved what nourished and ignored what didn't.

Interestingly this process applied not only to the harvesting of barley, which was comparatively easy, but also to the difficult process of our thoughts and emotions. We had to retain those thoughts and emotions that nourished and rid ourselves of mental waywardness and negativity. We had to control them by becoming aware of where they were going and then bringing them back, again and again, to a central focus.

Years later I was to look on this training as invaluable. It stopped the mind from being enticed endlessly by divergent distractions, bringing a greater focus and objectivity to what one was doing.

Ashishda had talked about plugging the leaks, so that the vessel of one's being could be filled with the rising waters of a higher awareness. Such an awareness, he said, can only be perceived when one is free of other preoccupations. Life in the Ashram forced us not only to accept that there were leaks, but also to become aware of our unregenerate personal sides. Any unchecked negative emotion, over-attention to food and clothes, or fussing over comforts and conveniences were among the inessentials.

Hunger at noon was a sharp, hollow cavity in the stomach, utterly ignored because there was no possibility of gratification in between. It occurred to me how much extra food I ate in the city because of its availability and due to the assault of sense-stroking advertisements at every corner. Now the food was wholesome, without tickling the palate. The clothes we wore were functional without a thought for fashion, cut or design. Gone were high heels or soft leather shoes. These were replaced by a pair of rubber slippers that were washed when they got dirty in the fields or the cowshed, and stood up against a wall to dry in the sun. When I cut Rajeev's hair for the first time it was a disaster. Two obstinate tufts stuck out on each side while the top of his head looked like a mowed lawn. Only I noticed it, no one else gave it a second glance! Appearances, unless one grew wings or horns, rarely came in for comment.

After a day in the fields, we often threshed the barley, stopping only when the evening service bell rang. Our physical self moved on as though it had an independent locomotion. I remembered Ashishda's words that the body could go on day-in and day-out without any pampering. It did just that, and I watched its momentum with pleasure. As we began pouring the threshed barley into sacks, I looked at my browned and rough hands with gratitude. I thanked them for serving me well in this new experience.

One evening after threshing, I was sitting at home. I must have dozed off, for I suddenly found myself out of my body, standing out in the open, looking at the night sky studded with stars. It was exhilarating seeing the same stars one saw every night but free from the confines of the body. I drew back into my body as unexpectedly as I had left it. When I got up to make supper, I was utterly refreshed.

It was a new kind of exploration that the body appeared to be allowing me, perhaps out of its sheer tiredness. When I sat down to meditate, I found my thoughts were widely spaced, at times petering out completely. Without the demanding restlessness of the 'body-mind', an uncluttered space of clarity formed. It was as though by distancing myself from the tiredness of the body, I could discover a small space from which it was possible to watch my participation in all activities. One night I had a dream:

I am standing in the tea verandah and from the window I watch Persis in the garden, Don going down to the dairy and Rajeev scrubbing the temple utensils outside the kitchen.

When I spoke to Ashishda about the dream he said, 'You're watching from above, so to say. The residents working represent the various aspects of yourself, which you are observing. It seems to me that you are participating and observing. That's good. But the question is—can you rest more in the observer than the observed?'

Two nights later I had another dream. It was different in its outward symbols, but its theme was the same.

My mother and I are walking under her favourite umbrella. Unexpectedly a large bird comes and takes away the umbrella. I am standing and laughing while my mother looks very crossly at the bird who can be seen in the sky carrying away the umbrella.

My mother's umbrella had been lifted from my head. Yet I didn't seem unduly perturbed. I remembered her, looked forward to her letters and was awaiting her visit in late summer. However, there was a difference. My life here was so absorbing in its challenges that my former life seemed like a dream—a dream I looked upon fondly but without the sharp, defining lines of immediacy.

The immediacy was here and now. In watching Ashishda cut the first stalks of wheat, walk up to the temple and tie them to the pillars that supported the altar dome. His face was tender with love and his glance rested on everything without singling out anything as if to say, 'Not with pride do you survey the fields of your achievements, but offer it in love at the altar of service.' That was the tone with which he undertook all activities. We had a mysterious fascination for this man who, having outgrown many of the attitudes we still struggled with, worked alongside us.

What was deeply attractive to us was that Ashishda's was not some hallowed philosophy that remained only in the realm of abstract thought seeming to lead nowhere in particular. It was a philosophy that had to be practised and implemented in every act of the day and through the night. A practical spirituality that demanded constant attention. He believed there was something real to seek and that a definite path led to it. There was no segregation in which the inner was exalted and the outer ignored, or vice versa. In the unmistakable poise of his life he had found the equicentre that illumined both aspects.

He never sought disciples nor tried to convert anyone. For those who came to him, he gave his all. What hit home was the other-worldly light in his eyes when he said, 'You'll never be disappointed in what you find if you genuinely seek. Give your life to it, for there is really nothing else worth doing.'

It was to this light that I had bowed my head. He knows, I felt. What he knew, I couldn't say. I realised there must be other men, greater or lesser than him, other paths as valid as this one, but for me Ashishda's formulation was compelling.

Whatever little I had tried to make of Ashishda's teaching had, without doubt, made an immense difference to my life. When he had asked me to be kind to my own rejected self, something had grown out of that experience. He had urged me to find the 'still point' in meditation and I was quite startled when I chanced upon it. When he asked Rajeev and I to be like twin stars who moved around a common centre of gravity, he had bound us together beyond the egocentricities of the personality. Now he was putting us through hard physical work, owing to which sometimes I would glimpse a freedom that set limits on nothing. When he spoke of an unimaginable mystery, I trusted him to take us towards it, giving my silent consent to whatever price I had to pay for it.

The price was absolute submission to the guru. On the face of it, it was a dangerous doctrine, full of paradoxes. If you argue and question, you cannot learn. If you don't question you may reduce yourself to a brainwashed automaton. However, it became apparent that in the guru-disciple relationship, the submission is of a more complex nature. The disciple is seeking the highest Truth that only the guru can guide the disciple towards. In turn the guru expects total, unconditional surrender. The ego, with all its wants and desires, must be offered at the guru's feet so that it can be moulded in the image of the highest. Even though I could see how the ego's desires and fears held me captive, robbing me of inner equanimity, my mind still baulked at such a sacrifice.

The mundane repetitive tasks assigned to us caused, at times, bursts of resistance, flashes of anger and knife-edged tensions. Working with compost all day could, for example, set off an internal tirade that could spill over into an interactive situation. When difficult situations arose Ashishda used them to relate to his teachings. Whoever raised the issue with him was usually made to see his or her side of the problem.

'But what about the other person?' he was often asked.

'You deal with your bit. If you get free of it the other side will cease to matter.

'I'm not saying don't be aware of what the other is doing. But where should your main focus rest? On the other or on yourself? Your anger, your irritations tell you about yourself, not necessarily about the other person. Remember finally no emotion is positive or negative, you must learn to use both, as a charge, to delve deeper into yourself.'

Then there was Dave, the community's hair-shirt, who periodically stirred the cauldron. This time, it was when Mike and Promila took over the running of the temple vegetable garden. Although they were an ideal choice—Mike had taught at an agricultural university, and Promila had managed a half-acre campus garden, raising fruits, vegetables, rice and pulses—Dave, who had himself appointed them for the task in the first place, seemed to disapprove of their decisions most of the time.

Immediately after tea Mike and Promila used to leave the harvest fields to work on the temple garden.

One evening, Mike was carting the last of the wheelbarrows of manure from the cowshed to the temple garden, when Dave stopped him. 'You're using too many wheelbarrows of compost for the garden.'

'It's essential. Since we don't use fertilisers, we have to upgrade the soil constantly.'

'Tell that to your students! I've worked with this soil longer than you have. Restrict yourself to seventy-five wheelbarrows per year from now on,' Dave said, walking away.

A thoughtful Mike said later, 'I think I'll reduce the area under plantation so that the effect of the compost we are allowed to use is concentrated in one area at least. We can afford to cut down, since we're producing a surplus of vegetables.'

With growing disapproval Dave watched Mike reduce the cultivated area of the vegetable patch; he had spent years extending it. Things came to a head over a pile of cauliflower leaves that Mike had kept aside. In the evening Dave told the village men to feed the leaves to the cows.

The next evening a flushed Mike confronted Dave in the workshop. 'If you've left the garden to me, why do you interfere all the time?'

Dave scowled but did not reply. Shutting the workshop door in a flurry, with Rajeev trying to scramble out in case he got locked in, Dave walked to the temple and went straight to Ashishda's room.

At one level these were the pinpricks of community life

and at another level they were pointers to our attitudes. So often Ashishda had said, 'When you find someone else's attitude profoundly irritating, you're probably attributing to the other all the motives which belong to you. So often anger is a projection of one's own complexes onto another person.'

Maybe Mike asked himself, 'Why does Dave irritate me so much? Are Dave's high-handed ways a challenge to all that I have masked under a social veneer?'

What of Dave? Did he wonder why he reacted so often and so strongly to people? His bristling exterior possibly hid a vulnerability. This new community was both a challenge and a threat to him. He now had to work with people, a new experience for him altogether. Don's intellect struck Dave dumb, Mike's professional knowledge of cattle and farming made Dave argue without listening, John's design skills and perfect carpentry made him competitive. Unlike the others, Rajeev chose another way in his relationship with Dave. He handed Dave all the credit in most things, giving him the acknowledgement and the authority he craved for.

I asked Rajeev, 'Are you doing this from real regard or expediency?'

'I'm following Ashishda's cue. Maybe unconditional affection can disarm Dave much more than a pitched battle.'

Such an approach was totally uncharacteristic of Rajeev and I wondered how long he would sustain it.

I suspected Dave's problem with the men in the community had to do with the way he had viewed his father. He had perceived his father as unjust and harsh towards him. Having internalised that feeling, when he grew up he projected that hostility onto other men. The sense of helplessness he had felt, as a child, in front of an omnipotent father was now inverted in his drive to dominate the men he came into contact with. When he did that, he was, in effect, saying, 'Now do you realise what I felt with my father? In my making you feel helpless, I feel less vulnerable.'

When complaints about Dave reached Ashishda, he recounted the story of the pike in the pond. There was once a farmer who bred fish. Thinking he would increase the cultivation he removed all the predators from the pond. But just the opposite happened. The fish became fat, sluggish and non-productive. He then put a pike in the pond and soon all the fish were moving around energetically again.

'So consider Dave the pike in the pond,' Ashishda said.

I saw the point of the story, since routine can very soon turn into complacency and inattention. Pinpricks help one to think and correct one's course. They are a strong reminder to become more watchful, more aware of oneself. Soft words and gentle nudges rarely achieve this. But what, I wondered, happens to the pike himself? While he is cracking the whip at others, does he ever subject himself to it? This thought crossed my mind again a few days later when Dave announced to Rajeev, 'You move out of Pandekhola today.'

'Today…?' Rajeev was nonplussed.

'Why not? You're getting a bit too comfortable there. In any case we need the place. You move up to Bhagiya's.'

Slowly, bit-by-bit we carried our luggage uphill. Bhagiya's was one of the oldest Ashram cottages, consisting of one L-shaped room, attached to which was a small dark room divided into bathing and kitchen areas. The one tap there had to serve us for bathing and washing utensils. The wood placed on the rafters had rotted and threw down occasional clods of earth, along with a scorpion or two for variety. Of course, this only added to the delight of a constantly leaking roof in the monsoons and the gleeful whistle of wind through the cracked windowpanes in the cold weather.

Two days after shifting in, we woke up with our backs stiff as boards from the chill that had seeped in through the cold cement floor.

'I think I'm beginning to feel really sorry for myself,' I said to Rajeev.

'What for? You'll get used to this place.'

'Oh, yes? You leave when it's dark and come back when it's dark. You don't live with rats and lizards as I have to in that black hole where I wash the dishes.'

'What can I do?' Rajeev said wearily.

Immediately I felt contrite. 'Nothing much, I suppose,' I said in a subdued voice, 'except hear me out.'

I walked towards our one-table kitchen wondering what was bothering me. I believed I had put more effort into adjusting to this life than I had into anything else. Maybe I had expected a pat from Ashishda, a word of praise. Instead, he had moved us to Bhagiya's. However, if he were to see me now, he would be appalled that I had not learnt the elementary lesson of overcoming self-pity. Another kind of submission was required—to live a life in which the ego was hardly ever stroked. The ego was now a thing you had to deal with, as it surveyed its starvation with angry eyes.

For me, things went wrong in quick succession after our move to Bhagiya's. Two cows developed mastitis. Early morning milking, instead of being a one-and-a-half-hour task, stretched way past two hours. When we milked one of them, she thrashed around enraged by her discomfort. If we didn't milk her, the udder became engorged and even more painful. We started squeezing antibiotics into the infected teats and treated the udder with warm water fomentation. Recovery was slow and most of the milk had to be thrown away.

One afternoon Dave came to the cowshed while I was struggling with one of the cows and said, 'Ask Mike to milk her tonight.'

I passed on the instructions. Later I heard I had annoyed Mike.

'What do you mean?' I asked Dave.

'He felt you were abrupt and officious.'

'What?' I was startled, for I thought I had conveyed the message in a matter-of-fact tone.

'Ashishda also felt you could have handled it better,' Dave said.

That was the final rub. This was the limit! I fumed all the way home—is this an ashram or a concentration camp? Rajeev made clucking, soothing noises when I told him about it.

'You're sounding like a nursemaid to a cretin,' I said crossly.

I flopped down and shut my eyes. The only way I knew how to get my act together was to withdraw and still my thoughts.

Had I been so relieved to hand over the job of milking that I had ordered Mike, in dread of any resistance from him? Or had my tone held all the resentment of 'I'm glad someone else will know what it's like milking a battle tank with four legs!'

By the time I began making supper I was feeling better.

That evening I found myself sitting next to Mike. What may have passed off as an uneventful evening suddenly flamed into a riot of thoughts in my mind. Arguments and counter-arguments in my own defence shot through my mind like a volley of arrows. There was a break in the talk and when I looked up Ashishda was looking straight at me and frowning. Suddenly he said to me, 'Will you please put an end to your non-stop chatter.'

Since I had not spoken a word, I was stunned. There was absolute silence in the room. My magpie-like mind now seemed open for all to see. Shortly afterwards, Ashishda put an end to the session. Rajeev walked comfortingly close to me on our way home.

At that point in time I felt a total loss of autonomy. If even my unexpressed thoughts were audible to Ashishda, what personal space did I have left to call my own? Were my desires and emotions no longer mine to direct as I pleased? As I mulled over this, I realised that Ashishda had really helped me by cutting into the spiral of my thoughts. A new challenge seemed to be emerging. While we appeared to have very few choices within the normal, work-filled day, at another level we were making choices all the time. I realised that in every response was an element of personal choice. Ashishda had said that you cannot separate thought from action, as action followed from thought. If the thought was negative and unchecked it would lead to a circle of action and reaction that once set in motion, bound us.

In the days that followed I was left with no time to think over this as another emergency took precedence. The pine forests on many of the surrounding hillsides caught fire. The only method to deal with a spreading fire is to clear the surrounding area of dry pine needles, twigs and leaves. Occasionally a fire, if assisted by wind, can jump this 'fireline'. The last recourse then is to retreat to the ridge of the hill and send another fire downhill; and wait for fire to meet fire and extinguish each other. Ashishda grimly recounted how ten years ago a forest fire had raged and come to just below the cowshed. They had worked through the night beating the fire back with sacks, and luckily managed to extinguish it.

We watched with growing tension as tree after tree

burned. We kept two-hourly night watches to monitor the spread of the fire. One night, when Rajeev and I walked down at two o'clock in the morning, we no longer saw individual trees burning, but just an orange red glow silhouetting the night sky. Fortunately, the fire burnt itself out before it reached our hill. The hill opposite, bare and smouldering, bore wounds which showed when the fire's rage was spent. As I surveyed the damage I realised how quickly something which had taken years to grow, can be destroyed, just as Ashishda had warned that a single negative emotion can destroy the inner-effort.

<h1 style="text-align:center">16</h1>

Piggy Rides Do Not Get You Very Far

Six months had passed since we had moved to the Ashram. The days now had a peculiar quality about them. There was no energy left to feel sorry for myself, or angry about anything. However, something kept me going. I don't know what it was, but I sensed that it was apart from the 'I' that I knew. While tiredness can produce emotions like irritability, real fatigue, I discovered, quietens the normal reactive self.

One afternoon, while cutting the undergrowth near the temple bridge, some plant or insect disagreed with me. I broke into a rash. My legs and arms burnt and itched endlessly. After work I went home and had a bath. That aggravated the problem and the discomfort became unbearable. Rajeev put some lotion on the rash and gave me homoeopathic medicine, but the burning did not subside. It took two more days for the attack to abate, leaving me limp in its aftermath. In the days that followed, I had to fight a peculiar lassitude. I felt apathetic, and all I wanted was to succumb to sleep, and not wake up for a long, long time. I then had a dream:

It is night-time. I see a full moon reflected in a river. Ashishda is rowing a boat upstream and I am sitting beside him. The night is quiet except for the sound of the oars slicing through the water. Ashishda rows in silence for some time, then looks up and says, 'Can you see that bridge?'

I look ahead and see a bridge that loops across the water like a semi-circle. Ashishda says quietly, 'After we cross that bridge you will be able to see the Great Men.'

I am taken aback at the statement. As we approach the bridge, I see a figure on top of it, raising a hand in greeting towards us. The face is hidden in the shadows, but I feel an immense love and luminosity emanating from him.

Ashishda says, 'That's him, the Great One.'

We cross over and go and meet him at the foot of the bridge. His face is bathed with a white calm, and I, instinctively, bend to touch his feet. He takes me by the shoulders and smiles. In his love-filled eyes I see the wisdom of aeons.

He says softly, 'Hold onto that awareness. Pinpoint it within yourself. Don't let go, for the road you're travelling on leads to something real. Keep at it.'

He talks with urgency about the Path, about the need for effort and the vicissitudes along the way. I feel mesmerised by his presence. Ashishda stands quietly next to me, listening with absorption.

When I awoke, I wished I could have remembered all his words. Yet more overwhelming than the words was his presence. Who was this man who had been following my struggle all the way? Where did this shimmering luminosity come from? A luminosity that had nothing to do with face or features. His voice had washed over me with a compelling intensity born of love. The dream had a transparency about it, like a film of light. Yet it was more real than reality itself. So human was that contact that I felt blessed by something otherworldly on that strange, mysterious moonlit night.

Later that morning I sought a private session with Ashishda. Before I even sat down he said, 'Something has happened, has it not?'

I recounted the dream to him. His face came alive, his eyes glowed. There was silence as he continued to look at me. Ashishda broke the silence quoting from the Victorian poet, Arthur Hugh Clough:

> Say not the struggle naught availeth,
> The labour and the wounds are vain.
> The enemy faints not, nor faileth,
> And as things have been, things remain.

And in that moment everything seemed worthwhile.

We were quiet again for a while, and then Ashishda interpreted the dream, 'Rowing upstream, means keeping the struggle alive. These Great Beings visit us sometimes, when we least expect them to, as though responding to the small core of sincerity in our strivings. At other times they grace our lives to encourage and reinforce our efforts. So, hold on, as you have been told.'

Some experiences leave indelible imprints on the psyche, as though they are meant to be the needles with which we knit together our life's perceptions. For me, that night was one such encounter. A sense of well-being followed. For days I was puzzled about the whats and hows of the dream. However, I did not think this was a psychological dream with the images as symbols that need to be interpreted in ways other than how they appeared in the dream. I was convinced I had actually met this man on the bridge and the impact of that encounter made a lasting impression on me. His words of advice kept coming back, 'Hold onto that awareness'. This new awareness seemed to be of a different order.

The teaching imparted in the dream lent a new impetus to the practices I was following, raising them above the status of learned techniques. And with those words had come the quiet, firm reassurance that this Path did, indeed, lead somewhere. I felt a strength of conviction build up inside, and suddenly the Path became synonymous with a single luminous feeling—love.

The next afternoon, as I was going down to the fields, I saw Ashishda standing outside the kitchen. He seemed absorbed in some work, so my natural reticence took over and I passed him by. At that moment, without looking up, he called out, 'Come here.'

I went over to him. He smiled at me and then took my hands and looked at them. Taking out a bottle he said, 'This is a mixture of beeswax and vaseline. It's good for cracked skin.'

He gently rubbed some of the mixture into my fingertips. I felt my body relax with the warmth of the gesture. I hummed all the way down to the fields.

Inwardly I knew I was changing. I now understood better why Ashishda had stressed that 'service with love' is the Path. In my dream Ashishda had taken me to meet a man who was the embodiment of Love itself. Love that gave without any self-consciousness. Just love. So large and all-encompassing, that it flowed naturally into everything. So huge that it took my breath away.

I searched for a connection between that love, emanating from a man bathed in moonlit calm, and the world I saw when I opened my eyes. The dream altered my vision of everyday reality. It now seemed immersed in this light of love.

This light was there in the wee hours of the morning

when we helped deliver a calf. How soft were its eyes, innocent and startled in the first glare of birth. One dusty light hung from the darkened beams of the cowshed, swinging in the wind; inside, the cows chewed their cud, snorting an occasional welcome to the newborn. The mother licked her calf with vigorous, enthusiastic strokes while Dave completed the drying by rubbing the calf with a sack. The calf-heifer suddenly began to thrash around in an attempt to stand. Dave held her up but in a minute she collapsed in a jumble of legs. Outside the rain and wind serenaded this coming of life.

Something in the sight of this newborn calf, wet and trembling, evoked a rush of reverence in me. I saw it as undefiled; in its eyes I read a memory of its true beginnings.

The next morning the calf was put out in the sun and she stood uncertainly in front of the garage. She flicked her tail and her rickety legs tried to follow Lama, the cowshed dog. Only a few weeks ago Lama had startled me when one night on opening the door I had found him lying in the bullock's stall with his head on his paws. The one-ton-plus bullock was licking Lama's back with slow, friendly strokes. Lama's eyes were drugged with the pleasure of being massaged. The bullock, who with just one hoof could snap Lama into two, was bending over him with the tenderness of a soul-mate. As I fed the cows their silage the heat of their bodies enclosed me in a sense of well-being.

I asked myself: aren't these also expressions of the love I had beheld that night? Doesn't reality reflect merely the state of our minds? How else could I explain my going into a rigorous maize harvest in September with such ease in my steps?

We hacked at the tall maize plants, placed them in neat bundles and carried them on our backs. From the lowest fields we walked up in single file with the green leaves of the maize trailing behind like peacock tails, unloading them with a swish on the threshing floor. At tea time we cooled our backs by resting them on the huge maize piles until Don would chirp, 'All those who cannot walk to their posts are permitted to crawl!'

At half-past-three the chaff cutter would start and we hurried to take our positions next to it. Ashishda or Dave with two other men pushed the maize plants through the rollers of the chaff cutter. Rajeev and John walked briskly back and forth from the threshing floor, carrying the next armful ready for chopping. Don and Mike vigorously forked the straw into the heap of chopped maize and then shovelled the mixture into the baskets. Parveen bent down to lift the full baskets onto our heads. With the hill woman's characteristic hip-swing, we walked up the rickety wooden staircase which led to the four silos, and in we dropped our load, returning from the other side to continue the relay system. After fifteen days of carrying headloads of maize I couldn't comb my hair. A small lump had developed in the centre of my head where the basket had cut in.

I saw Persis tap Parveen on the shoulder and say, 'If your shoulder is hurting, I'll do today's night watch for you.' Another cow was calving and we took turns to check in on her at night. The extra duty meant that Persis would hardly get any sleep. There was something about a community effort that made one's own workload feel like a just contribution.

Care and concern were present in so many unexpected ways. It was there in the face of Tilu, the villager who had worked in the Ashram since he was a boy. Now he was the foreman, his beard liberally sprinkled with grey. His gentle eyes looked sorrowfully at Rajeev as he said, 'I hear your mother is not well.'

'Yes, Tilu, she's got cancer,' Rajeev said.

'What does the doctor say?'

'It doesn't look good. We went down to Delhi for a week to see her. It was difficult.'

Tilu stood looking down at the ground, nodding his head in sympathy. Finally, he said, 'Like me you've given your life to the temple. Your strength will come from there.'

They walked alongside, hands behind their backs, keeping perfect step. How come Rajeev's youthful, impatient ones matched so well with Tilu's more sedate steps, born from the wisdom of accepting the inevitability of suffering?

I saw care in Ashishda's eyes as he looked at John's bent head in the evening session. John had hit a low and was trying hard to cope. Ashishda continued to talk, but ever so often his eyes kept coming back to John who had hardly spoken in the last four days. Ashishda's eyes seemed to say, 'You're not alone. I walk with you whether you know it or not.'

If I could sense Ashishda's silent reassurance reach out to John, it was because I had been made aware of such a support through my dream. Perhaps it was from the time of my last dream that something began to loosen up for me. My hold on my fears, anxieties and hopes seemed to slacken as I realised how illusionary these preoccupations are.

When Dave was going through a particularly difficult patch, he had gone to Ashishda and told him, 'I don't think I can do the morning service any more. My thoughts are so negative that it would be an abuse of the privilege given to me.'

Ashishda had said to him, 'Why do you think you need to offer only the best to "Them"? Offer "Them" your hurts, anger and doubts. Since they are also a part of you, "They'll" accept them.'

One day during the maize harvest I looked up and found to my dismay that Promila had fainted with fatigue. Around the same time Don, who was pushing sixty, had been protesting, not to the participation in the work but to the volume of it. He seemed to be asking for an acceptance of limitations that age imposed on him.

In fact, we were all being pushed to the brink of our physical capacities. And though we empathised when it appeared one of us had been pushed too far, we did not protest but maintained our silence. This was a grey and confusing area, one that was a source of many a doubt. Did unquestioning belief command such a silence? Was this strenuous and demanding work to be accepted, irrespective of personal limitations of age and capacity?

One autumn morning, when I was about to wake up I heard the words:

'There is a glow behind physical work—find it.'

I had lain in bed strangely charged by the thought. In pushing my body to its limit I had once crossed a threshold and had an experience which stands apart. I had had my dream of a Great Presence on a night when my body seemed to have been anaesthetised by fatigue. Now this new dream left me with a cryptic statement that there is a glow that can be found through physical work. Obliquely it suggested that the physical trials we were undergoing at the Ashram were important to the ultimate goal we sought.

I asked Rajeev, 'I wonder what or where this Path we are treading leads to?'

'If I knew I wouldn't be here.'

'Still, you must have some image or some thought in your mind?'

'Probably, to the source from which all life emerges. All of life comes from somewhere. But from where?'

A few evenings later Don asked Ashishda, 'What is the final attainment of the mystic? What does he "see"—a vision; a revelation; a light, or...what?'

I sat up straight. Others shifted on their mats, watching Ashishda with interest. Usually, we would be wise not to plunge headlong into a question of this nature, unless we wanted only a few grunts from Ashishda. He was mercurial in this respect. He would put himself out to explain the mystical significance of the number seven one day, and then a week later he would react with total blankness when someone else asked the same question.

Ashishda plunged into the answer straight off. 'What you have to appreciate is that your conditioning dictates what you see. The Hindus find their Vaikunt, the Muslims their Jannat and the Christians, Heaven. The inner worlds are plastic and reveal themselves in the form you expect them.

'Take, for example, the after-death state. What we see there has a lot to do with our cultural or religious bent. I knew a dear old Bengali lady who had been ailing for some time and died at the age of ninety-six. A few days before her death, she sat up and in a moment of great lucidity pronounced that her husband had come the previous night and had taken her to see the house they would stay in after her death. Her description fitted the archetypal Bengali village, complete with the pond and well-fed cows grazing peacefully around it. The house she described was a traditional Bengal mud hut with a thatched roof. She seemed very content when she died.'

'And I suppose had she been a Christian, she would've seen a different setting?' Don asked.

'Possibly. The religion of your upbringing does tend to colour your scenario.'

'Does this apply to what you see when you finally attain?' Don asked, adding, 'This isn't very encouraging, is it? You first spend your life searching for something, and then on finding it one would not know how much was subjective and how much was objectively true.'

'That's the point,' Ashishda swooped down swiftly on Don's thought. 'Do you want to see Reality as it is or as you expect it to be?'

'Obviously as it is. But how does one know the difference?'

'By constantly watching and knowing the difference between your wants, desires, hopes, and the essential You.'

'Suppose someone is successful in distancing themselves from pre-conditioned images. What would they find eventually?' Don asked.

'There is no standard mystical experience which I can describe. But in essence it is that you, as you know yourself, do not exist as you merge into the Universal Consciousness. There is no I and no you. No this, no that; no here, no there; no now, no then. There is no one to know and nothing to be known. There is no distinction of any kind. All is One. It is just a state of utter incandescent unity.'

'This experience...how does it happen?' Persis asked.

'How or when you arrive at that realisation is totally unexpected. What is important is the constant questioning. What is the source of my awareness? What is the ground of Being? What is this mystery? This sort of questioning should be going on at the back of your mind all the time, whether you are eating, milking, digging or meditating.

'No doubt, this questioning cannot be turned on to order. It is something that must genuinely perplex you, consume you. When the effort is sincere, the experience will one day just happen. This may happen in meditation, or while you're sitting, or raking the muck from the cow stalls, or anywhere.'

'Is that experience the end of the road?' Mike asked.

'I'm afraid not,' Ashishda smiled ruefully.

'What remains to be done?' Don asked.

'The work never ends. You've experienced something enormous. The question is—can you live up to it and integrate it into your ordinary life? It is one thing to have this experience in an altered state and quite another matter to live by it for the rest of your life. For, remember, when you come out of that experience all your desires, compulsions and hang-ups don't automatically vanish. You have to work at them by being ruthlessly honest in trying to bridge the gap between what you've seen and what you are. Seeing the unitive vision is only the halfway point. Being like it all the time is the other half.'

'Is there any other way of experiencing this unity? Can someone else induce a state in you to bring this experience on?' John asked.

'You mean a short-cut? Why take the trouble to quieten your mind, why look at your motives? Why be consumed by an enquiry and a search which takes long years to produce answers?' Ashishda retorted with fire in his eyes.

'What's wrong in at least knowing for a fact that this state exists? Isn't that better than merely speculating on it?' Don countered.

'Gopalda told me that once Ma (Gopalda's guru) induced a state similar to what she had experienced in one of her disciples. She did it without drugs, for she had that kind of power. After the experience was over this person said, "That was interesting. How did you manage it? Hypnosis?"

'Two things become apparent from this. What for Ma was the culmination of her search, when given to someone, who had not quested for it, amounted to nothing. Whereas, if it comes after a long struggle, then this experience puts a final seal to your years of faith and enquiry.'

'And the second thing, Ashishda?' Persis asked.

'You cannot be carried on somebody else's shoulders. The mists that shroud the mystery don't melt and yield their treasure to you on the strength of another's striving. This search is your own and you have to carve a way out of the labyrinth by yourself. Piggy-back rides don't get you very far.'

17

Dark Clouds

Towards the end of the year, when the fields were being tilled for sowing barley and wheat, a dream alerted us to an impending death:

> *Uma, Rajeev's mother, comes to me and taps me on the shoulder. I ask her, 'Ma, how are you?'*
>
> *She says, 'I just came to say good-bye.'*
>
> *I see her wearing a white saree, walking into a dark tunnel, and I know I cannot follow her.*

I woke up feeling very uneasy.

Uma's last letter to us had been short and cheerful. She was undergoing chemotherapy for lung cancer and the doctors were hopeful because a few patches in the lungs had cleared. She was coming to the Ashram the following week.

When I mentioned the dream to Ashishda he said, 'A tunnel in this context may symbolise the passage between life and death.'

A week later my brother-in-law came up with the message that Uma had been getting persistent headaches, and a CT scan had revealed thirty malignant tumours in the brain. In a state of shock we went down to Delhi. She was just coming out of a two-day coma. A month and a half later, one February evening, surrounded by her family she died. For a while no one moved in the room. In a hoarse voice Uma's eighty-five-year-old mother said, 'Open the window. Let the soul go out.'

Unwittingly our eyes turned to the window; why did the room feel as though everyone present was momentarily being allowed a glimpse of a gate opening? It was dusk, and when I looked up I saw Rajeev's eyes, dark with pain. It was a very difficult time for him. The death of a parent marks the final severing of the symbolic umbilical cord that connects a child to its parent even through adulthood. A separate existence, physical distances and independent lifestyles do not undo that essential bonding. Only death brings it about.

A very subdued Rajeev returned to the Ashram at the end of February. A definite tension was growing in the community. The issue was work and the heavy silence seemed the breeding ground. The older community members were finding the workload too much to shoulder, and had pulled out of many activities. This meant more load on the younger lot.

Mike had developed a bad back while Promila's blood pressure had shot up. Don and Parveen had withdrawn in the middle of the last maize harvest because they felt they were too tired even to walk home. Fatigue was writ large on everyone's face. The impasse continued, as though no one could afford to understand the other's point of view. If we attempted to, we would in turn forfeit relief for ourselves. If the older members realised how pushed the younger ones were they would feel obliged to help. If the younger members appreciated that Mike and Don had walked alongside all the way, but had now reached the end of their tether, they would have to accept the increased workload for good. Dark clouds of resentment were gathering over the community.

Some of the younger members discussed the problem with Ashishda. There were three kinds of work involved. First, looking after the temple, the Ashram kitchen, the visitors' accommodation; then the cowshed, the dairy and its products; and finally the work in the fields. And, of course, there was one's own cottage and garden to tend. 'We cannot manage all this on our own without the full help of the community,' the younger members complained.

'Why not ask the senior members how they might help?' Ashishda said.

When they were asked they politely refused. An uneasy limbo ensued. Then Chitra decided to take the initiative and called for a conclave. The community was to meet in the Library, but not for the usual evening session. Ashishda was not going to be present and neither was Dave, but then Dave hardly ever attended the evening sessions.

The smiles were strained as the community gathered that evening. Chitra sat in Ashishda's usual place. She cleared her throat and said, 'I think we should talk of this uneven distribution of work which has crept up on us in the last four or five months.'

A year had passed since our arrival and this was the first crisis we were involved in. In our day-to-day relationships most of us did not feel the disparity in age. There was a sense of equality in which no one pulled rank, yet there was an age spread of thirty-five years in the group that was gathered in the Library. Don and Mike were well past their mid-fifties, Parveen and Promila were over fifty, John and Persis were in their early forties, Rajeev was in his early thirties, I was in my late twenties while Chitra was twenty-three, with a seventeen-year age gap between her and Dave. Not attending the meeting was Savitri, truly the senior citizen at seventy-five, and, of course, Ashishda who was sixty-five.

In a cool tone Don began, 'I'll speak for Parveen and myself. We're finding the farm work next to impossible to cope with. We're just not in a position to take on any more.'

'It's not that we are expecting you to do an equal amount of physical work—but just give us a helping hand when we're rushed off our feet,' Rajeev said.

'I don't think you understand. Life at sixty is very different from life in one's thirties,' Don replied. 'Parveen and I find doing all the housework takes the stuffing out of us, and we're struggling to keep abreast with our temple duties.'

'Then how do people of your age manage in the West?' Chitra asked excitedly.

'I knew you'd say that.' Don grimaced. 'Do appreciate there are a lot of labour-saving devices and gadgets in the West. That's hardly the position here. We are out in the sticks with conditions that are pretty primitive. In the West, you turn on a tap and you don't have to worry whether it is drinking water or bathing water, for both meet WHO standards. Here, every morning, I have to hand pump our bathing water to the overhead tank to get some in the tap. And you know that we who live the furthest have to lug our drinking water uphill in jerrycans all the way from the temple. Anyway, I am sure we haven't met this evening to compare and contrast our lifestyles with the West.'

'We all hand pump our water every day, Don,' Persis reminded gently.

'I'm not making out a case that my problems are greater than yours. All I'm saying is that I've reached the limit of my capacity. Parveen has spondylosis that gets inflamed with heavy work. And I still have to complete our cottage. The other day I counted to Parveen nineteen major projects still incomplete in the house.'

Don stopped speaking abruptly. 'Why am I telling you all this? You know it yourself. All I want to say is that after three hours of planing I'm just done in. I get so tired that I don't even have the energy to walk down for the evening sessions that I love.'

'Don aren't you being a bit selfish? All the work you off-load falls onto us. Do you realise I too go to sleep tired and wake up tired every morning? For the last three weeks I've not managed to reply to a single letter. I just don't have the time. Have you considered that?' Chitra said indignantly.

'Listen, I'm not being unsympathetic to all of you. Also, I'm not trying to hide behind my years. I admire the amount of work you all are doing. I wonder if I were thirty or forty, would I cope as well as you all are doing? But that doesn't get us very far in this argument.' Don fell silent for a moment, before continuing, 'I would like to raise a question: Isn't there more work than we can handle? Is all this farming really necessary? We have to accept that some of us are getting old and the rest aren't getting any younger! Sooner or later we will have to confront this question of the quantum of work and our capacity to do it.'

'Promila's position and mine are pretty similar to Don's,' Mike said. 'We just don't have the strength. Both of us have learnt that at the cost of our health. We are clear that we can't do more than what we already have on our plates.' His emphatic tone was out of character with his normally mild manner and disarmingly gentle smile.

'That would mean twenty years of Dave's effort gone to waste! He has toiled for so many years to develop the farm and now you say we should drop it,' Chitra said, appalled.

'I think we should remember that for Ashishda the farm serves as a demonstration project for the surrounding villagers. He is trying to encourage them to see how scientific farming can be applied to suit local conditions. So I don't see how the farm can be dropped.' Rajeev said spiritedly.

The temperature of the discussion was slowly beginning to rise. The customary symptoms were drearily manifesting themselves—no appreciation of the other's viewpoint or difficulties.

'My dear Rajeev! I know all that. I do the work because Ashishda asked me to, and I'll always honour whatever he says,' Don reacted to Rajeev's reference to Ashishda.

Don was now resorting to his characteristic gesture of patting down the sparse hair on his head, an obvious self-calming gesture. He picked up the conversation in his normal manner—cool, rational and objective, 'Why don't we employ a few more men to ease the workload? We can all contribute to the extra expense.'

'Dave won't even think of it. That's out, Don!' Chitra declared.

'We seem to have drawn a magic circle of what we can do and what we can't,' Don retorted. 'All right, let's explore the possibility of giving jobs which don't involve physical exertion to those who are getting on in years. I go every morning to muck out the cow stalls. Instead, I could very easily take the men's attendance in the morning, or I could write the temple account books.'

Chitra, who maintained the accounts, suddenly bristled and said, 'The accounts are not just accounts. They are temple accounts.'

'Also we have to consider that often one couple is not in the Ashram. Then there is a mad scramble for the others to cope with a double shift,' Mike said.

'Instead of getting negative, we must remember why we are here. We are here to serve and obey,' Chitra's voice rose an octave as she ignored Mike's last remark. 'We mustn't resent the work we are given and neither can we refuse to do it. We've got to control our minds. We have to offer the work we do to the temple...'

'Let's go, Parveen,' Don stood up and began collecting his pipe and tobacco. 'I refuse to sit here and listen to this simple-minded account of religious doctrine.'

'Please don't go, Don,' Persis was quick to say. 'If this talk is upsetting you, then I'm genuinely sorry. One person's difficulties affect us all.'

Don sat down. Gone was his cool manner; emotion was choking his throat. 'Yes, we are all interdependent. In a community someone may be dragging their feet over physical work, but how do you know he is not trying to compensate in other areas? What would you say...'

Parveen cut him short pleading agitatedly, 'No! Don, don't! You promised you wouldn't say it. Please...'

'I have to Parveen,' Don said with head bent. 'We have no access to any market to buy vegetables. We are all dependent on the temple garden for our needs. I admit Parveen is a slow worker in the vegetable patch. All of you have been getting vegetables regularly, but for the last few months we haven't received any vegetables. On Dave's instructions Chitra has stopped giving us vegetables. Why? Because Parveen is dragging her feet.'

There was a stunned silence. The disclosure came as a hammer blow. We all knew that the land around Don and Parveen's cottage wasn't fertile. Only during the monsoon, maize was grown in those fields, as fodder, and the crop was usually pitiful. To grow vegetables there, without fertilisers and farmyard manure, would daunt anyone save the most determined farmer.

'And what do you think I'm supposed to feel when I see, a few days later, a full basket of overgrown cauliflowers being fed to the cows? They were the surplus from the vegetable garden that had gone over because there were no human takers.'

The silence became louder.

Finally, Persis asked, 'Don, have you told Ashishda all this?'

'Yes.'

'What did he say?'

'He didn't know about it. He said he'd find out from Dave.'

In shocked silence the meeting broke up. My head was pounding, my thoughts bewildered. How come none of us had been aware of this discrimination? We all worked together, and were such a small group that it should have come to our notice much earlier. Had we become so blind, turned so stone-like that we were letting things just slide by? Was this treatment intended to show Don and Parveen something that mere words could not, or was this just another exemplar of Dave's high-handedness?

And how could we absolve ourselves? Had we not questioned because we were afraid of the consequences? Questioning meant sticking one's neck out and paying the price for it. The price was Dave's anger at being crossed. Had it blurred our attitude towards justice and injustice?

It became apparent at the meeting that there were many more issues to be tackled than just those related to work. They concerned the philosophical tenets that guided this community. If discrimination was unjust and we did not speak up against it, was it because we believed that trials were part of our learning? We were constantly reminding ourselves that we had to get beyond our egos. By this logic wounded pride or a sense of injustice were opportunities for growth. Be watchful, be aware of these feelings—Ashishda had cautioned us.

Yet an instinctive voice warned me that there is a fine line between a dangerous path and one that can take you all the way. In submitting to the Path it was important to ensure one's inner voice was not snuffed out.

Next evening we had a hurried supper and left for the Library a few minutes earlier than usual. There was an urgency in the smudged darkness. As we neared the Library half a dozen torches were approaching. They seemed to be hurrying too. The tension was not only within us.

The light in the Library was already on. I wondered who all were sitting upstairs. We climbed the stairs to find Ashishda sitting by the lamp, with his palm on his forehead and elbow resting on folded knee. His eyes were intense as they looked at a point in front of him and there was a peculiar stillness in his bearing. We went and sat down in our usual places and soon the others came in quietly.

'This afternoon, my attention was drawn to a passage in this book,' Ashishda opened a black hardbound book lying beside him. He read to us about an esoteric group in which resentments and anger had become rampant. The teacher had warned the group that if this persisted he would dissolve the community and discontinue all teaching.

A chill ran down my back at what Ashishda was implying. If we could not get our act together he was not interested in continuing with us. Only a year had passed since this community had been formed and it was already in danger of dissolution.

'Problems and difficulties are always there. If it's not one difficulty it will be another. I'm not here to adjudicate on your problems since I don't see myself as a father figure. You must think on your own and decide what you want to do,' Ashishda said in a voice that was holding emotion in check. 'I'm not suggesting that you suppress all your uncertainties and doubts. Nor am I saying that professing to have faith is enough. Learn to live with these doubts, learn to use them as things that drive you to seek something beyond them. What you have to see is that these emotions have built up a charge, a heightened point of focus. Transmute this energy that has been generated, and rise above the personal situation. Only when you do that will you see what lies beyond yourself.'

He then talked of the work we had to do, the practices we had to follow. 'Instead of uncertainty and doubt being a hindrance, they can be a spur for you to vitalise your search. Bickering or negative feelings are a vortex; they dissipate this charge and lead you to the lowest depths of behaviour.'

Ashishda grew silent. He closed his eyes, and we all sat in quiet contemplation. After a while he opened his eyes and looked around the room, his gaze pausing fleetingly on each one of us.

'The choice is yours.'

Ashishda's talk left us holding onto a new dimension. He was suggesting that in being pulled apart by diametrically opposite tensions lay the ground for transformation. While he had not condoned Dave's conduct, he had drawn our attention to the manner in which Don and Parveen, and the rest of us, could transmute the experience, the tensions and use the heightened charge thus generated to go beyond ourselves.

As always Ashishda brought our focus of attention back to the work we had to do on ourselves. It was much later that I began to understand the full implications of the ideas Ashishda had introduced to us that day. While I had earlier believed that an acceptance of suffering was an important aspect of his philosophy, I now realised that in itself suffering does not guarantee transformation. It comes about only if we can stand back from our experience, view it as something apart from ourselves and so rise above our personal anguish.

Don and Parveen faced a bewildering dilemma. Their suffering was born out of the circumstances confronting them. On the one hand, they perceived that an injustice had been done to them. On the other hand, their yearning needed the guidance and direction that only Ashishda could give, and which they were unwilling to sacrifice. It seemed, Ashishda was saying that when challenged with an essential dilemma, where either option is untenable, it can lead to a deeper questioning—What is this all about?

In searching for answers we may go past personal hurts and hopes, beyond the apparent dynamics of the current situation to the most basic question—What is the purpose of our lives?

This kind of questioning if stemming from intellectual curiosity may lead to philosophising, but if it arose out of an existential angst it could lead to transpersonal Truths. Maybe that is what suffering is meant to do. Is that what Ashishda meant by holding and transforming one's tensions, hold...hold...hold till they yield to an altogether different state?

A quiet descended on the community. The tension was silently diffused as word went around that Don and Parveen were receiving their share of vegetables.

Ashishda watched, alert and expectant, as though waiting for something. Realising the critical phase we were going through, he appeared poised to move in, in case the need arose. Go on, he seemed to be saying, for I promise you, one day the road will clear.

18

Intensification

Don and Mike put aside their difficulties and quietly resumed work. Although life returned to its original pattern, the tone was different this time round. The initial spirited enthusiasm had been replaced by a quietude. Work went on as before but our emotions had settled into an even keel. This reduced the extent to which we felt burnt out because we were not expending energy in uneven bursts.

I think Ashishda wanted much more from the situation. He did not want to see a quiet passivity in us. He wanted us to understand the aim towards which he was pushing us. 'In a fire, each stick may burn well individually, but unless the sticks are brought together in a particular formation, you can't have a fire that roars. Each stick is a discipline, and together they make up the fire. Scattered they burn out, put together they create a blaze.'

Summer came dry-eyed, but was soon transformed by early monsoonal outbursts. Often the moonbeams on those wet misty nights were like whey dropping from the trees. Was it the moon or the mist which conjured up phantoms that swayed to the moan of nocturnal winds? Through our windows we could see lightning scissor the night-sky continuously. Its eerie blue-white glare often kept us awake.

Months passed, Ashishda spoke increasingly of keeping alive the intent with which we had come here, encouraging us to try and reach another octave of understanding.

'Hold that awareness,' Ashishda urged, cupping his hands together as though protecting something precious, 'cleave to it in ever increasing urgency. It is not a question of roaming around with pious, spiritual expressions, but of slowly transforming an inner intent into a state of mind and heart in which everything resonates from that sense of centeredness. This state of expectancy, the longing to be completely drawn within the centre of your being is like leaning on a closed door with your full weight, so that when it opens you fall in.'

Did this 'centeredness' come from identifying with the observer? Ashishda had often said that the inner journey is a process to try to 'awaken' to the observer, its discipline and its practises, an attempt to identify and remove all that blocks the path. In the rush of everyday life how was I to become the observer? It eluded me as my mind was lost in the incessant movement ahead, in my concerns, in what I had to do next, my feelings about it and the whirr of thoughts that were fully invested in them.

As Ashishda had said, the 'observing I' watches the 'participating I' and thereby helps centre the seeker beyond their personality. In these efforts meditation would become the chief tool to identify that which observes. The mirror of dream would unravel the complexities of the emotional nature to reveal the identifications that stop the observing process.

With renewed effort at the practices I realised whenever I became aware of what I was thinking, my thoughts were often rather fretful and childish. But by a few simple tricks of observation, I could see the kind of thoughts that were distorting and limiting my perceptions.

Deliberately and consciously, I tried to broaden and deepen the field of awareness to enable a new kind of experience to emerge beyond 'blind thinking.' Repeatedly I reminded myself that the world is not what we see, but how we see it. I realised that even with a fleeting awareness and focus on my habitual beliefs, my usual filter for perceiving led to the awareness of my mind and its vagaries. However, another step was needed to be taken beyond this. For although I might be conscious of my thoughts, I was yet to become aware of myself as being conscious. And when that happens the restlessness of the mind quietens and slowly the involuntary flow of thoughts and associations become distanced. They are still there but you are not them. Like watching your life play out on a screen. This process produced those rare moments when I became aware of myself. Then I was neither running ahead nor lagging behind, but just standing there present to myself and to something 'other'. I realised the very act of observation alters that which is observed.

In every age we try with almost bare hands to excavate the cryptic messages of Eternity. What vanity had gripped me to believe it was possible at all? But for the constant affirmation I received from my teacher, all my efforts may have been diluted with doubts.

I found that if I strove in order to achieve something I ended up confused. The right state seemed a selfless one in which the person was not there, as he or she ordinarily knew himself or herself to be. It was a state akin to melting wax, on which Divinity could leave its fingerprints.

They were days of simply living and soaking up ideas that pulled at my heartstrings. I was caught in the ambience of a strange pulsating power that called for greater commitment to its cause. The teaching itself became an elastic band that stretched and tightened to fit the entire range of our experiences.

'How many hours of sleep do you think you actually need?' Ashishda asked us one evening.

The answers ranged from six to eight.

'Nonsense!' he said, 'Five hours is all that the body requires to refresh itself.'

'But sometimes it is difficult to get up after a tiring day with only five hours of sleep,' was the complaint.

'That is because you aim for total oblivion when you sleep,' he said sharply. 'Making that small effort before going to sleep is important. Still your mind and hold that centeredness. This doesn't mean fighting sleep, but slipping into it, "wakefully". If you did this every night, then sleep would not be an eight-hour opium that you can't do without.'

Rivulets of feelings were collecting, rippling, rushing past me in an ever-increasing current. I felt as though I was throwing off an anchorage. This is hard to describe; individual events would tell only part of the story. For instance, when I was asked to cook in the temple, my task became part of a meaningful practice. The temple and its kitchen had an aura of serenity that enveloped you as soon as you set foot inside. I was not the only one who felt transformed in that atmosphere. Work in the kitchen was guided by Ashishda's instruction: cooking the meal should be an offering, and a feeling of reverence should accompany everything you do. All of us tried to hold to this while cooking and looked forward to the ritual offering that preceded the midday service. The person entrusted with the cooking was left to set out a thali of freshly prepared food, and sit in meditative silence for a few minutes while 'They' were invited to partake of the offerings. I was conscious of the fact that Ashishda not only ate the meal but seemed to imbibe the whole atmosphere that surrounded its preparation. The flow of feelings began to come naturally and with it a sense of moving in the right direction. Somewhere there was a feeling of repose.

One night after supper was over, I found myself alone with Ashishda. We sat quietly for some time before he broke the silence. 'What are you thinking?'

'Just sitting, Ashishda, hardly thinking,' I said.

He smiled with so much sweetness that I was moved. A few moments later, he closed his eyes and seemed to withdraw, though the smile still lingered on his lips. I watched him for a while, then I got up and quietly left the room.

Then there was the sheer pleasure of being taught the temple service. Rarefied by years of devotion, there was potency in the atmosphere of the inner sanctum. The heavy brass hand-bell, the conch full of water, the big copper-spout, the ochre cloth and the oil-laden brass-lamps were rich with symbolism. One monsoon evening, I opened the temple door and the mist floated in with its gentle balmy spray. In that moment, reality blurred as every sharp outline disappeared. In the inner temple the gauzy mist swirled its skirts in a diaphanous display. The dispersed light from the lamps seemed to spread its fingers in columns of cloudy gold. All these were part of the mischief of that night so that, if I looked from the corner of my eye, I saw life dance but if I stared directly, I lost view of it.

Another evening, after preparing for the temple service, I sat for some time in meditative quiet. Temporarily I lost cognisance of myself, and I saw Thakur (Lord Krishna) step out from the Image on the altar in the form of a golden outline. The outline changed into a ray of thick golden light that poured towards the centre of the temple sanctum. Suddenly the whole temple seemed alight in this golden hue. When I surfaced, I looked at the Images. Outwardly everything was the same as before.

Later I went to Ashishda and told him what I had seen. 'But I don't understand what it means.'

'You are being shown that the Images are only a symbol. The Truth behind the symbols is so profound, so majestic that it can hardly be encompassed within the symbol itself. So, through the form seek the Formless.

'Very early in my stay here, I was given an overwhelming vision of Radha-Krishna, shining in all their glory, but appearing much younger. Since my way of life was conjoined to the temple, I had seen "Them" as I saw the Images in the temple. Within a few days I was shown that this was the view of an immature boy. I understood that this early vision was asking me, who is Krishna? It was urging me to transcend a specific religious symbol and see the non-sectarian Truth behind it.'

He fell silent, withdrawing into himself, before he reflected about what I had seen. 'When Thakur appears in a golden outline and slowly dissolves into a beam of light, this is a way of telling you that the Truth itself is beyond form, even though, initially, we have to seek it through concrete symbols and defined shapes.'

'It was totally unexpected,' I said.

'That is how these things usually happen. But remember what you saw was given to you. It was an act of Grace; you had nothing to do with it.'

Suddenly the temple, its Images, the ritual and worship

took on a different significance. Each lent a form to my strivings, creating something that could become the focus. I remembered Ashishda talking about Gopalda, who had inherited a tradition of ritualistic worship and strict Vaishnav do's and don'ts from his guru. But Gopalda, fifteen years after his guru's death, had radically simplified the ritualistic aspect. For he believed that the form of worship must change in accordance with the times. Ashishda had further simplified this aspect, but had retained a few symbolic observances, whose focus centred on the Images in the temple. Ashishda when once asked why he continued the ritual worship in the temple although he had seen the Truth behind the symbol had said, 'It helped me at a particular stage. Why dismantle it? Why not leave it intact as it may help to ferry someone else across the river of life.'

The experience remained with me as a constant reminder that this search for the Eternal Truth leads beyond all forms and images. However, the formless nature of the Truth necessitates its representation in concrete symbols. The Images help coalesce our aspirations. They may also become the focus of a Light that otherwise has no limit or location. Symbols can carry or aid up to a certain point; beyond that the attempt is to face the mystery naked— stripped of all embellishments.

PART THREE

The Inner Compass

19

The Egyptian Mystery

We watched the approach of the second winter of our stay at the Ashram with greater ease. Its silence was now familiar and the sharp sting in the air felt less like an assault and more like a reminder of the demarcating lines of the hill seasons. The trees seemed to change their colours into shades of frosty brown and the ground under one's feet felt, as though it was preparing to go to sleep. The sun shone, but it had icicles at its fingertips, which prodded the tawny grass at the edge of the fields into stiffening and straightening up. The local village women were clearing the estate of all the dry grass for winter fodder. The wind seemed to whistle through the wide gap in their tobacco-stained teeth as a handful of them moved over the hillsides holding fistfuls of dry grass in their hands, cutting it with swift, sharp strokes of their sickles.

At one end, was the withdrawal winter brings, and at the other, a growing sense of undefined anticipation. When Rajeev went for a dream session, out of the blue Ashishda said, 'There are changes ahead, big changes that'll affect everyone.'

In late winter Dave announced his decision to retire. He

wished to give up managing the farm and estate, and lead a different kind of life within the Ashram.

'What sort of life?' Rajeev asked him.

'For twenty years, it's been work, work and more work. First it was setting up the farm, then maintaining it.'

'What will you do?'

'All I ever wanted was to potter around in the flower garden and harvest honey from the bee boxes. You'll soon know what the pressures of running this estate are because I'm going to hand over the responsibility of the entire show to you,' Dave stated firmly.

'What...why? I didn't leave the factory to run the farm.'

'Who said you can get away from anything? You just meet it later, in another form.'

'What's making you do this?'

'I was so busy proving myself outwardly that I never paused to think much about other things.'

'Does withdrawing stop one wanting to prove oneself?'

'Why not? I'm willing to make the effort. I'm pulling my energies out of farm work and redirecting them elsewhere; to read, to meditate more.' Dave said with conviction.

Ashishda seemed very pleased about Dave's decision. 'I'd hoped you'd come to this. I'm waiting for the day when I can give you the robe.'

To me, it seemed that Ashishda was looking past the man standing before him to a Dave with shaven head, ochre robe and wooden sandals on whom he wanted to place the mantle of his successor. Next to him, Dave moved restlessly as though Ashishda's image of him in the robe of renunciation was an imposition.

What an austere and humbling ceremony it must be when with a rough ochre cloth on your back, the sanyasi is handed the begging bowl to roam the streets to beg for food! Gopalda had done this for many months at a stretch, after his guru had conferred the robe on him.

With such high standards to meet, it was no small wonder that Dave shied away from this ultimate responsibility. Yet, Dave made his own smaller changes to mark the end of one phase in his life. Chitra and he gave up their cottage and moved into a small sunless room next to Ashishda's in which the old styled window panes and floors were dark with age. This had been Dave's room before he was married, and Ashishda's when Gopalda was alive. Ashishda's present room was just ten steps away, but how many years of walking would it take Dave to get there?

When Dave walked into his room did he wonder what had made him give away most of his possessions, to bring only what could fit into the tiny cupboard in the room? It is possible that his eyes searched the room for memories he was trying to outgrow. If he looked out of the window on his left, he saw the Library where his parents had lived and died. Maybe he wanted to make his peace with that memory by surveying it from the vantage point of distance. For, although it was a small room, the view outside opened up to the temple garden, to the fields and the mountains beyond.

Dave's decision to withdraw set me thinking. When we had moved to the Ashram we were young, full of energy and had many expectations. We had pictured a life devoted to inner contemplation in the traditional sense, anticipating our spiritual lives would blossom quite automatically. Neither of these pre-conceived notions had any bearing to the life we were actually leading at the Ashram. It was quite clear by now that on this Path, progress may not be visible either to oneself or to others for a long time. All of us who had joined the Ashram had to reorient ourselves and in some sense, unlearn a great deal. If for most people professional competence, fame, or money are standards by which to measure success, none of these applied to us and we had to learn not to judge ourselves against them.

I remembered a dream I had had when I began milking the cows. Nandita, a school friend, had made two films which had made her internationally famous. In the dream Nandita is saying to me:

'See what I've done for myself while you remained in the Ashram.'

Ashishda laughed when I told him the dream. 'You poor thing. While you milk cows, Nandita gets all the awards. So tragic,' he mocked gently.

'You're really rubbing it in,' I said, embarrassed.

'The dream is asking "Will the awards be enough after a point. Will she not ask the same question years later—Was this what I really wanted? Was it enough?" You're asking these questions now. What's wrong with that?'

I remembered Ashishda telling us that the first five years of his stay in the Ashram were spent in work, which left him exhausted and unable to do much else. The next five years were that mysterious span he talked about obliquely, but always with passion. He did not move out of the Ashram and was totally immersed in inward contemplation, which reached such a level of intensity, that when working he found it difficult to drive a nail straight into the wall. 'I was quivering with the magic, the power of it.'

He said that at the time his awareness of his surroundings was so acute that he saw light emanating out of everything: the trees, the dog, the food he ate and the wood he planed. This light suffused him. 'The body could hardly hold what it was receiving. I felt every cell in my body would burst with the charge.'

I had seen a photograph of Ashishda taken in that phase. He was in his early thirties then. His face was much thinner. His cheek bones protruded, but above all, his eyes stood out. They were so intense I felt they beheld a vision beyond mere sight. Even through an old photograph taken with an old-fashioned camera, the force was palpable. If Dave could catch that quivering magic within the cup of his in-drawn phase, it would mark a watershed in his life.

The clouds darkened in April, pelting down hailstones that destroyed most of the ripened barley crop and bent the green wheat. We tried to salvage the flattened crop but the attempt was hardly worth the effort. In addition, another wave of mastitis broke out among the cows. The milk yield dropped and the cowshed resembled a dispensary with medicines, tubes, bowls and cotton wool lying on an improvised table. The winds were cold and the leaves flapped nervously on the trees like trapped birds. There was restlessness in the air, as though nature was fretting. Often, I saw Dave pace up and down the kitchen flagstones at the end of the day as if he was holding himself back from coming down to the threshing floor to see the day being rounded up.

Three months after Dave had handed over the farm, Rajeev said to me, 'Dave's finding it difficult to keep away from the farm. Initially he would come to check whether I was doing all right. Now I feel he's being driven by sheer restlessness.'

'He comes down to the fields quite often?'

'Yes, but I don't mind that. It's when he fires six rapid instructions to the men that things go haywire.'

'You think he's aware of what he's doing?'

'I hope so. Yesterday when I went to the Post Office fields, the jeep got stuck in the slush and I was late coming down. Dave, sitting in his room, kept looking at his watch and worrying. He told me later that he felt that if I didn't bring the jeep down within five minutes I'd be late with the load. He was so gripped with tension that he started walking up to see what had happened. By then the jeep had started.'

'You mean he's given up the responsibility without giving up the control?'

I had always seen their relationship with puzzled eyes. Rajeev's was an energetic, full of ideas, ready-to-lead kind of personality. With Dave, he completely reversed this role. He was the recipient, letting Dave take the lead and be the senior partner while Rajeev played the apprentice.

In a good working relationship mutual respect and understanding are essential. In some areas one person takes the lead and in other areas the second person. Each acts from an area of strength and takes a back seat on weaker grounds, allowing the other to compensate. However, such an understanding did not exist in Dave and Rajeev's relationship. I had seen them tallying their accounts after a shopping trip to Haldwani. Dave who found adding and subtracting an impossible task was correcting Rajeev, with his engineering background, on how to total the accounts. And Rajeev listened without a murmur of protest. The situation seemed unnatural.

Unstable equilibriums cannot be indefinitely sustained, I remembered from my school chemistry. A lack of mutual respect can force a partner, sooner or later, to assert himself, and desire an equal relationship. This seldom suits the dominant partner who is unhappy at being dislodged from his position of control. Rajeev was now expecting equality and Dave could not understand why. Long kept silences were impelling Rajeev to speak while Dave struggled to maintain control.

This became amply clear as more and more frequently Dave would open his window and give instructions for the day's work to the farmhands, when they passed by the temple building.

Rajeev went to Dave to talk things out. 'I'm running up against a problem. I've no objection to your giving instructions to the men, but you must also tell me about it. I plan the day's work in the morning and when I tell the men about it, they just shrug their shoulders and say curtly that they already have their instructions from you. If you like I can come to you at eight-thirty in the morning. You give me the day's instructions and I'll see it's done.'

'Ashishda did the same to me. So I don't see what you're complaining about?' Dave said stiffly.

'Ashishda abided by whatever decisions you made. You can't have a situation where two people give orders. The farmhands will then play one against the other.'

'You have your ideas of how to run a factory; that kind of thing won't do here.'

Dave continued giving instructions to the men while Rajeev became more and more unsure of his exact role.

During that period I recorded a dream:

It's a festive occasion and everyone is in Ashishda's room, singing. Ashishda begins to read from a book and I'm sitting right behind him, back to back. Slowly he begins to recline and continues to move back, while I'm gradually being squashed with my face pressing against the wooden floor. Soon his entire weight is bearing down on me and I make a silent vow not to complain or ask to be let off.

> *Then, Chitra comes in and says that Rajeev is back from
> purchasing the cow fodder and is very tired. I go to look
> for him and find him at the stone quarry, breaking stone.
> I realise he's really pushing himself hard.*

When I spoke to Ashishda about it he said, 'Breaking stones
is hammering down solidified feelings, attitudes and old
ideas. It is often very difficult to do this by oneself. You
need an outward force or person to bear down on you to
bring about that change.'

At quite another level, Rajeev's reaction as he associated
with my dream was, 'I think my solidified, unquestioning
attitude towards Dave is changing. Earlier he was always
right and someone else was wrong. Now I think he's equally
to blame. He had limited Mike to seventy-five wheelbarrows
a year of compost in the vegetable garden. Now ever since
Dave has been running the flower garden he has instructed
the farmhands to deposit a mountain of compost in the
vegetable garden. This, of course, is besides the fact that
he never allowed Mike the use of farmhands to carry the
compost up to the vegetable patch—he himself has not
brought up a single wheelbarrow.'

'Do you think Dave is regretting his decision to
withdraw?'

'I think he's still struggling. He feels he'll lose face if he
retracts his decision. So he's fretting.'

Meanwhile, Dave began pushing us to move into our
cottage. Only the rough planing of the planks had been
done and there were no doors or windows, nor a staircase
to connect the two floors. In fact the inside of the house
was bare of woodwork, plumbing or electrical fittings. We
began going to the site after work to lay the wooden floor.
By some benevolent intervention, as soon as Rajeev had
finished the floor, a carpenter arrived. We asked Ashishda if

we could use the carpenter's help in the house and he agreed reluctantly, mainly because of Rajeev's farm commitments.

While the work on the house was still in progress, Ashishda called Rajeev and asked, 'When are you moving into the cottage?'

'There's no plumbing or electricity and neither has the carpenter finished yet,' Rajeev told him.

'You don't need electricity and it doesn't take more than two days to pull a line to get one tap functioning. Take a few hours off from the farm and do it. I am expecting fifteen visitors connected with the environmental work on the 16th of August so if you want the Griha Pravesh done by me, it has to be in the next four days.'

We worked late into the nights, clearing the construction rubble; improvising a water pipe line, polishing the floor and moving our belongings into the cottage. The large windows of the upstairs room looked down into the forest while the tangy smell of pine from the freshly planed staircase and the kitchen shelves pervaded the walls. I ran my hands with pleasure over the rough stone walls, the rolled-up mattresses in the corner of the room, the wine-coloured woollen rug. I wanted to touch everything that made up this home.

'It's a beautiful house,' I said to Rajeev.

Rajeev looking at the floor and said, 'I can't believe I laid this floor. You would have laughed if I'd suggested it to you five years ago.'

'That was then and this is now,' I said quoting Ashishda.

'It's been worth it, hasn't it?'

'Yes, these three years have been worth it.'

Suddenly my eyes stung with tears. 'What's wrong?' he asked.

'Why do I feel that something is coming to an end?'

Rajeev let my words hang in the air for a moment. 'Why not think that something new is beginning.'

A new phase did indeed begin when Ashishda blessed our personal image of Krishna in the temple and carried it up to our house. He placed the Image in its special niche in the stone wall. The dark God seemed to smile when Ashishda put flowers at His feet and lit the incense from the brass brazier glowing red with coals.

'May His blessings be with you,' Ashishda smiled warmly.

The clouds cleared as we looked out into the night. The stars almost felt an arm's stretch away. The little path made of stone slabs that ran outside our house up to the old iron gate was awash by moonlight. It was a full moon. Was it a good omen? Or had things come full circle?

The visitors arrived and settled into the Library and the other rooms. That night John came running up the hill to our house and said, 'Trouble! Big trouble. The Library water tank has run out. The hydraulic ram has also stopped, so there is no water in the temple either. Come quickly. You've been summoned!'

While Rajeev was connecting the temple supply from the mains to the reserve tank, Dave met him and shouted, 'Have you no sense? The Library water has run out because you didn't ensure a continuous flow from the upper spring.'

'I filled the tank this evening. Yes, I did make the mistake of diverting the water away from the irrigation tank, under repair, and didn't make sure that there was running water to the feeder tank.'

'Excuses, excuses. The fact is that you don't know the difference between your arse and your elbow.'

'Your shouting is not going to help get water into this tap,' Rajeev flung back.

'What is it that you're doing now?' Dave asked, as he

watched Rajeev put the temple on reserve supply. 'The reserve water is undrinkable.'

'But you've been using it for the last twenty-five years.' Rajeev retorted in exasperation.

Dave turned on his heels and left, clearly annoyed.

A month later, one evening when Rajeev was in Ashishda's room discussing the planting of wheat, Dave brought up the water incident and started to fume.

'You fouled up a very simple job that day. I wonder what you'll do next!'

'I've already apologised about that. There is no point in losing your temper again.'

'I don't lose my temper, I use it.'

'Use it for what?'

'To spur myself and others on. For I am in control of it.'

'If you lose your temper and then…'

Ashishda cut Rajeev short, attempting to deflect the impending onslaught. 'Also, one loses one's temper only with those whom one is fond of. Dave loses his temper with you because he feels you're capable of taking it.'

Dave frowned; Rajeev couldn't be stopped.

'If you lose your temper and then drop it that's absolutely fine by me. But if you carry your anger from one incident to the next, then it's just your personal hang-ups coming to the surface. And it's time you took a look at them.'

Ashishda sat back, resigned. What he had feared had come to pass. Dave buried his face in his hands. Rajeev, his anger spent, wondered whether he had crossed some invisible line.

The silence was broken by the gong in the temple, announcing the evening service.

'Something uncomfortable is building up.' I later told Rajeev.

'I know. I am just wondering which of my attitudes is making him behave this way.'

'Maybe outwardly you are in agreement but internally you are resisting. That kind of thing can easily be sensed.'

'What am I to do?'

It was the first time Rajeev had openly questioned Dave. The invisible line had been crossed and neither Rajeev nor Dave were comfortable with the transgression.

The following night Rajeev recorded a dream that had a strong impact on both of us.

> *I am looking at an old Egyptian manuscript. There is a tower, which has an internal staircase leading to the top, with windows at regular intervals. The number two priest is standing at one of these windows and is holding a man by his ankles and beating the man's head against the wall.*
>
> *I am expected to paint the picture.*

On relating the dream, Ashishda said, 'The dream seems clear enough. The head stands for the ego—that which we most pride in ourselves. The tower stands for established structures. The head is being bashed open not by the head priest, but by the second in command. The reference to that must be obvious.' He looked directly at Rajeev, choosing not to mention Dave's name. 'Also, you're expected to paint the picture. Which means you're being warned of something about to happen.

'There's no point asking why the number two is the one beating you in the dream. It does not matter who is instrumental in creating an experience from which you have to learn. Remember, Thakur himself cannot appear and give you this lesson. It has to be through the agency of another human being, who himself may not be perfect.

'I was put through the paces too, by my teacher. It was tough, very tough. Yet, every now and then, an encouragement came my way…or was it given? I held onto these signs through all the storms. I just held on and on… till the next one was given.

'I am not saying everyone needs to undergo this treatment. However, this dream has come to you. It means two things. One that it will happen and two you are probably capable of taking it.'

They sat in silence, Rajeev trying to digest all that had been said.

'Only overpowering love or suffering can break the boundaries of the ego. Fate has pointed its finger at you to take on this lesson. If you can use it well, it can take you beyond yourself to grasp at first hand the highest truth that can be apprehended.

'At points you will feel the whole thing is next to impossible to bear. You'll feel there is no justice or love. However, looking back, years later, you may perceive this experience as being a watershed—where you traded naïveté for deeper understanding.'

Seeing Rajeev's shaken expression he continued, 'If it helps, all I can say is that I got my suffering early in life. Maybe I was hit too hard; who can say? In retrospect, I feel, if it leads to the state which I now know to be a reality, I'd choose that suffering again and again, life after life.' His voice throbbed with intensity.

Silence, once again, filled the room. After some time, as Rajeev got up to leave, Ashishda said with great compassion in his eyes, 'Remember this: Hope will guide you when reason fails. Love will sustain you when all else is dismayed.'

Something about the dream and Ashishda's interpretation of it chilled us. There seemed a violent unreality to the prediction. Was I holding onto a slim thread as I consoled myself that there was an element of choice in the dream? Rajeev was expected to paint the picture. It was not an order. The choice was still his. He could refuse to comply. Yes, he could do that. But then why had we come to this remote hermitage in the first place? If we had wanted to lead a comfortable, easy-paced life we need not have left Delhi. We needed a sharper focus and the life here provided that. Pushing the body to the edge of fatigue, trying to align oneself to an inner centre during the day and in meditation, brought its own rewards. To me the magical experience I had had in the temple that misty evening had permitted a momentary glimpse past the veils of this mystery. Since then I had been trying to recapture that state of awareness, but could only conjure up its memory. While I continued to feel the glow of that experience, somewhere I wondered whether I had reached a plateau.

The climb ahead, according to Ashishda, had to do with the toughest part of walking this Path: that of challenging and laying siege to the ego until the way is clear for an experience of another Reality. So far I had understood the ego as only something from which pride and arrogance are born, but Ashishda had widened its scope to be the fount of our individuality, the sense of being an entity separate from others. He felt unless that sense was eliminated it would obstruct the route to the goal. The little experience I had of trying to get beyond my ego, through various practices, had shown me how harsh the internal rebellion could be. The only thing I tried to hold onto was that this phase was a part of most spiritual traditions. The practice of 'fana' or extinction is central to Sufism; the Zen method of Koan (or meditating on a paradoxical problem) is an attempt to tire the mind out completely, so that the Truth can be revealed; the Whirling Dervishes who continuously whirl during their dances attempt to blur the hold of our ordinary reality and spin into another one; and the total submission of the disciple to the guru in the Hindu-Buddhist tradition—are all illustrative of this common theme.

All these traditions and practices attempt a total destruction of all known and comforting structures that an individual lives by. This aspect of the training is intended to develop the disciple's yearning for the Truth to the exclusion of everything else. The intense perplexity that arises when the disciple feels vanquished by ceaseless, often unjust demands and circumstances, prepares him or her, as it were, for 'the great jump'. The Sufis call this dismay or perplexity 'hayrangi' which is 'a crisis when the mind comes up against its own limit'.

During this phase however the disciple, we understood, is confronted with the ultimate challenge—of holding onto his faith when apparently everything, including his guru, seem to turn their back on him.

I had read about Tibet's great yogi Milarepa's gruelling, almost inhuman experience at the hands of the guru who was testing him. I gathered from Milarepa's case and from other accounts, that the guru puts his disciple knowingly into a 'purifying fire' and suffers for him, awaiting a time when the disciple can emerge to fulfil his or her potential. Ten centuries later, here I was wondering how many gurus had followed this approach and honoured the eternal nature of their responsibility to their disciples.

At a personal level I was totally unsure of being able to withstand the intense suffering Rajeev's dream seemed to have predicted. We had no way of knowing what form it would take. My mind went back to the stories Ashishda had told of his own discipleship and the phase in which he had felt demolished. I drew hope from Ashishda's belief that no one is alone while going through such a phase, and that help is given.

Where would the help that Ashishda had referred to in his talk with Rajeev, come from—Ashishda himself, or through dreams, or...?

A process of contemplation on our past experiences began for me. It occurred to me that our dream lives, both Rajeev's and mine, were an important dimension, which we hadn't granted full recognition. Looking back, I could see that we had been prompted, reassured, guided and warned through dreams, which came to us at crucial junctures. There were many dreams, but some stood out like markers on our path. For example, my dream of being rowed by Ashishda to meet a Great Teacher who spoke to me of continuing the struggle, affirming that something real exists. I felt a growing conviction they could steer me in times to come.

While carrying a bag of wheat from the store Rajeev sprained his back. After two days the pain was just about bearable. He limped down to the workshop to try and start work on our woodstove. It was November and we were still without electricity or any other means of heating our room. In a month's time it would snow and the tin roof would turn the cottage into an icebox.

There had been little time between harvesting the maize and planting the wheat to attend to work on the house. The cycle of activity for the year was more or less over. The signs of winter's inturnedness were already in the air. Now only the dried grass on the hillside needed to be cut and stored for winter fodder. The women from the adjoining villages had come to cut the grass, an activity the residents did not participate in. Rajeev worked on the woodstove in the workshop and made periodic trips down the hill to check the progress of the women's work.

One afternoon Dave came to the area where the grass was being cut and said to Rajeev, 'Why aren't you cutting grass? You are not the manager here.'

'I've sprained my back and I find bending very painful.'

Dave looked at him coldly and said to one of the women, 'Put a sickle in this man's hand and let him cut with the rest of you.'

Turning to Rajeev he said sarcastically, 'Of course if you have any problems regarding that, you can talk to Ashishda about it.'

Rajeev began to cut grass at a painfully slow pace as his back muscles cramped up in spasms of pain. As I watched him I felt torn apart and utterly helpless. I couldn't bear to see him in so much agony, wanting to be his shield. On the other hand I felt my strength drain away in the face of the surrender we had acceded to. Rajeev, it seemed, was being tried and I did not know how to intervene on his behalf.

The next day, after work, Rajeev was summoned to Ashishda's room where a tight-lipped Dave awaited him. 'The women aren't cutting enough grass. So backache or no backache, you are to cut grass from nine-to-five with them. Also you can use the workshop only after five in the evening. Is that clear?'

'My cutting grass alongside the women will not increase their output. I have been keeping an eye on how much they have been cutting—on other days they were bringing in sixteen headloads while today, when I cut with them, there were only fourteen.'

'I am telling you that you have to cut grass with them.'

'What is more fourteen or sixteen?'

'You handle him,' he looked at Ashishda. 'I don't know

what to do with his justifications,' and he stormed out of the room, kicking the door open and leaving it flapping on its hinges, like an injured bird's wing.

We struggled more with the pain in Rajeev's back than with the growing chill in the atmosphere outside. Because of the bending and cutting his back had gone into spasm. Lines of fatigue and pain grooved his face.

As the grass cutting came to a close, Rajeev went to Ashishda to ask permission to go down to Delhi to get medical attention. Ashishda agreed. The next day Dave called Rajeev and in front of Ashishda said, 'You cannot go to Delhi now, for who is going to collect the pine needles for the cow bedding? We're running short. Another thing, you better start learning how to milk after five in the evening.'

Something primitive and dark was stirring. My whole axis was tilting so that I wasn't sure which way I was looking at things. A loop was tightening and we saw ourselves being knotted into it.

That night I had a dream:

> *I am wandering around in a large empty haveli (mansion). A man appears in traditional Muslim attire. He is wearing a double-breasted swirling frock. His name is Rumi. He takes me by the elbow and we go and sit outside the deserted haveli steps. In the fading evening light he says very softly, 'Die before thou diest...'*

I must describe my dream. I saw a man twirling like the Dervishes and, when he faced me, I knew that it was Rumi—the greatest mystical poet of Persia, who lived in the thirteenth century. I felt intoxicated by the joy of his presence. There was nothing morbid when he spoke the words, 'Die before thou diest'. Only a joyous buoyancy of those words could be understood and realised. Later I was to discover that this was a favourite phrase used by Rumi and attributed to the Prophet. Reading Rumi, I realised how effortlessly he surrendered to love.

By now it was December and the next afternoon it began to drizzle. Sleet soon followed. That evening the temperature plummeted and the house felt cold and dark. We found ourselves going half an hour early for the session, so that we could light the stove in the Library and warm ourselves. When we arrived Ashishda was already sitting there. He did not look up and we remained silent. The stove crackled. The silence stretched.

'May I tell you a dream I had last night?' I ventured.

'Huhh.' Ashishda said noncommittally.

I recounted the dream of the haveli.

'The true death is the death of the ego as opposed to physical death. It is a mystical death in which you are reborn to a higher awareness within your lifetime. Therefore die before thou diest.' Ashishda said in an impersonal voice.

Die to what? To a mode of perception which is filtered through memory and expectations. Expectations layered by social and personal indoctrination that never seem to pause. Die by standing aside, standing apart, by being an observer without investment in what is observed? Ashishda had said earlier, 'To find anything real, one must break one's identification with the body and all the things that go with the body. Only then can one find what it is that does not die because it was never born. What one wants is the true identity; "That art thou"—what is it that remains when everything is dropped.'

We had understood the shedding of identity to be an inner psychological process, but here something else was directed at Rajeev, bodily suffering being pushed beyond its aching limit. To us it seemed an injustice. I wondered if this was what my dream was asking: Die before thou diest.

If dying was being asked for, can the body be disregarded? In Rajeev's dream, the head is being bashed against a tower to achieve the dying. Were our apprehensions making us imagine the worst outcome? The fact was, however painful his back was, Rajeev was managing to work. Could we be pushed to do something which we were incapable of? The army officer in my father proudly maintained that while training commandos the limits of their physical endurance were tested and they were pushed even beyond that. Later in their career the transformation it wrought in the men shone from afar.

It was then that I chanced upon a quote from another Sufi mystic which read: 'When the heart weeps because it has lost, the Spirit laughs because it has found.'

In between the searching and the finding, I thought there is only faith, when all else is taken away.

Even the year was dying. The trees were austere without their leaves. The cold vapours of December were settling on the sun, which looked down upon the bare, brown earth. Dark clouds were gathering, but where was the shelter?

Three days later Rajeev was summoned by Dave and told to go down to Haldwani to get the jeep repaired. Rajeev said to me, 'Maybe it's a blessing in disguise. I'll try and get the stove pipes quickly fabricated there. I should be back in two days.'

When Rajeev returned he went to ask Ashishda if he could be given one day off to fit the stove pipes. 'Yes, I suppose you can do that. Also you can go to Delhi for your back trouble.'

Rajeev was relieved as he had resigned himself to living with a painful back. I noted that Ashishda was not unaware of the actual situation, in fact, he had kept it in mind.

We fitted the stove pipes by punching a hole through

the stone wall. Although, we couldn't use the woodstove till the cement was cured, it didn't seem to matter much since we were leaving the next day. When we woke the next morning, there was a foot of fresh snow outside. As we walked down to the village we saw pug marks of a leopard that had crossed our path during the night.

20

Suffering Is Behovely

When we returned to the Ashram, Ashishda greeted us briefly outside the workshop, with barely a smile on his face. We greeted Dave, but he turned his face away.

The next day Rajeev went to clean the anteroom of the temple. As he was picking up the broom to sweep the ramp, Dave said, 'You're not going to be doing any temple work anymore. You're out, brother.'

Rajeev, thinking Dave was joking, looked at him again. Dave's blue eyes were icy and his lips were set in lines of tension. Rajeev put the broom down slowly and walked down the ramp.

Any work connected with the temple was considered a privilege. To be able to serve was an honour. Conversely to be turned away meant you were no longer worthy. How had we failed and by what standards were we being judged? Hesitatingly, we decided to go and see Ashishda hoping he might tell us it was all a mistake, or that it was a temporary arrangement with a valid reason behind it. When we entered Ashishda's room, he was sitting in his chair looking out of the window. He turned impersonal eyes on us.

'Er...umm...I have been told not to do the anteroom by

Dave.' Rajeev stumbled over the sentence.

There was no response. Ashishda turned his eyes away and looked out of the window again. 'Yes, and that applies to your other duties as well. You are not to work on the farm anymore. Dave is going to look after that again. Stay in and around your house. No temple work, no farm work, no working in the workshop either.' Turning towards me he said, 'You are to continue milking in the three shifts. Otherwise the same applies to you as to him.'

We sat there looking at Ashishda's face in shock. His face was distant, his words sounded like a banishment. Why? Why? Why? The question formed in my mind but never came out. We found no words to break that silence. Finally Ashishda spoke, 'You can go now.'

Go where? Work and participation in community life was the daily living enactment of the teaching for each of us. Through it we affirmed our commitment to the ideal. Without this outlet, the ground on which we stood seemed marshy. What we had put so much effort into, now suddenly seemed null and void.

'I feel Dave is piqued, that's why we're in the doghouse. I questioned his judgement and this is the result. If he wanted to run the farm, he didn't have to throw us out. I would've willingly withdrawn.' Rajeev said heatedly.

'Ashishda wouldn't agree to it if it wasn't necessary,' I said.

'Necessary for what?'

I had no answer.

That day we just sat outside our house on the stone slab, watching the fading January afternoon turn into a twilight chill. As we shut the front door I felt we had been locked into the thick grey walls of the house.

Simple household chores kept us going in a mechanical

kind of way for the first few days. Rajeev went to fetch our milk from the dairy. Dave was standing on the threshing floor, giving instructions to the men for the day. He turned his back as soon as he saw Rajeev. The men looked on curiously.

Don stopped Rajeev on the way, 'How is the new house? It must be good to be out of Bhagiya's. Oh, by the way, just keep in mind that whenever one of the men is free, send him over to chop some firewood for us.'

'You'll have to ask Dave. He's running the show now.'

'Oh, that's all right. Just keep it in mind anyway.'

None of the residents knew about the recent developments. No one believed us when we tried to tell them. Slowly it became apparent to everyone that we rarely stepped out of our house. Persis asked me what was happening. When I told her she asked, 'Why, to what end?'

Our minds chattered uncontrollably. Meditation seemed like an activity we had never undertaken before. Mechanical and compulsive thought patterns took over and there seemed no way of stopping them. With our energy not canalised into outer activities the pressure began to build up inside us.

Fitfully, I paced the narrow path outside our cottage thinking I must stop feeling the injustice of it. I must rid myself of this unbearable tension. I tried to persuade myself that it is all in the mind. If only I could harness my thoughts away from their frenzy I might be able to perceive the situation differently.

I said to Rajeev, 'This whole thing may be an opportunity in disguise. We have been rushed off our feet all these years. Now we can happily withdraw. Why can't we see it like that?'

'It's hardly been handed to us as a privilege, more like a punishment. First we have to get past that before we can do anything else.'

Again the question was one of perception: how to decondition ourselves and not view the situation as others viewed it—as our being outcasts. When Dave had withdrawn from outer activity he had Ashishda's support and general approval while all we had was a curt dismissal.

Reminders kept coming our way as though to deepen our sense of isolation. Somewhere down the line even our share of vegetables was denied to us. We started digging the soil outside the house to grow our own. It was of very poor quality and we knew Dave would not allow us any of the cowshed manure. So, Rajeev often went to the area outside the workshop to pick up the droppings of the bull and smaller calves that sometimes grazed there. Once Dave saw him and stood watching. Then with a flick of his hand he indicated that Rajeev should leave.

The farmhands came after fifteen days to enquire how we were. In their wake came a message from Dave: 'Don't try and chat up the men to gain their sympathy.' Every time we went to collect our jerrycan of drinking water from the temple we wondered when we would be told to get it from elsewhere. When our provisions dwindled, we requested Don who was going by his jeep into town, to get ours too. We didn't know for which tiny lapse Dave would admonish us.

The passing of days found us living by ourselves. We hardly met anyone, except in the evening sessions where we barely spoke; nor were we spoken to. Outwardly we tried to structure our lives around the house. Rajeev began to make some more shelves for our kitchen. Internally we lagged behind in accepting the change. When the temple bell pealed for the service, we longed to walk down and attend. Often I sat with eyes closed, the ringing of the bells echoing in my ears long after the service was over. When we heard the tiny tractor chugging away, we knew we would not be there with the others to cut the wheat and plant the maize or potatoes. Each day we hoped that something would change. Every evening we watched Ashishda's face expectantly.

Ashishda smiled and laughed with the others but seldom ever looked in our direction. Whether we entered or left the room he hardly seemed to notice. Yet one evening just as we were leaving Ashishda called us back, while the others left. 'Your mind's chatter can be heard even in the temple. Do something about it.'

For the first time I realised that prayer was a refuge. I repeated my mantra automatically, mechanically, somewhere at the back of my mind, all the time. I wasn't sure what that would do. Hoping it may do something, I persisted.

Late one evening, the snow began to fall. By early next morning there was nothing to be seen or heard in the blanket of white silence. As I made my way to the cowshed I felt insignificant amidst such austere beauty. Maybe the snow's flawless purity reminded me of a state of detachment I didn't have. When you looked at the snow everything was painted with the brush of evenness—no colour, no flaws, no good, no bad, just uniformity.

I agonised about the purpose of our stranded state— in the Ashram yet not a part of it. Did these three years amount to nothing? Was the very pivot of our aspirations under question? Why was Ashishda letting this situation develop? Was it with a specific end in mind? Sometimes the dream of the tower came back to me. You were expected to paint the picture. We had to live through it, even if we could not comprehend why. Earlier, we had thought the de-husking of the personality would only be a psychological process and it was unjust if health and body suffered. Now we seemed to feel a greater sense of injustice when subjected to psychological suffering!

In the evening, in answer to a question by Persis on suffering, Ashishda said, 'Suffering is an essential part of life. It is the grindstone on which the individual is refined. It is largely due to the mind, which when thwarted of its desires and expectations produces what we call suffering. Silence the mind, and go beyond. Suffering should make you look for a state beyond itself, and therein lies its true purpose.'

The days passed; our lives mirrored no change. I awoke one night at about three in the morning and looked out of the window. Faraway an owl hooted while the sooty darkness covered everything. In my desolation I wondered if this was the end to all my aspirations. It seems that the opposite of life is not death, but fear, and I felt afraid of drowning in something very dark. This biting fear sharpened my senses, amplifying both sight and sound. Far below, I could hear the clang of a steel bar as a cow shifted her bulky weight in the stall. I knew in the morning I would go down, lift the steel bar and let myself into the cowshed. I would be alone, for Persis had gone down for a month to the city.

I recalled Ashishda's words, 'Though Persis has gone, there should be no difficulty in your handling all the shifts by yourself.' I had kept quiet. It was not milking five cows in the morning or four late at night; it was not the dripping rain or the cold, nor the lack of electricity that bothered me. What mattered was that I didn't matter. When my mind veered in this direction, I remembered that whenever I had met Ashishda privately he had never turned away. What if he were to withdraw this significance also? What would be left? Probably I would have to watch a dream being undone bit-by-bit.

I sat on the window ledge staring unseeingly. I knew I had to help myself. I quietly walked towards the temple. The darkness hid me and the bay of stars lit my dim passage till I reached the ramp leading to the shrine. I looked at the closed temple door and thought if I ask the same questions about suffering—'Why me? What have I done wrong? Did I deserve this?'—then I will circle back to the same point with no way out. What if I ask a different question? Is it possible that doors are often locked to present facts in a new light? Closed doors could mean: Stop looking at reality this way. Have the courage to see things differently, for the old way has outlived its utility and can present no fresh opportunity. I knelt down and bowed my head in the direction of the Images. I stood there for a few minutes. I found myself relaxing as though I had handed over a burden. I walked back slowly to the house. I slept soundly till dawn.

Such moments of peace were few and far between, and try as I might I could not keep away the waves of despair and hopelessness that engulfed me. Then one February morning I came alive. In a fluid state, half asleep, half awake:

> *I saw a Light to my left. It was a circular effulgent form, radiant in the semi-darkness. I felt no fear, in fact with a sense of joy, almost abandonment, I saw myself leave my body to go and meet this Light. It filled me with a sense of overwhelming love and without words communicated a message—'I'll come to you, every month, for the next two and a half years.'*

I was filled with wonder and awe as I was engulfed by a love that in one moment dissolved and in another moment filled my universe with light. For a while the Light remained and then was gone. I woke with a feeling of immense gratitude.

I grew quiet inside. The felicity of love that enfolded me in its magnificence completely altered everything else. It was a whisper from another shore, a benediction that gave life to a slackening heartbeat. I held this feeling close to me for a few days before knocking on Ashishda's door.

'There is something I would like to talk to you about.'

Ashishda nodded. Rather haltingly I told him what I had seen and been told. Ashishda's face immediately became alert and softened completely by the time I finished.

'You are fortunate.' His eyes shimmered like the sea catching the morning rays. He smiled, as he seemed lost in remembrance. When he looked again at me I felt the frozen outlines of distance dissolve between us.

'When did you have this experience?'

'Around the end of last month.'

'What date?'

I told him.

'Then "He" will come every month on that same day.'

'Will "He" really?'

'Did you doubt it?'

'I don't know what to think. It was so real and so unreal. So close, so out of my reach.'

'That is the great mystery. This force, or "They", just bless us in the hope that one day we may become worthy of "Them". The wonder is how we, with our greed, pride and smallness, still invite their compassion. For there seems very little in us worthy of it,' Ashishda said.

'What does the reference to two and a half years mean?'

'Probably you will encounter much pain and despair in the next two and a half years. Support and guidance from powers above us doesn't guarantee an easy life. It doesn't mean "They" will prevent or protect you against pain; only give you the strength to handle it.'

Two and a half years...would this phase last that long? If our suffering was an opportunity for possibilities that I could not even comprehend at this stage, then I had to accept the suffering on trust. A conviction was growing within me; that behind this circumscribed, limited world I lived in were unseen eyes which cared and loved. This was support at such a fundamental level that it moved me beyond the difficulties we were encountering. If only I could develop the capacity to hold onto that arrested moment, which had streamed with clarity, through the next two and a half years. As Rumi said,

> I am the Pure Awareness within your heart,
> With you during joy and celebration, suffering and despair.

Maybe I was being told that it was too early to despair.

This experience took away my excuses for not continuing to try.

21

Even the Elephant's Wounds Heal

March came and the bees buzzed over the apple blossoms; white and feathery, like the memory of winter snow. The peach trees dripped pink as they burst their buds, spring fulfilling the inarticulate promise of the quiescent winter earth. Even our tiny garden produced three or four narcissi and one sun-drenched yellow daffodil, which defied the poor soil and stood erect at the edge of the garden, undeterred by its solitude.

Life formed its own rhythm. Outwardly we had been banished, but internally we felt inexorably bound to the heartbeat of the temple and the community. The sound of the conch was still the measure of our time. Rajeev would light the hamam as the temple gong pealed for arati. The clang of the iron gate outside the workshop and the sound of the jeep starting meant it was nine o'clock and that the farmhands were coming in for the day's work. Instinctively Rajeev would begin to do some carpentry on the bench behind the house. It was as though by keeping to the outward rhythm of the work, we were maintaining our own sense of continuity with the community. At five-to-twelve Rajeev would come in, dust the wood shavings from his clothes, and sit down on the kitchen floor waiting for the temple bell to announce the midday service.

In the afternoons we worked in our vegetable patch. When we first ran the soil through our fingers, it glistened with mica. The topsoil was largely the construction rubble, so sandy that it would not have retained any water. We began digging clay from the fallow upper Post Office fields and bringing it down in sacks to mix into our soil. We spent many an afternoon gathering dried leaves to start our compost pile, adding the kitchen waste to it.

In the late afternoons when the sun slanted through the trees we usually went for a walk to the top of the mountain ridge and sat listening to the faint sounds which came from the valley below—the shout of a child, the voice of a village woman singing a folk song, or the bleat of goats being brought in for the night. We would watch the first cluster of lights come on in the valley before making our way home, en-route collecting pine cones and kindling for the hamam.

When it got dark, we would sit on the kitchen floor talking over supper about inconsequential matters. In doing so we were trying to distance ourselves from thoughts that had no immediate solutions. We talked about the kitchen shelf and when it would be ready; the pride over our first crop of radishes; how well the chilli and capsicum seedlings were doing on the warm kitchen window-sill; a letter from our parents; what was being planted on the farm. A small world no different from any other in the rhythm of its days.

There was an unaccountable fortitude in doing simple things without resentment. As our stock of wood dwindled, we combed the jungle behind our house and located a huge, fallen branch of an oak tree. We dragged it up the slope and gradually sawed it into small pieces sorting them out for the hamam or woodstove. When our hamam developed a leak, we took to putting two large pans over the woodstove at night and got reasonably warm water in the morning. We felt delighted when we managed to cure a cough or a cold by looking up homoeopathic books, as though grappling with these small matters helped to carve a way out for us. This period of isolation was in no way dull, for it required all our wits and attention to live under a new set of correlates.

The whistling thrush sang its tune somewhere near the oak tree outside our house. I listened, as the fire crackled in the kitchen stove's grate and the nutty smell of baking bread filled the house. The iron gate outside the house clanged and my head turned, instinctively hoping it was someone with news for us. It was Himmat, the farmhand going home. Whom or what had I expected? Ashishda, or someone else bringing news that the last three months had just been an aberration.

'I don't know why Dave can't talk about his upset with me,' Rajeev said.

'He's steamed up because there's been a change in roles. From being submissive, you've started treating him like an equal. Equals question, ask, discuss. He's not used to that. Besides, he believes talking never helps. Minimum communication brings maximum results.'

'It's all so confusing. I know those dreams did foretell this would happen. Somehow I presumed Ashishda would engineer the situation to fulfil the prophecy of the dreams by putting the pressure on us consciously. But what I can see is a Dave who is annoyed and Ashishda's coldness hardly seems contrived. His dismissal of us is so complete that if I ask him a question in the evenings he seldom answers it. If, at the beginning or end of the session, I greet him he ignores me. If we don't go for the session he never asks about us. Not a word, not a smile, not even a nod that we exist. It's quite eerie, as if we are dead.'

Die before thou diest. How, when every nerve ending is alive to the rawness of experience? I could not cauterize the pain, nor could I ignore it. 'I'll get used to it, I'll outlast it,' I said to myself as a self-calming exercise. But the feeling refused to be soothed, proclaiming its autonomy against all reason. It was then that we looked around to see if other thoughts could occupy our minds. We began reading avidly. The very things Ashishda had discussed in the evening sessions became our initial readings. To our surprise a wide variety of books were available within the community. Rajeev got interested in Darwin, Einstein and in astronomy.

One day Rajeev borrowed a book on Western Astrology from Kersy. He read the book steadily through the evening. By midnight he had cast his own chart and was fascinated by the accuracy of some of its details. That he spent hours calculating the Speculum and rapt parallels of charts was incidental, astrology became a means for him to grapple with what he was experiencing. Are certain events fated in our lives? If so, why? The birth chart mapped out the basic destiny of the person. Does that mean that the individual has very little choice in the way his or her life will unfold? Or is there a meaningful design that will lead to self-discovery?

Hope of a change in the situation kept us going. As March slipped into April, the clouds gathered, darkened and pelted down hailstones the size of small pebbles. We would rush out to cover our seedlings with anything handy— baskets, tins, broken pots and pans. I could not help wondering if next year while we were working on the farm, would we reach our vegetable patch in time? If we were working on the farm...

That 'if' came to pass in a peculiar set of circumstances. On a mid-May morning we heard a knock on our door. Ashishda was standing there. He came upstairs and got straight to the point with Rajeev, 'How about doing some work?'

'Yes, Ashishda, I'm willing.' His face lit up.

'We're short of leaves. You're to work on the periphery of the estate. Collect a trailer load, then come to the workshop and take the jeep to wherever the load is. I expect you'll make two trips a day; one at midday and another in the evening before five.'

Ashishda seemed excited. At last a breakthrough had been made!

'It'll be done, Ashishda.'

'I'll let you know when to start.'

Ashishda had gone as suddenly as he had come, leaving us stunned. After a few days, at the end of an evening session, Ashishda quietly told Rajeev, 'You be down at nine tomorrow.' Rajeev was ready long before nine. His excitement was contagious as he checked his watch every five minutes. It was five-to-nine when he stubbed out his cigarette decisively and announced to himself, 'It'll be just right if I leave now. Neither late nor too early.'

Half an hour later to my surprise I saw a confused looking Rajeev walking back.

'What happened?'

'Nothing.'

'What do you mean nothing?'

'I went down. All the men were surprised to see me. Even more than them, John, who was marking the attendance. I told him that Ashishda had asked me to come down for work. He didn't know what to do with me. I suppose he hadn't been told anything.'

'Then?'

'We waited for twenty minutes. John said, "Let Dave come—he'll decide." But Dave never came. So John told me to go back home.'

That evening Rajeev was asked to stay back after everyone had gone.

'Why weren't you down for work, especially after I'd told you,' Ashishda thundered, his lips tight with anger.

'Ashishda, I did go down at nine...'

'But Dave told me you weren't there.'

'I promise you, I was there at nine. I waited there for twenty minutes before going back.'

'Who told you to go back?'

'John. I asked him what I was to do. He didn't know.'

By now, Ashishda was clearer about what had happened. He pounded his forehead with his palm. 'Oh no! Oh no!' But he quickly recovered. 'Never mind, make sure you are down tomorrow at nine sharp.'

There were no glitches the next morning. Everything went smoothly. The extra hired hands were waiting. The regular workforce and the community members were busy with the wheat harvest. Rajeev and the temporary gang marched off with a dozen nets and two dozen sacks to comb the hillsides, starting below Mike's cottage. Rajeev would come for the jeep at eleven-thirty. The jeep with the trailer would be parked outside the garage, with the key hanging in the ignition. The temporary gang would know which area to sweep. He was expected to follow them, to the designated area.

It was becoming more and more apparent that Dave wasn't happy with Ashishda's decision to bring Rajeev back onto the farm. Dave's protest took the form of cutting off all communication with Rajeev. They would be standing five feet apart but if instructions had to be given, Dave would relay them to Rajeev through one of the men. If Rajeev wanted to clarify something, Dave would turn his face away, call out to one of the farmhands and answer the question. The old pattern was asserting itself again. Dave was creating a situation where there was minimum contact between Rajeev and him, preferring to operate by remote control.

Two weeks later Rajeev had brought up a load of leaves at midday and was helping to unload it when John delivered him a packet. It was a note from Dave.

'I've been sent a memo!' Rajeev said taking off his gumboots and entering the kitchen. He looked upset.

'What does it say?'

He showed me the note in Dave's handwriting. There was no beginning or end to the note. Just a curt message:

'Take green jeep and old trailer. Buy 10 quintals barley and 5 quintals rice husk. Enclosed 3000. Leave tomorrow.'

Rajeev was silent through lunch. After lunch he wrote on the reverse of Dave's note:

'Barley purchase delayed. Prices may be up. Indicate maximum purchase price. Confirm that the green jeep is capable of pulling up the load. Will leave tomorrow.'

The response to Rajeev's note was swift. Chitra intercepted Rajeev after work, 'Dave wants the three thousand back.'

'Of course. I'll be in the office in ten minutes.'

Rajeev returned from the temple in fifteen minutes. His demeanour betrayed a sense of shock. There had been a ring of silence around the temple. Chitra wasn't in the office, so he knocked on the door leading to their suite. She emerged after a few minutes, counted the money and Rajeev retraced his steps. Nothing was said.

'I think it'll take me weeks to digest this information overkill!'

Little did we realise the prophetic content of that exasperated utterance. It would take many months to understand what had happened during the space of those six hours.

Two days later, Ashishda knocked at our door.

'Good morning, Ashishda...'

He waved me aside by asking, 'Where's Rajeev?'

'Upstairs. Would you care for a cup of tea?'

He didn't answer.

I followed him upstairs.

'Hello Ashis...'

'Now look here. What's the meaning of this note.' Ashishda looked on the warpath as he ground the words out.

'I don't understand?' Rajeev looked puzzled.

'Why so many questions in the note. Are you looking for reassurances from Dave. Tell me what price to buy the barley...tell me this...tell me that...' Ashishda scowled.

'I have to make a decision on the spot there. If I know the last purchase price, I'll know whether I am being quoted an inflated price or not. The price is expected to be up now, as barley has been harvested two months ago and all the surplus has probably been sold to the brewers,' Rajeev said quickly.

'You are trying to stand on your abilities. We all know you ran a factory and can work the market. Here that won't do. If you are told to take the jeep and go, then do just that.' Ashishda's eyes were flashing.

'I got to know recently that the cylinder-head of the green jeep got cracked when Dave drove it without water. The stress of hauling up fifteen quintals may crack it again.

It was a reasonable guess that I would be blamed for it.' Rajeev said, flustered.

My heart sank as I looked at Ashishda's face flushed with anger.

'You are just being defensive,' Ashishda spat contemptuously. 'If you go on like this, I'll have to ask you to leave the Ashram.' He folded his hands on top of his head in a gesture, characteristic of bidding goodbye. 'You can get out. Go...' he repeated with force. A heavy silence followed. Rajeev leaned back against the stone wall looking drained and spent.

A few seconds later Ashishda left. The room seemed filled with his last words, 'get out...Go...' I looked at his retreating back from the window.

That day any footsteps outside our house made us feel that Ashishda had come himself, or sent someone else to actualise the threat which he had hurled at us in the morning. We sat huddled together, numbed at the thought.

We had believed we would convert our isolation into an opportunity to force ourselves to look at the dross within us. Now Ashishda was cutting at the root of that belief by telling us to go. So then what was this isolation and pressure all about?

The evening shadows stretched over the silence in the house. Finally I said, 'If they feel we are wrong, then we should apologise.'

'At the moment we are afraid. Are we apologising out of fear or because we believe it's the right thing to do?' Rajeev asked quietly.

'The only thing I know is that it might help us not get all uptight about the situation.'

The next day, without telling me, Rajeev went and apologised to Ashishda and Dave. When he came back from the temple he said, 'I went to meet Ashishda. Dave was also sitting in his room. I offered them an unconditional apology.'

'What happened?'

'Ashishda slowly nodded his head, while Dave kept quiet. I left immediately.'

We treaded with caution in those days. One wrong step and we may be out. If we had subconsciously hoped Rajeev's apology would make a difference to the outward situation, we were to be disappointed. In fact the reverse happened. The pressure began to mount from all sides. I was hauled up by Ashishda who, pointing to the milk register, said that the milk yield had dropped considerably, especially in the month I was milking alone.

'Ashishda there wasn't enough green fodder that month...' I protested.

'Was it that or was it the state of your mind resenting the work?' he asked.

Every morning we awoke with a leaden feeling of dread, not knowing which side the attack would come from.

I remembered Ashishda's words, 'Right, wrong, justice, injustice, good and bad are all relative terms. Those norms do not necessarily apply to this endeavour.' As Nisargadatta Maharaj had said: 'You need to blow the bulb. If an ornament has to be refashioned it has to be first melted into shapeless gold.'

I knew that what was being aimed at was far removed from the rational concepts of our known reality. I hung onto the thought that Ashishda was doing this for our good. At this point all I wanted was a shelter away from the storm. Even through the despair, I clung to the feeling that I was living through all this for a reason. Did the childhood rejection I had only partially dealt with, have to be relived in different circumstances for me to be finally free of it? I wondered whether this outward isolation was a part of my own isolated self that could only be reached by recreating the drama outwardly? Was it possible that fate presents the same theme again and again, till its captive ideas are released? If so then I was being given an opportunity. Earlier I had viewed this 'rejection' script as something I could only rework a few lines at a time. Now I felt the entire script had the potentiality of change.

I knew our time to leave had not come yet. Doing so would be tantamount to running away. But how were we to live through the day-to-day situation, and still make sense of it? I recorded a dream soon after, which gave me a clue to the answer:

> *A mahout (elephant keeper) is bathing his elephant on the bank of a river. The elephant looks rather forlorn as he is lead into an enclosure. The mahout then looks at me, his eyes shining with a strange light, and says:*
>
> *'Even the elephant's wounds heal,*
> *Only the airy space burns.'*

I took the dream to Ashishda for interpretation. 'The elephant is an animal which doesn't forget an injury. Neither does the ego. But the wounds will heal. There is a reassurance in that. The airy space is a reference to the higher mind. The dream is saying, don't worry about the ego whose wounds will one day heal. All that matters is that you hold onto the higher mind, which burns forever.'

In that moment I could have sworn that Ashishda's eyes looked like the mahout's eyes in the dream. I had thought we had been cast aside. But his look, indrawn yet penetrating made me feel that the connection was alive. Only it was at a far deeper level than the personality.

The same message was being conveyed again and again

through my dreams. Hold onto something higher. Even pain is transient. A lifeline was being given to make me understand what I had to struggle towards on this Path. It was not only a psychological understanding of the problem, where the mind is locked in arguments and analysis. Much more was being asked. A 'letting go' of the personality, and a concentration on that which doesn't dissolve with the passage of time.

All my arguments, to preserve my individual self with its particular desires, seemed of little concern to this airy space. It seemed a very impersonal power. Is the airy space that part which observes the personality without being identified with any of it? Maybe in times of greatest trouble, when the ego's integration is shaking that one finds its real presence. Through the suffering, would I find something that is calm and steady within, which watches the suffering without being unsettled by it, no matter how agitated my personality may have been?

Was Ashishda, by pressing down on me—like in my dream of Rajeev breaking stones—hoping to build intensity in our search to help make this crucial separation between the personality and the dispassionate watcher of it? If so, then viewing his actions only through the prism of justice and hurts would erect a barrier against his intent? Was that what the mahout was cautioning me about—not to tend to the wounds of the elephant but grapple with that which is beyond them?

What was it that passed like a flash in a dream, but didn't fade away? What were these strange encounters that breathed their ethereal vapour into my pores, yet left me isolated because I could not dissolve into their luminosity? What is it that looked through the dust of my body and proclaimed itself soaked in Light? Like the mahout, the other shining Presence came to me when I was half-awake, and rearranged the distorted contours of my mind with hands that suggested perfect symmetry. Who were these Revealers who came disguised in the cloak of the night and filled my dream-drenched eyes with something of the urgent Beyond?

22

The Dak Bungalow

Returning from milking one night, I heard the cry of a flying squirrel. I shone my torch on it and saw its pixie-like face light up. Its front paws were clinging to the branch of a deodar, its thick, chestnut-brown tail swishing as it peered down with golden eyes set in dark red fur. Further along the path two glow-worms danced ahead, accompanying me till our cottage gate. As soon as I crossed the gate, I felt something unusual in the air; a sense of protection engulfed me. So strong was the feeling that I stopped and looked around to see if there was a physical reality to what I sensed.

During this period, I seemed to hear things just below the threshold of sound, and sense things before they became visible. Held alert by inner tension, I walked the edge of two worlds. Often the gentle breeze put its fingers on the deeply etched furrows of my thoughts, smudging the harsh boundaries. Once in a while, caught by an inexplicable mood, I would feel myself ease into stillness, such that if I 'let go' I might be washed away by the incoming tide from another land. And if I held tight, I would remain stranded on this shore. Who was letting go, I asked myself? Who was helping me say not 'me', not 'mine'?

Subliminally I was clinging onto 'something' and that 'something' responded. As a part of me was being chivvied, another was simultaneously coming into being. At such times I felt myself dissolving, spreading, disappearing into an unseen land where secrets are whispered. Under the naked eye it seemed a static process but I knew that something stronger than the experience itself was being interwoven into my being. Something was standing aside and watching 'me'. Something was more widely aware than what I normally was. And to become more aware of this awareness, I had to become more and more still.

Yet outwardly, the old situation was recurring within the community. Most people had withdrawn from working on the farm, choosing to help only during the harvest. Ashishda was unhappy with the situation, and twice in the evening sessions he had commented, 'If you're finding a situation difficult, you don't withdraw from it.'

'What do you do if you feel something is unjust? It may not be towards you but to some other member of the community?' Persis asked.

Ashishda immediately said, 'In a guru-disciple relationship justice and injustice do not apply. Do you know the story of the Master who was giving his disciple hell? Nothing the poor fellow could do was right. The Master ignored him, nagged him, and ranted at him. One day the Master demanded some tea. The disciple brought it, but it was not to the Master's liking. He just picked the cup of hot liquid and threw it on the disciple's face. The disciple sagged with despair and began to weep. Immediately the Master's face softened and he said, "Can't you see, I don't have much time. Unless I shock you into a state where your ego ceases to matter, you'll never come upon that higher reality." It is difficult to see the Truth in your ordinary state of mind. Extraordinary conditions have to be created.'

Ashishda's words brought little solace. Maybe, they weren't meant to. In the story, the treatment does not appear to be contrived and the disciple felt its impact in the guts, leading to despair. And probably that is the crux of the matter. If the disciple feels the situation is contrived then there is that hope to hold onto. Was it possible that Ashishda had seized this situation and was letting it build up, not intervening, to let the situation peak? If he was doing that, then, I suddenly realised it couldn't be an easy task for him too. For as much pressure as he was allowing to be put on us, that much he had to bear on himself. To be tough on someone else, for a conscious purpose, is difficult; and the guru is forever conscious of the high level of responsibility involved in handling someone in this unconventional manner.

Did this explain the fact that while everybody else had drawn lines on how much work they would contribute, Rajeev was being pushed to work every day for eight hours with the men, weeding the maize crop. Inevitably, his back muscles cramped and the old ailment recurred. After lunch he started to rest for an hour before going back to work.

One afternoon he was back within half an hour.

'What's the matter? Are you alright?' I asked.

'When I went to the fields above Savitri's house, Dave was sitting there. He wagged his finger indicating I was not to work anymore. So I asked him—why? He said, "You'd better go and see Ashishda about that. He wants to see you." So I went to the temple where Ashishda was talking to a visitor. When I told him that he had asked to see me, he did not have a clue. I then told him what Dave had said.'

'Then?'

'So I'm here. Dave won't let me work saying its Ashishda's decision and the best part is that Ashishda knows nothing about it.'

An hour later Ashishda came to our house. 'Dave feels you should come for work immediately after lunch and not sleep in the afternoon. That's why he told you to go home.'

'My back has begun to hurt and I need to rest it after a bout of exertion.'

'Oh, I see.'

'Also, if Dave thinks I can work for eight continuous hours a day, it's not possible. There are certain postures I find very painful with my back, and weeding is one of them.'

'I don't expect you to do that. Just be around there to supervise the men.' While Dave did not want Rajeev to work on the farm, Ashishda seemed to be gently pushing Dave to give up his injured pride and face the situation. It was becoming apparent that earlier, when Rajeev had been removed from the farm, Ashishda had succumbed to pressure from Dave. Or had he let Dave have his way because of Rajeev's dream? The number two priest had to batter the ego. Paradoxically, Ashishda was constantly striving to bring Rajeev back on the farm. Why? Was he trying to bridge the gap between Dave and Rajeev? Hidden behind his attempts was there also some measure of concern for Rajeev? It certainly had kindled a ray of hope in us that our situation was not hopeless. There seemed more to what was happening than was apparent.

August had come with the plunge and thrust of dark clouds billowing with rain, which settled into a steady downpour through the day and late into the nights. For over a week our cottage had been insulated with cotton wool-like mist, making us feel as if there was no reality outside.

The oak trees outside our house were dripping like dark green fountains, with the chatter of rain still fresh on their leaves. The deep throated sounds of the frogs, the chorus of the cicadas and the faraway strain of a lonely flute from the cloud drenched valley below, were the seasonal offering of monsoonal music.

Later, on one such memorable night when the rain drummed steadily on our tin roof throughout the night, I felt some presence very close at hand. Through the thin veil of a dream:

> *A man talked to me of his years of discipleship and how rigorous and hard the training had been. He said that on looking back he never regretted a moment of it. For a second, I thought the face was Ashishda's, but it was someone else's, with a smile that was not unfamiliar. He sat on the ground near my pillow and then took my hand and said very gently, 'You have really nothing to worry about. Finally, there is always protection.'*

There it was. The tangible presence of love. So tactile was the dream that at the end of it I thought—it is a wet night, I wonder if he has an umbrella to take with him when he leaves. I woke up and looked around the quiet room, and then I flicked the light switch. There was no electricity. Outside the rain ceaselessly poured into the dark vessel of the night. I lit the kerosene lamp and searched the floor for the wet footprints of a man who had come from afar to help me through the long hours of the night. Those unseen footprints walked the pathway of my soul like a long-awaited friend.

Shortly afterward, Ashishda left with Chitra and Dave for a trip to Badrinath. In an ironical twist of circumstances, Mike fell ill and there was no one left to do the evening service. Mike asked me to take over, knowing that I had been taught how to perform the service. I was extremely hesitant since we were barely tolerated around the temple and I felt this might incur Ashishda's wrath. On the other hand, to refuse, when there wasn't anyone else, seemed an even worse option.

'What should I do?' I asked Rajeev.

'Ask for help, inwardly. Hold the question in your mind before going to sleep. Maybe an answer will come.'

Early in the morning I had a short dream:

An elephant is walking on whom stones are being thrown. Children are troubling him and dogs are snapping at his heels. The elephant neither alters his pace nor looks back at the object of his discomfort. He quietly walks on with unconcerned dignity.

I woke up and made my decision to perform the service.

I felt a 'quiet' take hold of me, as though doing arati fitted my present moment perfectly. It was a reprieve, stolen and precious. From a thick haze of impenetrability, things lit up and grew transparent for those few days. It was as if in his lines in 'Tintern Abbey' William Wordsworth had captured my present sentiments:

...that blessed mood,
In which the burthen of the mystery,
In which the heavy and the weary weight
Of all this unintelligible world
Is lightened:—the serene and blessed mood,
In which the affections gently lead us on,—
Until, the breath of this corporeal frame
And even the motion of our human blood
Almost suspended, we are laid asleep
In body, and become a living soul:
While with an eye made quiet by the power
Of harmony and the deep power of joy,
We see into the life of things.

Soon enough, Mike recovered and took over the service. A week later Ashishda returned. After three days I was summoned to his room.

'I've been told you did the service in my absence?' He asked grimly.

I nodded my head.

'And why did you not tell me?'

'I felt it was up to the person who asked me to fill in for him.'

'Well, he didn't. I got to know from someone else.'

'I am sorry,' I said feebly.

'Only those I give permission to, do the service. No one can take the law into his or her hands,' he said angrily.

'But there was no one else to do it besides me.'

'Yet you chose not to tell me.'

Ashishda looked at me intently and then took a small book that was lying flagged next to him. This gave me the impression that the whole thing had been planned in advance. He began reading from it. It said that if an instrument's string is beyond tuning, then it should be taken off. In the same way if a disciple is not in tune with the guru, he or she is cast away. There was more, but my mind had stopped registering. I felt frozen. I thought I was being punished disproportionately to the crime. If I was so unfit what was the use of my hoping or trying for anything?

'I did the best I could under the circumstances. I had a short dream which helped,' I ventured.

'What dream?'

I recounted the dream.

'It does not actually give a decision. What gives you the feeling that you will get guidance every time you ask for it?'

He seemed indifferent to what I was saying. The flow of words had kept up a connection with Ashishda. Now even that was being withdrawn. I made my way home not knowing what I passed for my eyes were full of tears.

I hit rock-bottom after that. I finally experienced what is termed the dark night of the soul. No clear thoughts separated my day. A thick black cloud enveloped me. Time suddenly lost its sense of continuity with its hope for change. Rajeev tried to reach me but I felt I was mourning a loss too precious to name. Is this the longest part of the journey, this fading hour? Nothing had been born, yet everything was breathing its last. I felt I was sinking into an abyss without end.

'I know it is difficult but we have to take this,' Rajeev said.

'Why?'

'Till the two and a half years mentioned in your dream are over. If we have been warned about bad times we can't hope to be released before our time.'

I suddenly felt humbled by Rajeev's acceptance. His words calmed me with their simple truth. Maybe such an acceptance was not a form of defeat, but a calling forth of strength. If I tried to reject, or prematurely shake off the process, I might never gain the self-confidence to be equal to what we were being put through. I realised that if I now turned my back on it, I would always remain afraid of the darkness I was being asked to coexist with. I had to let it walk alongside me without letting it overpower me.

How and when I decided to pull myself out of it, I do not know. As I blinked awake, I resented the glare of light outlining details I would have preferred to remain blurred. What kind of trial was this in which we had begun doubting Ashishda, but still considered him our teacher? After a while I knew I had to do something about the way I felt. My days were spent locating and shoring a clear uncluttered area within myself. My eyes bored into the darkness to vivify what I had glimpsed in some unforgettable moments.

We don't attempt to delve inwards because of the fear of losing the familiar security of the known world. My outward world was far from secure. The little I knew of the inner one had offered me far more support than I could have ever imagined. So I waited, remembering and holding. A significant dream during this time helped the process:

> *A practise session of Judo is in progress. Many students wearing the traditional dress are doing various exercises. I am part of a group that is running up and down staircases and tackling minor obstacles, in an effort to increase our stamina. Unexpectedly, the Judo Master appears. He is Japanese and a very venerated figure. He looks at me and says, 'Come here.'*

> *I go and stand in front of him. Before I know, he raises his hand and brings it down in a swift painful crack at the base of my neck. The impact is so strong that I faint. When I come around I see him standing near me, watching. I am very angry and say, 'You knew I couldn't handle that, yet you hit me.'*

> *'I did it, so that you are never caught unawares again. Be always in a state of readiness. Now I will teach.'*

> *He paused and looked at me gently. 'The first rule is that when a blow is coming, go soft, go plastic. Let the blow glance through you like air. The impact of the blow must not be such that your own resistance rips you apart.'*

> *He comes near me and demonstrates. The motion is so fluid, yielding and graceful that I feel awed. I bow my head with reverence.*

The dream challenged the common conception that suffering is best avoided by resisting it. The judo master was teaching me an important lesson: Don't stiffen up with fear and anxiety. Let go of those constricting knots of self-worry which never lead anywhere and only perpetuate themselves in endless cycles of fate and compulsion. Go fluid, become pliant, and yield. At its best in Judo the mind and body are relaxed, there is no desire to win.

I was amazed at the timing of these dreams. They offered me guidance when I could not see which route to take. I believed in the dream, for in it I learnt a significant lesson. It was out of love that the teacher in this dream had hurt me, so that I learnt the simple but profound truth: that the assaults of life are best taken by yielding, not resisting them. More than the external situation, perhaps, our internal resistance could break us. Like the willow bends under the weight of snow and straightens when it melts.

Maybe training in Judo is meant to relax the body and mind, to let go. One throws, holds and wrestles but without strain. The Master in my dream calls for effortless action, which comes from breaking free from the tyranny of the ego, to a state beyond thought. Only then can you become fluid and elastic, neither clinging to the past nor fearing the future.

Each month passed with the feeling that we were being held, almost carried by a strength greater than our own. Unseen, it came with a fullness of love till it became more real than Ashishda himself. Its reassurance stretched to simple things. On one occasion Ashishda had gone away for a few days and had said he'd be back on a particular date. I do not know whether it was the same Power, or something else, which made me see in a dream, Ashishda come back two days earlier than scheduled. I was amazed when Ashishda did actually arrive two days earlier due to some unforeseen circumstances.

It took me a while to realise that my questions and

concerns were being answered and explained in numerous small ways. I chastised myself for wasting an opportunity. Instead of asking this Power about the greater truths, my wayward mind stayed locked in limited preoccupations. As time went by, I began to trust this inner source completely. Its teachings unerringly relevant, and its instructions inspirational. Whatever it was guiding me towards was worth waiting for. If love and reassurance were what I needed, it would bestow them on me. If I wanted to seek something beyond these, it seemed to be waiting for my request.

The cherry trees were bursting with their blossoms in November when I asked Ashishda if he would interpret some of my dreams. When I finished, he asked unexpectedly, 'You were taught the temple service before?'

'Yes.'

'This time I'll teach you the service myself, when you return from Delhi next month.'

Sometimes good news can be as stunning as bad. I shared my relief with Rajeev who said, 'First he gets annoyed when you do the service because Mike is ill. After that you tell him a few dreams and he changes his mind and promises to teach you the service. Quite perplexing.'

The confusion deepened when a week later Ashishda called Rajeev to the temple and said, 'I'm not saying the farm is not running well. But from now onwards Dave wants to handle it entirely on his own. When you return from Delhi start learning how to milk.'

'I feel like a yo-yo. Sometimes we are up and then down.' Rajeev frowned.

'What happened this time?'

'It's obvious. Dave has wanted me off the farm ever since Ashishda brought me back.'

'Perhaps we are feeling this way because our attention is locked in refusals and confirmations of ourselves. What the Judo Master had highlighted was that we withdraw from hurts and hopes and look beyond them,' I said.

Ten days after our arrival, soaking in the family's warmth and the Delhi winter sun, I had a dream that gave an interesting recap of the past year:

I am trekking in the hills. I start off with a crowd of family and friends but we soon part company. The terrain is unfamiliar and I realise the sun is about to set. There is no sign of civilization as I thread my way through the thick forest. I begin to worry for if I don't find a place to spend the night I will be truly lost. While wandering around I chance upon a fork in the clearing ahead. One is a path similar to the one I'm treading while the other is up the steep side of a mountain. Both are unfamiliar, and both have ends unknown to me. I begin to climb the steeper one as I feel this may get me faster to my destination. While I am inching my way up, the sun dips behind the mountains. I struggle with footholds, sometimes sliding back while at other times levering myself up with the aid of any small root or shrub. I lose track of time as I try to maintain course in the semi-darkness. My hands and legs are bruised and I feel giddy when I look down. Finally, as night falls I reach the top of the hill and I see a Dak bungalow with a light burning. I sit down and weep with relief.

I knock at the door of the bungalow. It is opened by a man who says to my surprise, 'We were expecting you. What took you so long?'

I realise he is a guide who has come from the higher reaches of the snow-clad mountains. He asks me to rest saying, 'We'll wait for a day before climbing. You can visit some local sites here if you like.'

I toy with the idea of setting off on my own the next day but realise I have no idea of the path in the higher

<blockquote>

mountains. I would get lost in no time. After a day's rest we set off early in the morning with haversacks, the guide leading the way. We wind our way up the mountain tracks while faraway we can see the faint silvery outline of snow-clad mountains.

</blockquote>

What was this steeper climb, this fork in the road? The dream was a clear reminder that I had chosen the more difficult path to reach the resting spot faster, and that I had parted company with a 'crowd of family and friends'. Such a choice would inevitably bruise me. Yet, something kept me climbing. The dream shows that the initial yearning to set off on an untrodden mountain track in search of an inviolate sanctuary is tested again and again. At every point a barrier appears which can only be crossed if something is let go off. Inevitably, by the evening hour doubts creep into the heart, and I wonder if this search is just a myth. The dream assures that the Dak bungalow will be sighted, where a guide awaits. One can only weep with relief. Was the dream suggesting that climbing is a metaphor for the raising of consciousness to reach a 'still point'? Guidance is assured if I persevere. The next part of the climb would not be as lonely as the first leg, where I had to make choices— the steeper path and the ability to keep going. In walking behind my guide towards reaches familiar to him, I could perhaps let go of everything. The dream left me joyful.

Thirty years later I had a similar dream:

<blockquote>

I am leaving a celebratory gathering of family and friends. I walk alone into the hills. This time I know where I am going. To meet Ashishda. I walk for a long time and reach the door of a small cottage. I knock. Ashishda opens the door and enfolds me in his wide-open arms.

We walk companionably down a solitary mountain trail till we come to a clearing which looks down into a small

</blockquote>

lake which has hippos and crocodiles inhabiting it. He points to the edge of the lake and says, 'You can build house there.' He watches me intently for my answer. I turn my back to the spot and begin climbing. All of a sudden Ashishda is ahead of me and brings down a ladder from thin air, and begins ascending it. I follow him up the ladder.

Again, like in the earlier dream, family and friends are left behind. But this time I knew where I was going. Ashishda offered me a choice, to build home in the pool of instinctive, habitual behaviour patterns (hippos and crocodiles) or climb higher with him. Maybe this time I was more familiar with the terrain, more capable of making a conscious choice both of the climb and my certitude in my guide.

23

Get Out of the Way

We returned to the Ashram in the second week of January. The cows were dozing in the afternoon sun outside the cowshed. On crossing the threshing floor, the men greeted us as they looked up from shelling the ripened maize for next year's seed. Looking at the fields that had been tilled and planted with barley and wheat I was struck by a paradox. Last year when we had returned from Delhi we had assumed that Rajeev would be working on the farm, this year we had accepted that he would not. Had something changed within us?

We entered Ashishda's room. He looked up from the book he was reading, the hint of a smile on his face. 'Settle down and then we'll see,' he said enigmatically.

His fairly warm greeting made me presume that he was giving us a day before he would teach me the service, as he had promised. I wondered who had been doing the temple service while we were away.

Soon enough we came to know. That evening Persis invited us for supper.

'Is Ashishda doing the morning service himself?' I asked.

There was silence as Persis and John exchanged swift glances. Persis looked distressed.

'No he's not doing it,' she said.

'Who is doing it?'

'I am. He taught it to me ten days ago.'

I opened my mouth and then shut it.

'I know, I know he promised to teach you the service. When he called to tell me he'd teach me the service, I reminded him of his promise to you.'

'What did he say?'

'He just said, "Trust me. I know what I am doing."'

'Why do you think he changed his mind?' Rajeev asked.

Persis stared at the lamp on the floor for a few seconds. 'With him you can never make out the real reasons. One only guesses.'

In the next few days, we waited for Ashishda to call us with an explanation. He never did. I could not rest with the thought so I went to see him. I related the dream I had in Delhi of trekking in the hills. I was using it as an excuse to see him in case he had something to say. As a disciple I could hardly demand that he teach me the service nor could I ask him why he decided not to.

When I finished narrating the dream he said, 'It's good you are still climbing in the dream.' His look searched my face for clues. 'Has something happened in meditation?'

'Nothing extraordinary.'

'Some extraordinary effort has been made. For one is helped only if one is trying.'

Then why are you not teaching me? I wanted to ask, but the practice of obedience kept me silent. All at once I wanted to ask him many questions but was unable to focus on even one that was clear enough to voice. I just stared at him. Ashishda seemed faraway.

'Anything else?' he asked finally.

I shook my head and left.

Ashishda's refusal to teach the service was a greater sorrow to me than even our seclusion. Denial of arati seemed a negation at a more fundamental level, while refusal to let us work was, to me, a personality issue. Here he was cutting at the root of our sustenance. The foundation of the guru-shishya bond is based on the belief in the Imperishable. In seeking that state, the disciple finds its echoes in the relationship with the guru. If what I am seeking is eternal, then the bond with the man who is showing me the way is also indestructible. Ashishda's distance had left us very much on our own to deal with the next step. Could we walk this Path without him?

Rajeev said to me, 'Our beings are saturated with Ashishda's teachings, and we cannot take his withdrawal as a perverse self-judgement and give up the climb.'

I felt I may not have understood the full scope of his intentions. Earlier, I had felt it unjust when demands had been made on the body—Rajeev's back. Then when we had been excluded from work, we had suffered because the mind, through a belief, had been targeted. Now the heart felt under siege because my aspirations were being questioned. Was Ashishda asking that I step away from the outer and rely on something deeper within? Was he asking us to take greater responsibility for our search? For he knew that suffering is an opportunity which can turn the person to seek within for that which is inherently free from suffering—that which observes both pleasure and pain, but is untouched by either.

More importantly, my dreams were warning me time and again to turn my attention inwards. They repeatedly reinforced Ashishda's teaching to go beyond the travails of the personality and rest in something beyond it.

How could I accept the love and reassurance that flowed

abundantly in my dreams and forget the role of my teacher in guiding me towards it?

How would I answer myself, or look straight into the eyes of a luminous Being, I had met on a moonlit night who had told me, 'Don't let go, for the road you're travelling leads to something real. Keep at it.'

Would I continue to turn angrily on a great Master, who had cracked me on the base of my neck, to say, 'You knew I couldn't handle it, yet you hit me?' In the Judo Master's look was my reason to hold on. 'I'll teach you how to handle it,' he seemed to say.

In our 'isolation and separation' from Ashishda we had found an inner guide and 'He' relentlessly directed us to hold onto our search. Irrespective of outward circumstances, internally I now perceived that the search was not dependent on anyone or anything. I felt I had found a pathway that I could, if I had to, walk alone.

As far as our outward life was concerned, within days of our arrival Ashishda left with Dave for Delhi. Rajeev began to learn to milk and was none too happy with the experience. Somehow the phrase 'being in the doghouse' and 'being in the cowhouse' had become interchangeable in his mind. He cut a rather morose figure as we walked down to the cowshed, his head bent and shoulders hunched.

'Who knows, you may just grow to love it,' I teased.

'Why don't I stay at home till that ecstatic feeling floods me,' he countered.

His flippant remark became a painful reality when he burnt both his hands. I would light the fire in the dairy in the morning when we came to milk. A very large and thick iron kettle was left on the fire to give us warm water to wash the cows' udders, and later our hands. That day, after the milking, Rajeev picked up the kettle and put it under the tap to top it up with water. He didn't realise that, by mistake, the kettle had been left on the fire completely empty. As soon as the cold water hit the bottom of the burning hot kettle, steam rose and scalded his hands. He didn't drop the kettle immediately fearing it might break the wash-basin. By the time we got the kettle off his hands, there were ten large blisters on them. The pain was so intense that he kept flapping his hands in the air to ease the burning. The blisters were filled with water and the only small measure of relief came from walking outside the house in the cold air. He paced up and down till lunch time. I ran down to Mike's cottage for a homoeopathic ointment. The burning began to subside. It took a week for the Cantharis ointment to clear all the blisters. Without transport, or a doctor nearby, we were lucky to have hit upon the right medicine.

Rajeev seemed more rested after this incident. As though something that had been wearing him down was expunged by the physical pain he had borne. And with the healing he had quietened himself internally.

The incident and Rajeev's reaction opened up a fresh dialogue between us. One evening, he said contemplatively, 'I think we can learn to align ourselves with suffering. It seems to me that if you can't rise above it you can at least, walk with it.'

Promptly I said, 'I feel we must change the way we have been reacting to our situation.'

Rajeev responded eagerly, 'Are you reading my mind? Since I burnt my hands I have been thinking of nothing else but what you are suggesting—to try for a complete change in our attitude. If we continue to react with disappointment or anger to the outward situation, we are setting up a chain reaction from which there is no way out. Our lack of acceptance could be contributing in creating the very conditions that upset us.'

'I think I know what you're getting at,' I cut in warming to the conversation. 'Like in some of my dreams, the Teacher uses the medium of our current situation to point towards a level of awareness which transcends it; showing me where my attention should actually rest. Remember the dream of the mahout, the reference to wounds that ended by pointing towards the airy space?

'But, can we shift our attention, consistently, when the sandstorm continues to blow grit into our eyes?' I asked.

'We did it once before.'

'Did we?'

'When we went to visit Nisargadatta Maharaj. All we heard was his voice and words. Do you remember how surprised we were when we replayed the tapes of his talks? Then we heard the tinsmith banging in the street, the horns, the cries of children—sounds we had not heard because our attention wasn't on them. We may have to do the same thing with our mind; shift our focus of attention away from our thoughts to that area within, which is still and quiet.'

'Use any method but learn the trick which works for you,' Ashishda said swiftly in response to Don's question about stilling the mind.

'Maybe thoughts are just an illusion,' Mike said.

'It is difficult to still the mind by these arguments. You just have to drop them. You must've heard the story about the courtesan who danced as long as the King's attention was on her. She stopped as soon as his attention was taken away. Your thoughts are powered by your attention on them. As long as that is not withdrawn, they will continue to dance.'

Rajeev and I gave ourselves completely to building an inner focus. We discussed how to hold on to the observing state without getting entangled with the personality. Day after day we worked hard, fighting the compelling pull of the outward situation. Slowly our over-wrought emotions seemed to be settling and a measure of peace descended.

While trying to maintain this equilibrium, Rajeev and I drew each other back every time the mind drifted. With growing wonder, we realised that although it seemed that our circumstances presented us with no alternatives, in truth, they contained several viable options. To our relief, we had found that freeing our minds allowed us the space to explore those options.

Thoughts about our situation no longer gripped us but floated past, as if they did not belong to us. We felt as though we had been drilling the ground and hit a depth where clear and uncontaminated waters run. The calm had a fullness. When things feel right the flute of the winds, the quiet of late sunny afternoons, the shaded trees, the creatures of the forest all seem to hum with peace.

At the end of April, Rajeev woke me one night, and with urgency pulled me towards the large windows. Pointing to the night sky he said with wonder, 'Look at that sight. The sky is carpeted with birds!' I was bleary eyed with sleep, unseeing, uncomprehending. I went back to sleep. Next day he wrote in his diary:

> I woke at 2 a.m. and saw the sky covered with birds flying northeast. They had enveloped the sky from horizon to horizon. They were flying high and appeared only as specks. The sight was majestic and awesome. There was no sound. There were so many birds flying that each took up the spot where the preceding one had been. This gave the impression that they were stationary amidst movement. Woke up M. to show her. She couldn't see

anything and went back to sleep. I watched them for a long time. Drifted off to sleep. Awoke shortly afterwards and they were still there till four in the morning. Then there was a last flight in formation—a single line of these birds—and they were gone.

Rajeev went to see Ashishda who mused, 'What you saw can be interpreted like a dream. Birds usually represent thoughts. And these birds are still. A still mind can be awesome and majestic as you saw them. Yet the actual search begins only after the mind has become quiet. That is the platform from which the jump is made.'

'What do you think the last flight in single formation suggests?'

After giving it thought Ashishda said, 'I can't make anything out of that.'

'Ashishda, what lies beyond the quiet mind?'

'That you must find out for yourself. My telling you will mean nothing. After all, any words I use to describe a state will have severe limitations, and you can't, through them, replicate or know the true nature of that state. It has to be experienced directly. I am not trying to be secretive. I am only telling you that some things on this Path are taught while others are caught. What you may have to do is to intensify your enquiry. Go deeper and deeper into the stillness until you let go of everything.' He paused. 'All that can be said—align yourself in the right direction, and get out of the way.'

What is this getting out of the way? Initially, when I had begun to quieten myself during meditation I had, perhaps, taken my first shaky step towards withdrawing from the outer world of events to my inner dialogue—my internal chatter of wants, desires, hopes and fears. Psychological analysis had helped me to observe the patterns of behaviour and thought that knitted my psyche. Japa (repetition of the mantra given by Ashishda at initiation) had helped in focusing myself till the automatic flow of thoughts had slowed down and I seemed to float in the pause between the end of a thought and the beginning of a new one. I had then tried to lengthen the period between these pauses. Was this the free space where the 'I' is in abeyance and may have 'got out of the way'? It meant more than this, I soon learnt.

Ashishda had told us that if one is in a state of dhyan (inward concentration) then the japa has served its purpose. One evening he had given an analogy, asking us to focus on the candle burning in the middle of the room.

'See this candle—the outer world of objects.

'If your attention isn't wandering then you're only watching the candle.

'Now, pause. Become aware that you are watching the candle.

'You can then take one more step back into yourself: by becoming aware that you are aware of watching the candle.'

He then removed the candle from our view, asking, 'What happens if the candle is no longer there? You are now only aware of being aware.'

Is this what Ashishda meant by 'get out of the way'? Could it be that if Rajeev got himself (the ego) out of the way like in Ashishda's example of the candle, the sense of being 'this' or 'that' would disappear? Then the awareness, not having anything to focus on, may reveal the essential Self.

'Go deeper and deeper into the stillness until you let go of everything.' Ashishda had said. It was surprising that even in the stillness there was more to be let go of.

Earlier I had tried to widen my awareness by becoming conscious of my thoughts, by trying to separate the observer from them. Gradually, I saw that the act of observing was more important than what was being observed. It made me wonder who or what observed? It seemed to be a lit concentrated point of light, which when looking outwards could observe my thoughts. When it turned its attention away from them, it was just a focus of awareness without any content. Was this what Ashishda was referring to as taking one more step back into yourself? I could only describe it as something at rest, an alive stillness, an iridescence...

A Sufi has summarised this process thus:

> The first stage of dhikr is to forget self, and the last stage is the effacement of the worshipper in the act of worship, without consciousness of worship...

The 'dream' of the still formation of birds was a watershed for Rajeev. There was now a clearer framework and context in which he could both locate and loose himself. To me, as a bystander, it emanated a powerful beauty. How much more for the beholder?

The tempo of our life changed. The book I was reading, Rajeev cleaning the oil lamp for the evening, the leaves scurrying up our stone path chased by the winds, all nestled next to me with their quiet companionship. No longer did I walk the path outside our house with rapid, preoccupied steps but throbbed with the heartbeat of the setting sun as it caressed the top of the pine trees with its promise of warming them another day. I felt reassured that a strong interface exists between the reality I know and live in, and that which I had the occasional privilege to glimpse.

24

The Long and Winding Road

The weather had turned warm by end-May when Don, walking vigorously downhill waved cheerily at us. 'The Malhotras have arrived, bag and baggage. I'm going down to meet them. Coming?'

With flecks of grey salting their hair, the Malhotras were well into their late fifties. Ramesh had taken premature retirement from a foreign assignment to make the Ashram their home. Pandekhola was the house they had renovated. The Malhotras now joined us in the minority group of Indian couples. We arrived to find John, Persis and Mike already there. Don had his arm draped affectionately around Ramesh's shoulder teasing him as only old friends can. 'So Ramesh, I hope you're ready for some hard work ahead.'

'With your valuable experience to guide me Don, I can't go wrong,' Ramesh said with a straight face.

'My first disciple. I'm overwhelmed.'

'No, you should be worried. Haven't you heard the saying—Those who can, do. Those who can't, teach.'

We all laughed companionably, just as we had four years ago, when we had first entered Pandekhola to share a cup of tea. Waves of nostalgia washed over me as I noticed

Persis' baggy sweater similar to the one she was wearing when we first met here. This one was darned on the side, with little pretension at matching the original wool of the sweater. By how many shades did it fall short of the original wool, I wondered irrelevantly? And how far was my present moment from the time we first came here? That time was marked by the goggle-eyed enthusiasm of youth, while this moment contained all the sobriety that comes of learning that life has much bigger lessons to teach than those one is prepared to learn.

My current phase was presenting me with new lessons every day. Often, I felt all my energy was bunched together. And at other times I found I could slip into another state of awareness, so potent was this charge. It was impersonal, self-contained. I was merely the instrument on which it strummed its vibrant tune.

Was this the real point behind many spiritual practices? To shore up the energies, to build a centre, which would then brook no hindrance on its way to ascertain the Truth? Perhaps, a powerful focus develops and the searcher and what is sought come together in an upsurge of attraction. Is that why men and women choose seclusion to address themselves to one burning question?

Curious things began to take place. The psychic layers seemed to have been shaken up with the build-up of this new energy so that it was easy for me to disengage from my body. One night I felt myself leave my body, and begin to fly above treetop level. Slowly I rose higher into the cooler reaches of the mountain tops. I passed oceans and strange lands before I reached a place that for some reason, I knew was Netherlands. Later I began to fly again and went higher and higher till I saw the world getting smaller and smaller. I tried to focus on one tiny city that appeared as a point on the globe. Even that point seemed to get fainter, the further

I travelled. I remember feeling afraid and, in an instance, was back in my body.

When I told Ashishda about this he said, 'During his Cambridge days Gopalda had an astral projection in which he found himself soaring out into space. There was a guide with him. They were rushing out into empty space. Out, out and out...After some time Gopalda turned around to see some twinkling objects far below him. He wanted to identify our solar system so he looked questioningly towards the guide, who pointed to a small shining object in the vast distance and said, "That's your Universe!" Gopalda was so stunned by the immensity of the statement that he felt afraid. The fear brought him back into his body.'

For me a door had opened. I walked in and out of it, not out of conscious volition, but with little choice in the matter. The opening of this inner space extended according to my capacity to let it. The vastness of this new universe I now inhabited made me feel if I walked too far I might disappear forever in its blue midnight shades. Then, one night I dreamt:

> *There is a tall range of snow-covered mountains. I see myself being dropped on one of the peaks. The landing is soft as I sink into the snow. It is misty and a fresh snowfall begins. After a while I can't make out the difference between the speckled mist, the peaks and the clouds. I know I am at a very high altitude, very far away from any world at all. Everything around me seems to merge and melt into the whiteness. Through this, a voice asks me, the words echoing everywhere,*
>
> *'Where did you come from?'*
>
> *I am deeply puzzled because I can't answer the question.*

I emerged from this dream shaken by my own insignificance amongst such limitless immensity. I felt I had travelled into a space without boundaries, only to be shown that I was just a tiny fleck, almost indiscernible in the picture.

The white uniformity of the snow crystalized the relevance of the question asked: What remains when every identification is dropped? The snow-covered mountains, the mist, the fresh snowfall may perhaps be an appropriate metaphor for no differentiation, no duality and the place where the answer to one's true origins may be found. Where did I come from? What is the source of my arising? What is my true identity?

The question posed enhanced my perplexity, heightened the utter urgency of finding an answer.

I had felt I had reached some high point and while my mysterious wanderings made me soar, I was soon to be reminded that the events of my life were no less significant. I had a dream warning me of that:

> *I have to face an examination. The first test is scheduled for the 27th of June and the second for the 4th of July. The one on the twenty-seventh, I find I can tackle without much preparation. The one on the fourth is a different matter, for my examiner says, 'You better prepare, it might be very tough.'*

I had this dream in mid-June. Rajeev and I felt it was a premonition of some unpleasant events to come.

On the 27th of June we woke to find the sky overcast. We waited and waited, for what, we couldn't say. When the postman came my heart sank as I held my mother's letter in my hand, anticipating bad news from her. I relaxed when it turned out to be a cheerful letter. At supper our relief was palpable when Rajeev said, 'Nothing has happened. Let's hope the fourth is the same. Maybe the dream is not what we think it is.'

The 4th of July was as clear a day as the monsoons

permitted. In the late afternoon we went for a walk up the ridge where there was a small, not-so-frequented teashop. A villager or two strayed there and sat on the old wooden bench talking to the owner about his land, the price of potatoes, the money he had borrowed to repair his house, the state of his cattle…On the mud-coated chula an old kettle rested, which I had seldom seen on the boil. The old blackened beams of the teashop had once served as a shelter for wayfarers from far-flung villages in the valley.

As the sun dipped behind the mountains we felt relieved that the day had ended without any drama. Later, we walked into the evening session and had barely sat down when Ashishda and Dave entered. Dave seldom came to the sessions and I wondered what warranted this visit. I was startled to see Ashishda looking angrily at us.

'You think you both can sit there and waste all the Ashram wood. You come to milk at quarter-to-six in the morning and light the cowshed chula. The fire burns continuously for nearly two hours till half-past-seven, when Don comes to separate the milk!' He glared at us. Rajeev next to me was bristling. Dave had a smug smile on his face while I was trying hard not to erupt. Others in the room instinctively recoiled from the hiss in Ashishda's tone.

'How dare you think you can waste so much fuel? You may have money to burn but we don't. Urmila is not to be blamed for she has only just started milking. But you, you should know better,' Ashishda fumed.

When he had finished with us, Ashishda opened the book he was reading and commenced the next chapter. I closed my eyes and tried to quieten my thoughts. Quite unexpectedly my mind went quiet very quickly. When I opened my eyes Ashishda was still reading. Outside the moon was high above the temple dome. Everything was quiet as though it had found its reason to be so.

I could not help thinking that my mind had quietened because I had been warned by my dream. I was overwhelmed by a silent joy at my unusual response and was filled with a deep sense of gratitude.

Once, long before, I had asked Ashishda, 'How is the timing of certain dreams so perfect?

'Think of it like sharing a balcony with God.'

I had laughed. Ashishda had teased. 'Stretch your imagination. The strangest people can be found together! Well, what do you think you'll see?'

'I've no idea.'

'Probably what you may see are millions of small lights twinkling down below in the valley of the cosmos. Those are the evenly burning lights of human souls in the ocean of the world. They are a sea of glistening lights as may appear on a clear night from an aeroplane. These lights are burning with more or less even intensity. As long as they continue to burn evenly they appear homogeneous. But if one day one of those lights begins to burn with more intensity, it will stand out. Your attention will be drawn to it.

'Now don't think I'm suggesting that this is the actual view from up there, or even anything like it. This is just an analogy to help you comprehend how it may be possible for that Universal Power or Divine Being to recognise when one particular person has intensified his or her strivings, in an effort to know. The glow-worm in the valley begins to twinkle more brightly and attracts attention to itself. That is when instructions in dreams and visions can take place.'

While we lived in one frame of reference, forces built up to create its very opposite. Our isolation began to create a stronger reaction in the community. Persis said to us, 'This phase can't go on forever. You don't expect Ashishda to call you. Why don't you break this cycle by offering to do some work?'

'It's not so simple, Persis. Ashishda would call us if it was necessary.'

'Isn't your pride that's preventing you from going and starting work? Why would Ashishda object?'

'On the contrary, our pride is taking a beating by staying at home. We've offered more than once, and would like nothing better than to be back at work,' Rajeev said.

'If that is so, do the opposite of what you are doing now. Push for a change. It might help,' Persis said with a troubled look in her eyes.

Gently, one or two other community members suggested the same. The underlying feeling was—a change was necessary. Something had to give way. Thinking over it, we decided to follow the suggestion of offering to work again. Ashishda had, I recalled, said, 'At chaff-cutting time we prefer all hands-on-deck.' If we could quietly slip in and begin work at that time surely no one would object to an extra pair of hands.

One September afternoon, the day the cutting of the maize started, as the diesel motor chugged away, we slowly made our way down to the threshing floor. With each step I wondered whether we were doing the right thing or not. Nervously we stepped onto the threshing floor. I walked ahead over the maize covered floor to take up position near the chaff cutter. Dave was coming out of the milk room when he saw Rajeev.

'What are you doing here?' he raised his voice. 'Who asked you to come? You are not needed here.' He wagged his finger up and down in a signal to go away.

The men and the residents watched as Rajeev turned and slowly made his way back. The chaff-cutter's chug-chug suddenly became deafening in my ears.

Dave ignored me and I worked in silence that day. I did not return the next day.

That evening, I watched Rajeev across the room absorbed in a book he was reading. I reached out to him in thought. Our experiences had made me realise that a thin line divides pain from love. The depth of one feeling spills over into the other at some point. We had shared the pain to the fullest and realised in the process how it only helped reinforce the love further. In our stumbling, struggling efforts we had accidentally chanced on something far more profound than either of us, and it had linked us inextricably together. I could not regret one moment of this journey, for in it I found that the bonds of a relationship deepen in direct proportion to one's own capacity to grow. Then it becomes a truly shared path in which one person's clarity becomes the measure of the other's step forward; one partner's doubts become the other's reason to understand.

Eighteen months had passed since my dream had warned us about the trying two-and-a-half-year period ahead. Would it come to an end then? What was this strange web that was interlocking us all together, as though these circumstances were necessary for each of us, for different reasons? How long would it take for the lesson of this experience to be learnt?

A week later I had a dream:

I see a very old castle near the seashore. As I look at the castle from outside, I know that in it reside the world's best musicians. I slowly walk towards the castle and up a carved stone staircase to reach an open corridor. I look around and see a man approaching me. His grey hair touch his shoulders. He is wearing a flowing white gown and his face has a calm beauty to it. His eyes are like pools of light. With a soft smile on his face he says, 'I'll teach you music.'

He takes me into a room that is bare. The stone walls rise up to a high ceiling with two long narrow windows on opposite sides. In the centre of the room is a music stand on which a score rests. A single beam of light from the window illuminates it. I walk up to it and read the first line on the score, which is 'It's a long and winding road that leads me to your door'.

Besides the man who brought me into the room there is another man watching me. I know he too is a musician and a resident of the castle.

'I don't know how to sing.' I plead with them.

'Try,' the grey-haired man says gently.

I try to sing the first line; it comes out so badly that I hang my head in shame. I continue singing despite my acute embarrassment. I am conscious that the castle is full of top-class musicians who must be listening to my dismal attempts. The two men are pacing up and down in front of me. At one point I look up and the man with the grey hair smiles at me. Love pours out of him and tears come to my eyes to behold such compassion. I continue to sing for hours, each time starting afresh. I think to myself, 'How can you train a person to become a musician if the aptitude does not exist? The training must start when you are much younger, not when the voice is too old.'

Soon afterwards I receive a note that comes from another part of the castle. It reads, 'We expect you to make it. Nothing must stop you. At one time you unselfconsciously made the right gesture. You must follow that up, without letting up in your effort.'

I resume singing and as I look again at the score, I realise it is evening and the light has become faint. My two teachers do not seem to be tired and each time I start singing, they begin pacing. Looking at them I realise it is not the effort that tires them, only the lack of it.

My eyes were wet with tears when I awoke. My clumsy efforts and embarrassment did not deter the teachers.

Making mistakes, starting over and over again seemed perfectly natural to them as they energetically paced the room participating in every attempt made. The talent to sing did not matter. The effort to sing became an outward expression of a quest which demands no special talent or abilities, only the willingness not to give up.

25

If Mistakes Have Been Made,
I'll Pay for Them

Over the last two years I'd had recurring trouble with my teeth. I would have them attended to whenever we went down to Delhi. A desensitising dental cream had been recommended, which occasionally proved beneficial. Not this time though. Rajeev tried a few homoeopathic drugs but to no avail. A week had gone by, but the pain grew. One facility sadly lacking in these remote areas was a dentist. Mike mentioned to us that a retired military dentist had recently started practice in the nearby town. And he wasn't bad. At least he'd be able to diagnose the problem and prescribe some medication.

'What a happy coincidence,' I told Rajeev. 'Ramesh is going into town tomorrow and has agreed to take me too.'

Rajeev was equally relieved. He filled in for me at the night watch. One of the cows was due to calve any day now and two-hourly night watches had begun in case she went into labour. Strictly speaking, Rajeev was not allowed to do the night watch but that day I felt entitled to this concession. I also decided not to attend the evening session and rest at home.

It was midnight when Rajeev came home. I wasn't asleep and I sensed this feeling of heaviness around him.

'Is your tooth hurting? Why aren't you asleep?'

'What's wrong?'

'Try and get some sleep. You'll need it.'

'What is it?' I persisted.

He fidgeted around and then burst out, 'Ramesh came to the cowshed after the session. He was very apologetic but said that he wouldn't be able to take you into town.'

'What...! Why?'

'Apparently, Dave also has a bad tooth and needs to see the dentist.'

'So?'

'Well, Ashishda suggested that Ramesh take him tomorrow, or rather today.'

'But why can't he take me also?'

'That's what Ramesh told Ashishda, that he'd willingly take both of you. But Ashishda prevailed on him that there wasn't enough room and Dave has to go.'

I was aghast.

'Ramesh was upset at having to make this choice, but felt helpless since Ashishda was being so firm about it. Ramesh came to apologise to you.

'Never mind the ride. I've had time to think. The first bus leaves at half-past-seven. It'll get to town at about ten. The last bus back leaves at three in the afternoon. That'll give us enough time with the dentist and we'll be back for the night shift. I've asked Urmila and Persis to do tomorrow morning's milking. We'll make up the next day.'

His energetic delivery gave me the fillip that I needed. 'What about informing Ashishda that we won't be here for the day?'

Ashishda wasn't in his room in the morning, so Rajeev

asked Ramesh to inform him that we'd caught the early morning bus to town. There was briskness in our step as we covered the two-km-plus walk to the village. Our minds raced ahead worrying whether the dentist would be in town; I didn't have an appointment, would he be able to do something or not?

The early morning bus didn't arrive as scheduled. Nor did the next one due at eight o'clock. Rajeev tried to find out from the shopkeepers if they had any news. There was talk of buses not plying that day as a token protest against some driver's dismissal from service. Someone told us that one bus had gone past, the evening before, and should be returning any minute now.

The minutes ticked away. Our anxiety grew as we indulged endlessly in mathematical calculations. If the bus arrived at nine, then two and a half hours into town; half an hour's walk to the dentist; if we hurried, maybe twenty minutes; we'd have to leave his clinic by half-past-two to catch the three o'clock. That gave us a comfortable two and a half hours with him. If the bus came at nine-thirty, then how were we placed?

The bus did not come at nine-thirty. Just then, Ramesh's car sailed in and they stopped to do some chores. The shopkeeper, whom Rajeev had been badgering about the arrival of the bus, heaved a sigh of relief, 'Your troubles are over! You can get a lift with your friends.'

The polite smile on our faces froze as we rigidly stood where we were. Ramesh and Urmila came over to us—he helpless, her eyes brimming with tears. Dave stood aloof rolling a cigarette making a studied show of ignoring us. Five minutes later they were gone, while we had been rooted to that spot for just under three hours. We tried another iteration of our abstruse calculations with an initial value of ten. Yes, we could just manage to squeeze through the time barrier, and hope surged afresh in us.

Time dragged on, in its relentless march of tick-tocking. Now...now...now. Where in hell was the bus? Ten-thirty. Even now, we could manage it. Something inside me told me it would swing round that corner in two minutes. Many minutes came in twos and went, but there was no sign of the bus.

At a quarter-to-eleven we abandoned all hope. Beaten and dejected, we started walking back towards the Ashram. We reached the dirt track and our pace further slackened to take the uphill climb, our minds raging furiously. We'd barely climbed fifty yards when we heard the drone of an engine. The bus! No, it couldn't be. The sound didn't have the full-throated roar of a heavy engine. But I was already running back. Rajeev shouted after me, 'It's no use. I saw it on the last bend, it's a jeep and it's loaded.'

Wild horses couldn't have stopped me. I knew mine was an act of desperation, 'No harm trying.'

The jeep came into full view. There were three people in front and a few in the rear. I thumbed a ride. The jeep went past and then ground to a halt some twenty or thirty yards ahead. Rajeev was running behind me. We discovered four people in the rear, making a total of seven in the jeep. The driver smiled, 'Of course, we'll take you. That's what a vehicle is meant for. Squeeze in at the back.'

The engine roared and we moved forward. I felt I was being ferried on the back of a swan. So great was the relief at being aboard a vehicle that I became oblivious to the time trap we were in. As we neared town, these worries resurfaced. Our heaven-sent transport had covered the distance in an hour and a half, and we were seated in the dentist's office a few minutes before one. Dave and three other people were already waiting there, while the doctor was busy with a patient.

Ten minutes later the next patient went in. How long would he take? Five minutes passed, then another five and yet another five. It would probably take the usual half an hour, I thought. That meant my turn would come around three. By that time the last bus would be hooting its departure. While people idly turned the pages of their magazines, I kept looking out of the window. A woman in her mid-fifties was hanging out the washing. The midday sun was strong and I mused that the clothes would dry in barely two hours. But my bus would have left by then…My mind jumped back to the woman. She must be the dentist's wife! That was my only chance. I quickly went and apprised her of my dilemma. She was sympathetic and marched into her husband's clinic. She was out in a few minutes saying that he would see me out of turn if the other patients didn't object. She requested the three people waiting, including Dave, each of whom gave their assent.

I was out of the clinic by a quarter-past-two. I suddenly relaxed for the first time that day. The tooth was pretty bad and needed a root canal treatment, which the dentist wasn't equipped to handle. It would have to be attended to by a Delhi doctor. He had, however, prescribed some antibiotics to take care of the infection and the pain. We bought the medicines and boarded the bus ten minutes earlier than we had originally predicted in our frenzied attempts at higher maths.

'Ashishda is very annoyed with you.' Urmila said to me, when I went to the dairy to collect our bottle of skimmed milk the next morning.

'But Rajeev went to see him before we left. I thought Ramesh had passed on our message?'

'He did. Ashishda is upset because you jumped the queue over Dave at the dentist. He said you behaved discourteously. You should have asked for Dave's consent.'

Something in me snapped when I heard this. Milk bottle in hand, I walked into Ashishda's room and confronted him, 'Why did you have me offloaded from Ramesh's car?'

He sat silently in his chair, the book he was reading still open in his lap. 'Dave had been holding the pain for ten long days. He was in agony.'

'Does his agony rank higher than everyone else's?' I questioned recklessly.

'How long has your tooth been troubling you?'

'More than a week.'

'Why didn't you come and see me about it?'

'You knew about it. Were you able to do anything for Dave's tooth?'

Again he was silent, all through this conversation he gave me the feeling that he was slightly amused at my outburst. 'But you left early in the morning, without giving me time to arrange...'

'You had all the time last evening to make alternative arrangements! Another thing, if you pulled rank and got us offloaded don't you think you had some responsibility? You could have asked Rajeev to take the temple jeep into town to get my tooth attended to. But I guess Dave wouldn't have approved of that, would he?

'How come the story repeats itself again and again? If Dave does not want to work with him, Rajeev gets chucked off the farm. I wonder if it was for the same reason that you didn't teach me the temple service. Now Dave does not want to travel in the same car as us so I get offloaded!'

The smile of amusement had vanished, replaced by a grave look. I knew I had overstepped on all counts. My voice had risen a few decibels, but I carried on regardless. 'And what's this you've been saying about my being discourteous by not asking Dave personally to let me jump my turn?'

'Dave felt you should have asked for his consent.'

'Is that what he's been telling you? How the world rides roughshod over him? He was asked by the dentist's wife and he gave his consent. There is more than one witness to verify that. Forget about all that, Ashishda. It is because of you, that Urmila and Ramesh could not take us even when they met us at the village and realised there was a bus strike. One nod from Dave, and Ramesh would have happily given us a ride. But he never did. Why? Because you,' I said pointing my finger at him, 'are feeding each of Dave's neurosis by giving into them. What kind of man are you turning him into? Your so-called therapy with him is not working. You're producing a man who cannot bear to hear a single word of dissent and who is incapable of feeling anything for anybody but himself. And what he feels for himself is only self-pity.'

Ashishda listened intently but said nothing. I felt very certain that all this was news to him. I left him deep in thought while I descended the steps on unsteady legs.

I learnt later that Ramesh and Urmila had been called for a talk by Ashishda that afternoon. Oddly enough, Dave appeared outside the dairy room in the evening after I'd finished milking. He kept tinkering with the firewood outside for some time. He then came into the room looking slightly sheepish, as if he wanted to say something, but was finding it difficult. I dilly-dallied with washing the utensils to give him time, but he said nothing.

A week later we were on the bus to Delhi and something struck me about my confrontation with Ashishda. It seemed to me that he had not been contradicted for a long time. And despite that, he had actually been listening to what I was saying. The thought gave me some hope for a possible change in the future. I had a dream around that time which seemed to say that we were not in a hopeless situation:

I've finished five years at medical college and begun an internship. I'm attached to a hospital with a good reputation and a team of highly qualified doctors. The day I join, a patient dies. I ask the attending nurse, 'Has the body gone for post-mortem?'

Her answer is very evasive. I then go to a doctor and ask him the same question. He is very terse and edgy as he answers. I begin to wonder whether something is being hidden. I question the medical superintendent, the operation theatre staff and the staff from the ward where the patient had died. Finally, a senior doctor tells me off. 'Why don't you mind your own business? A lot of harm can come to your career, and who are you anyway to question senior doctors in this fashion?'

I persist in my questioning, and soon discover that the patient had died of an overdose of drugs, administered out of sheer negligence by the hospital staff. I am walking towards the wards when I realise that a threatening band of senior doctors, nurses and other staff members are encircling me. A top official says, 'We will blackball you and make sure that you can't work here or practise anywhere else either.'

'I'm not interested in exposing anyone. All I want to do is to ensure that such a mistake is not repeated again.'

The next day my name is up on the notice board, expelling me. I find myself standing alone in a darkened ward, where everyone avoids looking at me. Slowly I start to walk down the corridor at the end of which is a large, oval mirror. It suddenly begins to shine with brilliance. As I'm staring at it, I see one of 'Them' appear. Then another face, replaced quickly by another. Finally the last one of 'Them' appears, touches the brim of his hat with his fingers in greeting and disappears when I try and look closer. Each of them was characterised by a face and features from which an otherworldly light shone.

What I saw in the sometimes misting and at other moments clear mirror was the swirling epiphany of light. I'm so overwhelmed by what I had beheld that I fall on my knees and weep with gratitude for the support.

It took me a few days to go and see Ashishda. I sat opposite the window with the view of the willow tree. He sat on his chair, engrossed in pulling out burr-seeds from his woollen socks. I recounted the dream. He didn't say anything. We sat in silence for a minute or so.

'How long has it been?'

I knew what he was referring to. 'The two-and-a-half-year period is just about over.'

'Curious. Very curious.' He muttered more to himself. The socks lay unattended on his lap. Suddenly he was all there and very serious.

'An overdose has been given...an overdose of pressure... something may have died.' Again, he repeated the words as if thinking aloud. He looked out of the window, absorbed in his thoughts. I don't know what he was gazing at. After another ten minutes of silence, he said very quietly, 'If mistakes have been made, I'll pay for them.'

26

The Rhizome Remains

Once again, the plum trees were in blossom, marking the end of winter. A floating leaf brushed my elbow as I stood outside the house feeling I had aged many years in the last few months. I felt like some dusty sand dune that finds itself repositioned after the storm winds have blown over. On looking around I was surprised to see how much my internal scenery had changed.

If five and a half years earlier I had surrendered with faith to Ashishda, I now felt that the form of my surrender had changed. My last dream had shocked me awake, so powerful was its imagery that I became aware that I had reached a turning point in my perceptions. Although the 'overdose had killed' my uncritical response to Ashishda, yet I still saw him as extraordinary. As a teacher he had, until now, never failed me. On this I had no misgivings. I questioned Ashishda because I had been torn apart by a perplexity whose opposing pulls were created on the one hand by his unfathomable behaviour, and on the other, by my inherent belief in him.

The patient had died of an overdose, emphasizing that the wrong medicine had not been administered, but that someone had exceeded his brief. Could this mean that the pressure put on us was not altogether wrong? Besides the significant message for me, I felt the dream also mirrored my compelling need to understand all that had transpired at the Ashram over the last few years.

My great fear was that without any answers, I might succumb to the external pressure. Later I realised this dark and stormy phase, which lasted thirty long months, was to be a period in which I received the most invaluable teachings of my life; that this very perplexity was a chariot on which I could traverse a distance I had not dreamed of.

Two strands emerged as I reflected on the events that had so perplexed me. The first was to understand the guru-disciple relationship, which had its own compelling logic. The second took me back to my inner life and my dreams. They had helped me view my daily struggles from an altogether different position. I looked at each of these strands separately, together and, eventually, beyond them.

I had seen how following the practices Ashishda had outlined had culminated in my seeing the golden-etched outline of Lord Krishna melting into a streaming Light. Ashishda had said that that extraordinary moment had happened because of Grace. 'I' had nothing to do with it. His words rang true when I found in the following year that even though I persisted with the practices I could not reach that state again. I could not help but wonder whether I was just marking time; the skills to cope with the farming lifestyle at the Ashram had been honed, the discipline of the practices had borne some fruit, and a few sporadic illumined moments completed the picture. Had I plateaued because my initial yearnings had been satisfied and I was content? What I had not realised was that these were only the warm-up exercises. The climb was yet to come.

Perhaps, there had to be an urgency of aspiration if I had to get off the plateau. For, I had realised that our strivings, which had stood us in good stead till then, could take us only up to a point. Against this dilemma, I explored our experience with Ashishda from a larger perspective, free from the bind of the smaller, once agonising, details. The issue was complex.

Perhaps the most important factor was Ashishda's own beliefs that governed his role as a guru. The training he himself had undergone. Ashishda had completely surrendered his ego during his discipleship, which had helped him break his identifications and made real a state that is beyond our everyday consciousness. This had led Ashishda to believe that our true centre lies at the root of our being, somewhere within our awareness. That which allows me to look out at the world and participate in life, and yet has the capacity to also observe myself. But what is this observing awareness in itself? When the operations of the mind are stilled, then what is left is pure Awareness. The journey then becomes a process of trying to 'awaken' to that Awareness; its discipline and practise, an attempt to identify and weed out all that stands in the way. But how is this separation between the personality and that awareness to be achieved?

Our social conditioning, upbringing, and our religious beliefs all mould our conception of the 'I' we call ourselves and we get entrenched in our ingrained perceptions. To get past them, different methods have been devised by various mystical schools. One such method is to shock, stun, or paralyse the ego; by subjecting it to emotionally charged situations which perplex or tear the person apart so that an opportunity is afforded to detach from the personality and rest in the calm of a witnessing awareness. To aid this process, the guru challenges the 'normal' world-view and thereby the ego. The inferno, into which the ego is thrown, is set ablaze in the hope that the flailing disciple would gather the charged emotions in an effort to go beyond them.

Ashishda's own guru had hauled him over the coals. During that five-year period of intense pressure, Ashishda used to have a recurrent nightmare of being lashed by waves in which he would bob up and down, gulping, sinking, drowning...With every nightmare came a fresh bout of outward pressure. One night the dream started in the usual way, but this time he touched and stood on firm rock. Ashishda believed that this period of his training, though utterly impossible to endure, had transformed his life, making him rest in an inner certainty he had not known before.

As I looked back, I wondered if all the stages in Ashishda's teachings had been building towards this intense period we had had with him. What strongly supported this feeling was that under the untidy surface of our personality traits, ran the silent and compassionate flow of my dream life through which I became conscious of a pattern in the unfolding drama. From time to time my dreams had revealed what lay ahead. Implicit in them was the idea that our experiences had been both necessary and purposeful. Through them, I felt the unravelling of a precious teaching that I tried to imbibe. Their recurrent message was that I swing my attention away from the daily occurrences to an 'awareness' that is untouched by events. They suggested that turbulent events were like surface waves, below which were the calm, undisturbed depths of the ocean. Although my dreams indicated that I had to alter my perceptions, and hinted at how this could be achieved, I had to struggle with the 'doing'.

And in the struggle with the 'doing', the real wonder

was that my dreams became a personal document addressing my situation directly, and indicating precisely how I could replace my frame of reference and change my focus of attention. Let go of the perspective from which you view reality, they urged, and then discover what exists beyond. Not to look at the known, but towards that which Knows, and untiringly emphasized that any real knowledge rests only in the Knower. Through the years I had seen how difficult it was to act in consonance with the Knower, without any experience of it. So to say, the goal ahead lay shrouded in the mists of a mystery, while in the here-and-now Ashishda's voice urged us to shed excess baggage—emotional and mental—so that the ascent to the snow-clad mountains is made unencumbered. But how was this to be done within the clamour of my beliefs and ideas?

Perhaps, I would have to initially let go of my beliefs about myself. Was this what the ten-year old daughter of a numinous figure demanded from Rajeev? It was after this dream that Ashishda had decided to let us stay at the Ashram. The focus of our stay would be defined by the exploration of the question 'Who am I'?

Other dreams followed that pointed in this direction—my having to jump from a plane without a parachute. It was as if saying the jump can be made by letting go of my beliefs about my identity. Then two dreams showed how I was to gradually let go of basic ideas about myself: my mother's umbrella (ideas inherited from the parents) is taken away by a bird; and my watching from the window the residents working required that I view myself from a distance, apart from my beliefs.

In a rather severe and violent rendering of the same process, Rajeev's dream depicted the number two priest holding a man by his ankles and beating his head against the wall. The head stands for the ego, the centre of the personality, the part of Rajeev that he prides in himself has to be prised open, dismantled, bashed. But why such an extreme step? Would it not leave scars that might outweigh the results? Are there any soft answers if one wants to find out what remains when every identification is dropped? In the Naassene document it is said, 'Greater Deaths do greater lots obtain'?

In answer, my dream had quoted Rumi's injunction, attributed to the Prophet: 'Die before thou diest'. Put another way, the only certainty we possess is that 'I am'. But we define ourselves as 'I-am-this' or 'I-am-that'. We then convince ourselves 'this' or 'that' is mine. The relinquishing of 'this' or 'that' is the asked-for-death. And strangely enough the challenges in my outer life were pointing in the same direction. Since I was resisting them, Ashishda was bearing down with his full weight on me, as in my dream of Rajeev breaking stones, perhaps asking a voluntary surrender of me. The breaking of stones signified the hammering down of solidified attitudes and ideas.

All this may seem a heartless process. However, it is seldom without help. Someone is there to break the fall, to pick one up, to inspire, as I was lovingly reassured by a radiance, one February morning, that 'he' will be there every month for the next two-and-a-half years. As Ashishda had clarified, it did not mean that 'he' will prevent or protect you against pain; only give the strength to handle it.

Handle it how? I soon began to perceive that it was no longer 'my' strength that was capable of holding me up. Something 'other' was doing so. In one dream, that 'other' was the shining-eyed mahout, the guide who took a forlorn looking elephant into an enclosure to bathe it, and said, 'Even the elephant's wounds heal, only the airy space burns.' Perhaps, the 'airy space' (a metaphor for the higher mind) may be revealed only when the boundaries of the ego have been hammered down and are no longer there to shield it.

In another dream, I was instructed by a Judo Master about how to take a blow on the ego. Not by resistance, not by bunching up in fear and anxiety but by dissolving myself. When there is no resistance, the 'blow' goes fluidly as though through air.

The implication seems to be that once these ideas of 'who I am' and 'what I want' have been relinquished, only then can we dive deeper into ourselves in the attempt to discover our essence. As Ashishda had said, the learned practices do not automatically guarantee fulfilment; they may make the seeker more disciplined, mature the emotions and focus the mind. If the highest is the goal then the disciple must be consumed by an intense fire, in which everything becomes subservient to the Truth that is sought. But how is the disciple to generate this charge? Where does the fuel for such a charge come from? Even between the most sublime desire and the desire-less state, there is an abyss, a chasm that must be crossed.

Maybe, it is here that the guru steps in for what could be considered his most controversial role. He has to find a way to engender this yearning in the disciple. One of the ways by which the guru can generate this charge in the disciple is by creating strong emotions that will stun the ego. The disciple should be truly caught on the horns of a dilemma: the utter faith in the teacher, which makes the disciple persevere; and the teacher's actions which time and again make the disciple question him. If the faith is absent, the exercise cannot be continued as the disciple will walk away. On the other hand, if the situation appears contrived to the disciple, the intended impact will be missing. Maybe the teacher has to seize on a situation in the disciple's life and create the necessary perplexity. This perplexity, or 'hayrangi' as the Sufis call it, can make the disciple yearn to know the truth not only about this situation, the guru, but the Truth that supports the ground of Being.

One way of creating this strong charge is by isolating the disciple, restricting the energies which will bounce back at him or her from the artificial walls that have been erected. In our own case, since we had been isolated, there was nowhere to go, nothing to do, no guru, no context, no acceptability, only an increasing desperation. The energy finding no outlet, like in physical work, could only swirl around us. Frustration, fear and anger bubbled up within us, and we felt hemmed in as we tried to form a life within these changed circumstances. Had Ashishda, allowed us to become comfortable, it would have dissipated the charge. He attempted again and again to shake us, so that we shift the focus of our eyes from the outward situation to another centre of awareness. The guru is trying to accelerate a process of enquiry which otherwise may take a very long time to come to fruition. Is this the steeper path that leads to the 'Dak bungalow'?

This is the role of the guru—to point towards that free space within all human life where the light of awareness shines, shorn of any entanglement with the ego. The purpose of subjugating the ego is to bring the disciple to such a point that he or she is forced to seek answers that endure beyond all dualities—of life and death, heaven and hell, subject and object. For now, life or the guru is pressing on the disciple to practise what he or she has been taught. The guru goads the disciple with injustices and unfairness. The more the guru bears down on the disciple, the more the structures crumble, known habits dissolve and securities are wrenched away. No more can the disciple find solace in conventional formulations of God, peace and harmony. He or she begins to question all that was taken for granted, including the guru.

By now he or she is actively, desperately seeking answers as their whole life depends on it. Time is running out; if the relentless outward circumstances catch up with the pupil before he or she can reach the 'Dak bungalow', then the disciple is well and truly lost. It is a race to locate an inner foothold before the outer situation overpowers the seeker. In this desperation sometimes a leap is made in which something essential is grasped and held onto. That was the guru's aim from the very beginning.

Had Ashishda stepped in for what seemed his most controversial role, in order to push us to make a jump we may otherwise have been incapable of making? Was he guided by inner perception and an appreciation of our situation? Had he judged Rajeev's dream of the tower as an indication that our time for being pushed had come? Was the creation of a hostile outward environment an act of kindness from him? Undoubtedly Ashishda created a sense of urgency in us by demolishing every outward structure with which we could identify. The only way to survive this experience was to turn inwards and find a new point of reference.

There were indicators that Ashishda was conscious of what he was doing as he seemed aware when the two-and-a-half-year period was drawing to a close. It was as though he himself was keeping count. He chose not to protect us in the conventional sense, yet he strove time and again to bring Rajeev back on to the farm. Also, whenever Rajeev or I went for a dream session with him, he always rang true. He talked to us offering objective advice, urging us to hold on to our aspirations. Those words came from a man who was giving us strength to handle ourselves. Yet, he never revealed his true intentions and so we never had the comfort of knowing that the situation was being created for our own good. We questioned his motives, and at that point, the last security was lost to us.

In the intensity of those days, a fundamental shift in perspective did take place. I was learning to accept suffering as a necessary part of life. We, each of us, have our share of suffering at some point, and our attitude to it determines in which direction our next step will be. Suffering, confronts us with choices—we can either run from it, or walk with it, and finally, if we are lucky, listen to it. Suffering often is the inability to let go of something within us that we no longer need to hold onto in the old terms.

In the final analysis, even that is not important. What counted ultimately was what the experience meant to us. If we had felt no ostensible gain had taken place, besides the defacing of our confidence, then outrage would have ensued. On the contrary, strength was gained and something tangible of the intangible was passed on in the experience. If I had gone to the Ashram with doubts about the validity of this Path, my experience with Ashishda dispelled them completely.

What Ashishda had been pointing his finger towards is real. He was never wrong about the 'still point', or untrue in affirming that Inner Compass which pointed towards the greater mysterious Beyond. For me those moments are more authentic than anything else. The rest is a post-mortem of human frailties that have to be a container to those moments. Most importantly, when Ashishda's assumptions were challenged, he did not hide behind the ochre of his guru-mantle, but owned up to his responsibility—'If mistakes have been made I'll pay for them.' At that moment he was not a guru, but a human being who dispassionately viewed himself, as only an extraordinary man can.

Had he not stood with conviction time and again for this greater life, we would have given up in our endeavour. He gave our early stirrings, words; he gave those words meaning, and most of all he imbued them with his conviction. I do not doubt that the truth that stirred me emanated from the truth of his experience.

Time and again I have wondered, had the situation not been so charged would we have felt the magic and beauty of this ethereal dance? A dance that said, 'Soak your half-closed eyes with this sight so that when you open them to the world you live in, they are not limited by the boundaries of separateness.'

When I think of that, can I reject an experience that brought me glimpses of the possibility of such a unitive rendering of life? For if the outward situation had not been so utterly fragmented, could the Inner Compass have stepped in to show a totally different point of view? It danced on the crumbling bridge of a situation that allowed the eyes to change their focus, permitting me the possibility of true inner freedom. And, is that not worth paying any price for?

There was something else I began to perceive beneath the wavy ups-and-downs of experience. It was the sense that something indestructible lives and endures within the changing seasons of human existence. That each human life, including mine, was linked to this point, gave me a great sense of inner continuity. Carl Jung writes in his autobiography, *Memories, Dreams, Reflections*:

> Life has always seemed to me like a plant that lives
> on its rhizome. Its true life is invisible, hidden in the
> rhizome. The part that appears above ground lasts only
> a single summer. Then it withers away—an ephemeral
> apparition…Yet I have never lost a sense of something
> that lives and endures underneath the eternal flux. What
> we see is the blossom, which passes. The rhizome remains.

As for myself I cannot claim any startling breakthroughs. However, one thing shone for me in those dark hours and that was Grace. It came in many forms but it had a particular quality that made it stand apart. It was no faraway, impersonal, cosmic truth that was handed down to me but a personalised answer to one individual's call in her hour of need. The love that shone through that experience asked for nothing more of me than my allegiance to its cause. And for that I felt both humbled and honoured. I recognised it because it stood out with such clarity in the muddy stream of happenings that it became a space I could look upon without ambiguity. And this Grace brought a natural reverence leaving me no option but to trail its vanishing footsteps. It is at these points that any individual realises that alone she couldn't have sustained the struggle. So what was the purpose of the support given? It was hardly given to one person singled out for special treatment. Possibly, it was given as a confirmation that there is something real and objective worth struggling for. If no confirmation is given at an inner level the disciple may turn back and say, 'There's nothing there. It's only a rumour.'

Maybe, finally, this Power was nudging me to seek directly what it was a representative of—our numinous beginnings.

27

Malcolm

One more year passed. Six and a half years in the Ashram had made us feel as if we had no other life but the one we had lived here. All the days and months condensed to this point, where sitting in the sun I seemed to be recovering from an exhausting climb. At the end of that year I recorded a dream:

A production of Shakespeare's Macbeth is under-way. The finest actors and actresses from all over the world have gathered to rehearse for the play. I am standing at the back of the hall, in the shadows, watching the floodlights come on as Macbeth and Lady Macbeth appear in dazzling costumes made of silk and brocade. There is a general bustle of excitement as the props are being put up. Actors are waiting for their cues, and prompters flipping through the script. Suddenly the director appears and hands me a copy of the script and says, 'Play Malcolm's role.'

I protest, 'I'm not an actress. I can't even audition, let alone play the role.'

My words remain unheard as the director vanishes. I read the lines of the part and feel at a loss. Where do I start, what are the cues, where do I fit in? Days pass, months pass and I go on practising. Occasionally I manage to persuade someone to practise with me. One, two, three, maybe four years pass. Slowly I begin to get the hang of the role. There is activity all around me but I seem to sense it only through a peripheral vision. I am so involved with the role now that I rehearse it every spare moment I get.

One day someone announces, 'The day after tomorrow is opening night.'

There isn't an empty seat in the auditorium and the air is alive with expectations. The play begins. Malcolm is to appear towards the end of the play and I see myself coming onto the stage, to fight Macbeth in a one-to-one combat. The next minute, Macbeth is lying dead even though I, as Malcolm, made no move to kill him. (In the Shakespearean version it is Macduff who slays Macbeth.)

At this point, Malcolm makes an impassioned speech, and calls upon the Powers above to protect, guide and nurture the highest in himself so that he never comes to the same end as Macbeth. There is a moment's pause at the end of the speech before the audience breaks into spontaneous applause. The curtain falls and I walk back unnoticed to the corridors behind the stage, tired but not unhappy. I suddenly sense the director behind me. I turn around and he smiles, 'That was good. Remember what ultimately counts is the sincerity of the effort—the impassioned giving. The rest is immaterial.'

I had seen him so rarely throughout the production that I'm very pleased to be with him. He says, 'I am going to cast you in another role, another play.'

'Oh no!' I protest. 'Not as yet.'

He just smiles indulgently, 'Another play, another role.'

There were many ways to interpret this dream. Clearly, according to it, one phase was over and another due to begin. I felt a surge of confidence after the dream for I felt that it signalled a new role within the Ashram, and an end to the trying times that we had been through.

It also left me feeling that I was in possession of myself and would no longer be pulled down in the same way by my old fears, many of which had been my companions from childhood. They, like Macbeth had simply 'died' as though time had exhausted them of their life energy. This realisation made me feel a great sense of release, a new sense of wholeness.

When I asked Ashishda about the dream, he did not say much except, 'It sounds very much like an archetypal dream. Why did you hesitate to say "yes" to the new role?'

'I don't know. What new role can it be?'

'We can only wait and see.'

Six months later, circumstances developed in such a way that we were confronted with a choice. Quite unexpectedly, some of the members of the community were asked to sign a legal document which stated that a minimum number of hours of work had to be put in by each member; that the cottages would belong to the Ashram; and that the rules laid down had to be obeyed even when Ashishda's successor took over. We had already agreed and lived by these conditions and no one had ever questioned them. Refusing to sign the document would mean having to leave the Ashram, agreeing to it meant a compromise. Each choice was difficult to abide by. We could not say yes and we didn't want to leave. Finally, we made it clear we would not sign the document.

More than seven years ago, we had sat with Ashishda to hear him say, 'Yes, your time has come.' Now we sat with him in silence. 'Say it, say it', the silence in the room seemed to goad us. How can we be sure when sometimes the most irrevocable decisions are made in states of mind one might later regret?

'Maybe we should leave?' Rajeev finally uttered the words, his eyes asking Ashishda to contradict him.

'Think about it,' Ashishda said hesitantly. Then he changed his mind and said firmly, 'Maybe it's for the best, your moving on. Hold onto what has been given to you. Wherever you are, the Path will always be with you. The effort you make is never lost.'

We bent down and kissed his feet. He rose and hugged us.

'You've given us so much, Ashishda,' Rajeev said, his voice unsteady.

'Free yourself of everything, and the rest will follow. When I am in Delhi next, come and see me.'

We left, not really knowing what we were going to do.

On the last evening of our stay at the Ashram, as we stood in the temple anteroom, the circular ring of fire from the pradeep seemed like a benediction on the past and the present.

'Your leaving is a tear in the fabric of the community. We'll all feel it,' Don had said.

'I know Don, but our time has come to go.'

Initially we were just people who had randomly come together to form this community. We had stayed on to become friends. I had seen Persis more on the other side of a cow than face to face. Yet, through lugging milk pails together and seeing her groggy-eyed and silent in the milk room, I had communicated more with her than I might have through many a polite conversation. What of Savitri, who lived alone, yet ever so often made three portions of a dish to share with us, and Urmila whose enthusiasm for water-colours made me see the cherry tree afresh.

The conch, full of water, was being offered and my mind held onto each moment, unwilling to let it go. At the age of eighteen, I had travelled up to meet a tall Englishman who had helped shape fourteen years of my life. How was I to walk away from it all?

I felt as though a riptide was drawing me back into the sea of uncertainty. Without Ashishda as guru, without the centred atmosphere of the life he had designed, and without the single-minded focus we had been afforded, where would I stand? I was not the person I had been when I first followed in Ashishda's shadow. I had gone from straining to understand his every word, to discovering the quiet confidence of an inner voice. And yet, I was assailed by doubt as I wondered if, without a guru and the canalising currents of the life he offered, my internal conviction would lose its momentum?

The thought of returning to city life made me feel strangely threatened. Would it take me away from what I held so vital? Would it make me lose what I had gained?

For the moment, the only reality I had was the Ashram which was a whole way of thinking, believing, and living for us. How were we going to contemplate another way of living, when this one was so deeply imprinted on our psyche?

A curtain call had been made for this phase of our lives, as indicated by the words in my dream: 'Another play, another role'. I had not understood the full implications of that statement then, but realised now that it heralded our leaving the Ashram and the beginning of a 'role' set in radically different circumstances. Ashishda, it seems, had honoured the dream by not insisting we stay.

The service was almost over. The whisk was being put away and the drum beat ended on a sombre note.

What had life at the Ashram been? A pilgrimage, or

a living out of emotions that hadn't run their full course? Was it a seeking of a fresh canvas on which to repaint an old picture?

When a canvas cannot be painted on any more, the eyes seem to memorise every detail of the picture so that its colours, lines and texture become the means to preserve its essence. Like the blue shadows of the evening, encircling a garden full of narcissi in bloom, against the long strips of silvery clouds in the sky. Why, even the tall deodars seem to be pointing their green fingers at the first sprinkling of stars over the grey dome. I watched as the evening closed its drooping eyelids on very much more than just a single day in our lives.

As I walked down the ramp towards the Samadhi, I knew if I was leaving something behind, I was also carrying something away with me. What was mine was not only the conviction that there is a transcendental Reality, but also that there is a way through which we could meet that Reality. This 'way' was open to us all.

The director in my dream spoke like a true Master when he said that the outcome of a role itself—with its possibilities of success or failure, reward or loss—was of no importance. The manner in which the tasks of the role were fulfilled was what mattered.

I think I had valued this teaching, instilled by Ashishda and restated in my dream, but knew that it would be a struggle to make it work in the various aspects of my life.

In such a struggle, I now believed, we are never alone. The Inner Preceptor stands quietly in the wings, like the director in my dream, stepping into the light when his presence is most required. This Presence brings the reassurance that someone is always watching over our faltering attempts to play the role. Where the shadows stretch their arms to meet the light, where sleep struggles towards wakefulness, where the edge of a teardrop catches the sunlight, there 'He' sometimes smiles in wordless greeting.

28

Exhaust the Content of Experience

Where does a story begin or end? Not only in the first and last pages of what is told, but more in the echoes of what remains untold. We trap experience within words, when the real story of any individual life lies just below the threshold of sound.

What words can define was that we returned to Delhi in April when the first hot breath of summer was drying the last of the winter salvias and dahlias. We stood in a twilight zone, cloaked in memories of another life which intruded into the present, with their remembrances.

'We left all this once,' Rajeev said with downcast eyes. 'This time round will it make more sense than before?'

It was the same place, the same life but possibly we were different people now. Ultimately, meeting the future is usually a story of how we deal with past memories. I felt I was living with an amputated limb still not believing in the reality of its being cut off, convalescing from something that had to heal.

In the first few months I could relate to little around me. I functioned, and probably even made the appropriate responses outwardly, but internally I remained uninvolved and this worried me. I knew my lack of involvement did not stem from detachment, but from an inability to connect in a meaningful way to the environment I found myself in.

Everything in the city seemed to be harnessed to trade one's immediate reality for an idealised fantasy. Advertisements beckoned one from every corner enticing one to dream of a lifestyle not one's own. Magazines were swamped with a celluloid reality and the television portrayed the lifestyle of the affluent as though that was the norm everyone lived by. It felt unreal to wake up the next morning and catch the bus to work.

A hungry tension seemed to be everywhere with most people wanting to earn more, elbowing someone else out of the way in the process. Even the traffic seemed to have doubled its satanic drive, hurtling to and fro like an animated puppet show without a theme. In all this frantic activity where was the time to remain in touch with oneself?

I remembered Eliot's words in 'Burnt Norton':

...Only a flicker
Over the strained time-ridden faces
Distracted from distraction by distraction
Filled with fancies and empty of meaning
Tumid apathy with no concentration
Men and bits of paper, whirled by the cold wind...

It frightened me to see how everything in the city was geared for the rush of activity, without the tempering quiet of reflection to balance it with. Accustomed to the deep-wooded silence of my mountain home, I cringed at the disruptive noises that shattered the morning and unceasingly coloured the day. In the late evenings when the noises of the city were a ceaseless drone, I would be reminded of the mountains where the winds would be soughing through the pines and shades of lavender would be streaking the evening sky.

We were like waves that had rolled onto other shores to return to the old ones with a sense of bewilderment. Possibly we needed these old shores to understand what had happened at mid-ocean. But suppose, in time, we deeply regretted leaving the Ashram, would we be stranded in shallow waters, spending our life sighting ships at mid-sea?

How was I, without a supportive framework, to continue what I really believed in? As my mind thrashed around in a state of quiet desperation, I could not help but wonder whether I was seeing the world this way because my heart was bleeding.

> *'Humankind's biggest sorrow is that they cannot see the Reality behind the separateness.'*

I sat up alertly out of the semi-sleep I had been in early one morning. Whose voice was it that spoke these words to me? The words were like a small jolt from another level of awareness. This statement tore through my sleep-soaked mind, cutting a passage through the heavy veil of confusion that had shrouded me. What did they mean?

I instinctively knew something essential was being talked about, and my thrashing mind rested in it. In time I realised that like my dreams in the past, this statement was a teaching that addressed my personal dilemma and also pointed to a larger, transpersonal question. These words spelt out a simple truth. That higher Reality knitted the whole of life together, irrespective of place, people or circumstances. For that Reality there were no distinctions, no better places or inferior ones. If I felt that life in the Ashram had a quality to it which city life did not, I was wrong. If I felt that all I had received within the confines of a geographical place would disappear once I stepped out of it, I had missed the point.

This statement was pointing to that divisive line I had put on my experiences, which isolated me from its very essence. To seek that Reality meant to find its living connection in the life one lived. A connection which sews all life together with a common thread. That substratum which gives meaning to all the separate parts, that unifying power that holds and informs the diversity. Only such a shift in perspective would make my present life more intelligible to me.

This teaching was a real pointer for me. I saw that in the acceptance of my present circumstances lay the real challenge. I realised that if the inner voice is kept alive, in time, it becomes the reference point. The mind divides, the heart unifies.

Hermes Trismegistus says, 'If thou but settest foot on this Path, thou shalt see it everywhere, both when and where thou dost expect it not.'

As I came to accept my life more, I began to comprehend all that stayed within me as Ashishda's legacy. He led us by the hand, for as long as we needed his support. He prepared me and helped me find an ally so that I could walk alone. In retrospect I now saw what I could not see then—a process began when we were in the Ashram that made us direct our attention away from every conceivable crutch to the goal itself. That conviction became the light that guided our footsteps.

Outwardly and inwardly I entered a new phase. Outwardly, I had a full day, as I took up writing and meeting the demands of everyday life. Inwardly I continued to think about the statement I had heard and felt it was addressing the most fundamental human question. We take for granted that we are separate individuals functioning and surviving by our own will and strength. Our life and our concept of meaning is then built on this hypothesis. But are we separate entities, self-propelled and autonomous? And separate from what—from the ground of our being, from the source of our arising? Our thinking of ourselves as this individual 'I', separate from the oneness of life, is actually humankind's biggest sorrow. If this is not addressed, all other sorrows follow, because we have denied our own origins. Can a river maintain its full flow if it is cut off from its source?

Maybe the greatest human tragedy lies in not realising our deep and abiding connection with this Reality. We suffer pain and isolation, feel defenceless against life's assaults, battle against odds which baffle us, believing we are totally alone. That is the real sorrow. Of not being able to connect or perceive the unifying principle of life, of remaining trapped by the separate, divisive, alienating forces of human thought, which narrow the individual focus to such an extent that they exclude the vision of that Reality.

Somehow this thought excised the personal-feel of 'my' sorrow. It was not my sorrow alone. It was humankind's sorrow. Whatever maybe the specificity of our individual sufferings, its generic basis is that we fail to perceive our arising from and connection to that Reality. If I were to try and understand that Reality, what would I say to it? That I am you. You are 'me.' When I try to know you, you seem to be separate from me. But when you look through me, I cease to exist.

All these years my search had been without a clearly formulated question. It was just a looking, a seeking for something without a name. Ashishda had defined it for me by calling it the Ultimate. But those were borrowed terms of reference. Now for the first time I felt the question was there within me, slowly filling me with its import to seek the essence of that Reality. This questioning arose on its own like a phoenix from the sum of my past experiences. It spread its wings and flew above my personal dilemmas to become almost an impersonal, inner puzzlement. In fact I never put any effort into either ignoring it or increasing its intensity. It just walked alongside me as a companion, reminding me of its presence at the most unpredictable moments, drawing me back to itself, becoming my compass, leading me to where I needed to be led.

The June tarmac-melting heat eased into monsoon showers making puddles in the depressions on the roads. Young lads laughed and kicked with glee as they splashed their feet in the water. I watched them and wondered about the play of life.

Heat and rain, joy and sorrow, youth and infirmity, ever-changing seasons of human experience. My mind was thinking about that Reality where all these distinctions are meant to merge, but how I wondered?

> *'Find out what remains when you exhaust the content of all experience.'*

Clear and strong, the words imprinted themselves upon my consciousness as I drifted between sleep and wakefulness one night, a state when the conscious mind least interferes. Again and again the force of this sentence shook me. The words had the same quality as the ones earlier. Paying attention to the earlier statement had offered me invaluable direction at a time I needed it most, and had compelled me towards a new perception. So, I readily attempted to unravel the meaning of these words. They were not like a stray thought, but a continuation of the teaching given earlier. It was a complex thought and I needed guidance to understand it. Eventually I decided to write to Ashishda for his was an interpretation I could hope to follow. He replied:

'It is only when you find out what remains when the content of experience is exhausted that you discover a state which in no ordinary sense are you, yourself.

'Don't try to pre-empt or know what the state beyond exhausted experience is like. At present you do not even know if there is such a state, still less what it really is.

'Follow the instructions and "die" to yourself. Drop your identity—not only your identification with your body but with your thoughts and memories—everything you think of as yourself. Then see what follows.'

When I received Ashishda's response I happened to be reading Nisargadatta Maharaj who said, 'Question every urge, hold no desire legitimate. Empty of possessions, physical and mental, free of all self-concern, be open for discovery.'

I grappled with the statement I had heard, with Ashishda's interpretation of it, and Nisargadatta Maharaj's teaching, but continued to feel puzzled. I felt I had not fully grasped the intention of the statement. As time elapsed, I came to my own understanding of it. The statement suggested that I had to empty myself of everything. Initially the attempt had been to remove all the blocks and obstructions of the personality that could impede one's onward journey. Implicit in these attempts was the fact that only certain aspects of oneself had to be transformed. This present statement seemed to be saying that all contents of experience—not only the blocks and difficulties but the joy and the contentment, in fact all sense stimuli, all thoughts, all self-concern, everything that constituted experience had to be exhausted, dropped.

Would that not be an annihilation of all that constitutes

my 'self'? Was this not what Ashishda had tried to point us to—the witnessing awareness? 'Break the shell...Cease being fascinated by the content of your consciousness...Blow the bulb,' Nisargadatta Maharaj had insisted. And we thought we were being annihilated by the injustices. I understood in clearer terms the direction Ashishda had been guiding us to. He had wanted us to 'get out of the way' and become 'aware of being aware'.

I did not have to negate my experiences, nor suppress or run away from them. I just had to empty my mind of everything—the past, the present, or the future and become like flowing water which clings to nothing, collects nothing.

'Let it go...let it go', the airless September morning whispered. I realised it was not that I stopped thinking, feeling and reacting. It was just that I felt less compelled by the contents of my thoughts and feelings. The rains had stopped and winter had not yet stepped in. The pause between the seasons seemed the measure of distance I was feeling between my experience and my rush to hold onto it. There was a rest, like the quiet breathing that keeps time with life without lagging behind or rushing ahead. Old memories were slipping past me and new ones were not holding me.

I met a quiet October dawn with thoughts that drifted in, not to intrude but to join hands with the moment.

One February morning as I came awake I observed that my mind was totally immersed in the one question that had stayed with me all these months: 'What is this mystery, what is it...?'

What followed may have lasted a single moment or a full lifetime; I do not know. Any words I use will fail to capture this unveiling, where everything dissolved, disappeared, freed of the burden of all distinctions. If there was no blue of the sky and the seas, if the hurtling galaxies did not exist and the stars and this earth had not been born, then, what was there? When the fragrance of life was not conceived, when the secret of all unfoldment was not even known…then what was there? When no thought or act or deed existed, what was there? Suppose there was no container and no contained, then what was there? Nothingness…full to the brim. An eternal potential, majestic in its fullness, dimensionless, rolling out into endlessness…

When I came around I felt hard put to make sense of where I was located. Soon after I felt a sense of joy suffuse me and my being sang for days after that. In those moments I had known such utter freedom.

Is this where we come from? Is this what we belong to, I thought with wonderment.

For some time, I felt there was nowhere to go, nothing to become. It was not a passivity born of the fear of making choices. It was more a state where there were no choices to be made, since none existed. Rumi had said:

> I look inwards,
> And the beauty of my own emptiness filled me till dawn.
> I took a sip and saw the vast ocean
> Wave upon wave caressed my soul.

So, in the larger scheme of things there are no right roads or wrong ones. No good and evil, no death and birth. There is only one Reality from which other realities are born.

It was one timeless moment…a glimpse, no doubt only a glimpse but so vast in its immensity, so utterly conditionless. In it nothing existed, for the existence of anything would be a limitation to that limitlessness.

So utterly different was it to anything I could conceive of, that later I wondered how the world I normally inhabited could have anything to do with that experience. Without Ashishda, would I have even known that such a state existed?

I know memory erases the worst and best in experience and that the mind-stopping wonder and joy I felt at that time will ease into gentler, softer tones of remembrances. Yet, it will remain the cornerstone of my life. It is to that tune, heard one February morning, that my heart still beats. And I continue to look for its nuances in the life I live.

Soon after it happened, I was to acknowledge that by itself it would not free me from the dictates and limitations of my own nature, nor from the tensions and concerns of everyday life.

I also came to realise that the experience put before me the biggest challenge: the unceasing effort that had to be made through the rest of my lifetime to find a way to merge the sense of that experience with everything in my life. This would demand of me constant work towards freeing myself of all that may obstruct the filtering through of that experience into the life I live.

29

What Remains?

Years have elapsed since Ashishda passed on. Many things have changed in Mirtola. Dave succeeded him as the Pradhan Sevak. He also passed on six years ago. Over half the residents are no more. From among the disciples, a Managing Committee emerged to oversee the administration of the place. Chitra, the resident sevika, who now lives there alone, maintains the traditions of the place and attends to the steady stream of visitors and darshanarthis who have started to come after a twenty-year hiatus. Perhaps, after three gurus and their intense effort with the disciples, the place needed to go to sleep, and is coming awake again.

For many years, after leaving the Ashram, we did not revisit it. I then had a dream:

> *We are standing outside the mandir with Ashishda. He is aglow, a bright, shining presence. He looks at Rajeev and me with the tenderness of love. He puts his arms around both of us, kisses me on the forehead and takes us into the temple.*

Shortly after this dream we visited Mirtola.

Was the dream anticipating an event, or would the expression of love so palpable in the dream allow us to let go of our trepidations of the past, alongside suggesting that a change of perception toward suffering provides a compelling opportunity to grow, and would permit a letting go of the way we had earlier viewed our difficulties? Rather than see suffering as a frightening dragon opposing us, we began to sense that it may be guarding a treasure. For suffering can perforce make one search for answers within and drive one to take refuge in a deeper level, to seek confirmation of faith in experience, to coalesce one's practices in daily living. A combination of these, along with acceptance of pain rather than merely wishing its removal, alters the view of suffering itself.

Sattal

We now live in a cottage we had built a thousand feet above the lake at Sattal in the hills of Kumaon. We spend the better part of the year here. Looking back, life seems to have come full circle. We left the wooded, remote life of the Ashram to live in the city, and two decades later we are in a similarly quiet, remote place. Here, in such moments, there is no past, no future approaching, only the unknown awaiting recognition—a place where normal purposive activity does not exist. Each day seems like the last, with no rush to go anywhere, to become anything. Only the rhythm of a daily routine—a walk, tending to the garden, reading, a paragraph written, a short conversation between silences as you look up to see the clouds changing shape as they float past your window.

A process that had begun in the Ashram remained with me and gained greater clarity in the years to come. After leaving Mirtola, I tried to hold onto what was taught and slowly separate it from the circumstances in which those lessons had to be learnt. This struggle is significant as it represents a movement in my way of engaging with the world. Instead of outward-looking, my mind has begun to dwell more inwardly. And gradually I learnt that the difficulties on the path of self-discovery are usually not out there but lurk in one's own mind.

As the interior domain gained greater importance a series of dreams came, which depicted subtler states of awareness beyond the sphere of personality. The outer events that occurred since I left Mirtola, however significant, began to pale beside interior happenings which involved states between waking and sleeping, and in some cases a kind of 'wakeful sleep'. Having been privy to these experiences I wondered how to relate the story of recent years as I continue to try and fathom their import. Mainly what I will now recount is this inward movement and how the deeper part of the self was being reflected in my dreams and introducing me to altogether different states of consciousness.

With me was Ashishda's affirmation that dreams are also a way of self-enquiry in the disciple's journey. They are the 'switch-points' that allow a two-way view of the outer and inner realms. Different types of dreams occur that increasingly step away from the personal and allow glimpses of subtler states of being that are 'beyond' the ordinary. This realm is not divorced from the everyday but is at the heart of it. As Nisargadatta Maharaj said: Like a hole in the paper is both *in* the paper and yet not *of* paper, so are these states in the centre of the self and yet beyond it.

Ashishda had urged us to 'still' ourselves by constantly watching oneself, and by trying to self-remember. The idea being that one must dig within to find the cause of whatever happens to one. It was a way of going from the outward to another part of oneself. Increasingly, I came to believe that Ashishda's real intent was to introduce us to this part of ourselves, the deeper part, in which only inner values count. I remembered his words: 'In meditation one is not trying to *be* calm. One is trying to find the *thing* that is calm, stable, constant...' This was the legacy of my years in Mirtola.

The two levels of myself

My pursuit has been to try and understand my inward experiences which introduced me to two levels of myself, and find their relevance to my life. Normally I am much more familiar and comfortable with the level that is conscious of an outer reality and which invites me to participate in it. The inward level often remains concealed. Since any given experience is an interweaving of these two levels, the challenge was, and continues to be, to find a bridge, create an isthmus between the two levels of myself and search for the causes within me that inadvertently abet their estrangement. What credence and value I would ascribe to these intimations, would depend on how much I knew myself and was able to recognize when the shadow of the surface 'me' fell upon them. Slowly these inner experiences changed the way I viewed my practices and my self-perception, giving a different meaning to my life.

Watching myself

Earlier I had unwittingly seen self-observation, or watching myself, as a form of self-assessment, weighed against a 'should', or an 'ought' of what I was thinking or feeling. As a result, I was not actually observing my thoughts but inadvertently judging them and often finding myself wanting. This at times made me stop observing altogether, as I felt the more I observed, the more 'wrong' I saw. Then, one day while walking up the hill, a medium sized stone rolled down in my direction. I stepped away. Immediately thoughts of bigger and larger boulders falling, of an avalanche, then of the road being blocked, our not being able to go to Bhimtal to get our provisions raced through my mind. Amidst all this, a part of me spontaneously watched the escalation of anxiety these thoughts were causing. I realised, my mind could create a story, making the trivial and the important share an equal sense of urgency, without momentarily knowing the difference. In many such cases facts get lost amidst the fear. But I also sensed 'something' observed this process and it was free of both—the facts and the fear. I tried to flow with this part of me. But other thoughts, or rather affects, intruded even when I attempted to be still. Rather than slot these intrusions into categories, I tried to just observe what arose—tiredness, boredom, vague unease, mild irritations, or elation. I felt they were connected to hidden parts of myself. The more I was able to do this, more the practice of watching myself intensified. Surprisingly, it was accompanied with an unexplained feeling of relief. I felt I had chanced upon a way of getting in touch with myself.

What I gained from this incident was a closer look at the two levels of myself—the surface and the deeper. I sensed it would require a quantum jump in perception to contact this deeper level. What these insights did help me with was to gain familiarity with the 'I' which observes the world, and the 'I' which can observe my mind, its mental contents, and can go even deeper than that. And isn't it that only when we dive below the surface are we afforded a glimpse of the deep, where the tumult of the surface subsides into calm. And if we dare to look deeper still, we may be afforded a totally different view of ourselves and of everyday reality.

A Dream takes me deeper!

I got a taste of what it means to go deeper into myself, not by thinking it over, but in a dream. I have written about this dream in greater detail in my book *The Logic of Dreams*. Here I will render it briefly:

I am in an old Rajput fortress. I am standing in a room with the door ajar. I see a large hall where a woman is dancing, with her red gauze and silver spangled skirt in full flare as she whirls around. Beyond it is the market place.

Sita enters the room and says with urgency that the rebellion (of which I was a part) had failed, 'They will capture and behead you. Your death is inevitable. I don't want you to die in pain, so I will give you some sleeping pills. You just go to the other room take them and slip out.' I go into the adjoining room, draw the curtains, swallow the sleeping pills and lie down.

In time I felt drowsy. Then gradually my breathing slowed down and the thought came to me: So, this is what dying is. After a little while my breath became almost imperceptible. Then I felt a sharp constriction in my chest; I was sinking, lower and lower into a darkness that was in no way either frightening or uncomfortable. I stopped breathing, followed by a gradual stepping down into a vast darkness in which there was no object, no thought, no image, but only the sensation of sinking. The only thing that remained was awareness of the experience. Yet it was not filtered through the person I normally know myself as.

> *Gradually this awareness began to ascend and slowly*
> *I found myself coming back, first a dim recognition of*
> *my body lying prone on the bed, the eyes still closed,*
> *the curtains drawn, the twilight hour. And then the first*
> *thought, 'Death or dhyan?'*

The dream was presenting me with two distinct forms of awareness. It struck me that in doing so, this dream was answering a question that had been posed in an earlier one: 'Find out what remains when the content of all experience is exhausted.' To me a cessation of experience was the same as death. And appropriately here, the metaphor used to create a boundary between the two forms of awareness is death! Why? Because death not only marks the end of all experience but also marks an erasure of all that had been gathered in life. All that remains, the dream said, is Awareness—an altogether different kind of awareness. Though we all know what awareness is, it is difficult, nay impossible, to define it. Carl Jung contends that awareness must have an object to be aware of, for how can it be aware of nothing and still exist? In contrast, all mystics affirm that awareness has two aspects, one through which we cognize the world with its people, objects and myriad experiences, and the other which lies behind it, in silence—a contentless awareness, needing no object to be aware of besides an awareness of its own self-existent nature.

Two types of awareness

The earlier part of the dream reflects what we consider as normal awareness—I am sitting on the bed aware of what is happening outside as I watch the market as well as the dancing girl. At the same time, I am also aware of the choices open to me given the circumstances—either beheading or swallowing sleeping pills. At first, I presumed that the awareness in the latter part of the dream and the earlier are one and same. For what can awareness be but awareness!

But the dream portrays them to be different. How? The awareness I felt while sitting on the bed is that which enhances and defines me. My awareness of choices open to me is who I am, my upbringing, what I hope to be, my experiences, predilections, memories. In the other awareness, everything is being sloughed off, till there is nothing left of me, not even my breath. One could characterize the first kind of awareness as a personal awareness, and the second as an impersonal awareness—there is no personal element in it, no 'I', no thoughts, ideas, images, there is only darkness. I was taken step by step from normal awareness to a state without any content beyond which awareness seemed to exist by itself. As though I was brought to the very frontiers of the known and made to face the immensity of the unknown. This experience was beyond my knowledge, beyond my known self. 'I' had been replaced by something else—an awareness, in which the 'I' ceases to exist because it has been dissolved. This impersonal awareness was distinct from the state of quiescence that sometimes washes over one during meditation.

Though my mind appreciated these differences, internally I was still mystified about how there can be two types of awareness, and that the impersonal awareness remains even though it is eclipsed by the everyday awareness. Then I recalled my dream (given in the chapter 'Even The Elephant's Wounds Heal') about the mahout who had said: 'Even the elephant's wounds heal/Only the airy space burns.' Possibly that dream was also alluding to two types of awareness. One in which we get hurt, have our highs and lows in the market place of life, and the other is the 'airy space' in which the impersonal awareness steadily burns.

Was Ashishda hoping we discover this through the practices recommended by him? More than once, I found myself mentally referring the experience to him for greater clarity.

Another dream of the impersonal awareness

Something deep within responded to my plea, giving another glimpse when I had fallen asleep one afternoon. A noise from the direction of the roof jerked me 'awake'. I have no way of verifying whether there was actually a noise or whether it represented the jolt of becoming 'lucid'. I was still enveloped by sleep but something in me was 'awake':

> *Suddenly consciousness, an impersonal awareness, rose from the depths of sleep. Quickly and rapidly, it rose, till it came to the borders of wakefulness and then it attached itself to my personality. I first became aware of myself, and a split second later, my waking integration had taken over—cognizant of my surroundings, the room, the house.*

I did correlate this impersonal awareness to that in the earlier dream of 'death-dhyan', in which the 'me' had dissolved to reveal a featureless awareness, which then sank into the darkness, only to rise and again become the known 'me'. Here, there was only the ascent of awareness back into the known.

I also wondered if the rising of awareness was metaphorically expressing what happens when we wake up from the 'blankness' or 'darkness' of deep sleep (a kind of death), where there is only an impersonal awareness without any content. Then in that split-second, the boundary of 'blankness' is crossed and the bundle of all that is 'me', the personality emerges into the everyday world of my surroundings, the room, the house.

At another level, were these dreams attempting to depict what remains when one passes beyond the surface to the deeper levels? After all, I asked myself, what did I expect to find at the deeper end of the pool? The same sticks and stones as seen in everyday reality?

However, a niggling doubt persisted. Why had I not looked at these dreams as psychological commentaries or as a metaphorical comment about myself, but had treated them as allusions to the deeper part of the self? Because they were 'lucid' dreams, they came when I became 'awake' while asleep. Also, they were not sourced from memory, and did not appear to be a manipulation and recombination of it.

A memory

This dream made me recall an incident early in my association with Ashishda. I mention it again because of its unusualness. I have related this in the chapter, 'You Have To Be Ripe For It'.

I was all of twenty-one years then, and like my peers restlessly involved in my desires and aspirations. Because of Ashishda's suggestion, I had begun meditation. On that day, I had been given a dressing down by my boss along with a threat of termination. Most unfairly, I had felt. Expectedly, my mind had churned uncontrollably when suddenly the 'I' as I knew myself took a backseat and in its place was a calm state hitherto unknown to me. The experience had a quality of a silent repose that had no pulls in any direction. As unexpectedly as it had come, it dissolved. It left me wondering why I chose to live any other way. Yet I could not will it back. Only a memory remained as a reminder of the contrast between what that state was and my ordinary one.

I was puzzled that it had come in the most turbulent circumstances. Not when the mind was relatively quiet or when my anxieties were in abeyance. It did not seem to come from the person I knew myself to be, it seemed independent of me. I had always thought of this experience as a heightened awareness without exploring it any further. Now I regard it as being akin to the mysterious impersonal awareness.

Were these dreams and states showing me the difference between the surface and the deeper levels of myself? The only way I could make sense of all this was by believing that shorn of all specifics this unknown depth in me is 'Consciousness', or 'Awareness'.

Normally we perceive awareness (or consciousness) as a dependent process. We are aware or conscious when we see, touch, smell or hear something external to us. Not only that, we are aware of our own thoughts, emotions, and feelings. We can also be aware of ourselves as if watching ourselves from outside us. This leads to the belief that awareness needs an 'object'—external or internal—and a subject who is aware. The dream contrarily was suggesting that there can be awareness without an 'I' or any other container.

I don't know why but with these dreams of awareness, a feeling of liberation came. As though my life had been building up to realise its simple truth. Like while walking on a path in the hills, you are merely engrossed in climbing. Suddenly you pause and look up. The clouds have parted and your breath catches at the sheer beauty of the pristine, snow-covered mountains. They had always been there but you had never seen them before. Then the clouds descend and the view has gone.

Recurrent Facets of Awareness

In no way am I suggesting that I own these aspects of awareness because my dreams were thematically repeating images of them. I believe that whenever a recurrence happens in dream states, it could be showing their message from different points of view, as when mulling on perplexing issues, we often state, restate them, and repeatedly want to discuss them. For me with these experiences a process was underway. I was being asked to step further inwards but before doing that I had to grasp the many modalities of the 'I'. For in these experiences this 'awareness' was so different that I could not find its correlation with the ordinary 'me'. Then other dreams came expanding on the recurrent theme.

One morning in between sleep and coming awake:

I saw the waking personality as a faraway distant point. In that moment arose an awareness of an impersonal, utterly calm observing self, unconcerned with the distant personality.

In this dream, the impersonal awareness is not concerned with the personality. I also recalled something that had happened a few years ago.

Early in the morning betwixt sleep and wakefulness:

I found myself spontaneously puzzling over the relationship between the Observer and thoughts. For a fraction of a second there flashed before me the Observer, the still centre, imageless, unbounded. In a blink, outpoured an effulgence, like a thick cascading stream, which, as yet, had no individual characteristics, thoughts, shapes or particularities.

Here, the Observer has been equated to the impersonal awareness—still centre, imageless, unbounded—and the personality to thought. In the earlier dream, the impersonal awareness had attached itself to an already-existing (by implication) personality; in the one that followed, it is a distant point, while, in this dream, the as-yet-unformed thoughts (personality) are shown as an outpouring of an as yet contentless effulgence. However, I, the individual, appropriates the effulgence, the outpouring becomes the 'me' and the 'mine' of the personality. To me it seemed they were depicting different aspects of the relationship between the two types of awareness to give a fuller picture.

In another instance, early in the morning, embedded in the quiescence of sleep:

> *I felt a lit awareness, a disc of focused light, which was aware in an impersonal manner.*

Another aspect playing on the same theme—the impersonal awareness is now shown as a lit, focused disc.

I puzzled over-and-over again about the state in which these dreams or experiences happened, in which there is lucidity of an impersonal awareness amidst stillness.

Strangely enough while I was reflecting over all this my mind was slipping into semi-quietude. And at the heart of this quiescent state was again present that intangible awareness. Deeply silent. In the foreground were thoughts floating past, slower, without their usual whir, having no relationship to the 'presence' in the background.

Next morning, I tried to re-enter that state. It was not the same. There was stillness, a concentration. After a while, thoughts floated by seeming like happenings 'out there'. Then I realised that as soon as I invested in a thought, I was pulled out of the 'still' state. But that implacable 'presence' in the background I had perceived the day before was absent.

Sort out these dreams!

Another dream gave a greater fillip to understanding these impersonal dreams and states:

> *I am back in the Mirtola Mandir. In the inner sanctum of the temple just below the altar of Krishna and Radha's images, many offerings are lying on the floor—fruit, flowers, honey, large copper vessels of prasad, milk, fresh ghee, bananas, tulsi, rose petals. And the offerings are still coming in, wherefrom I don't know. The floor is quite full by now. Suddenly Ashishda comes out and says to me, 'You better sort these out, find places for them, make sense of them.'*

The prasad is a metaphor for what has been 'given' to me by way of the impersonal dreams and experiences. The offerings are scattered on the floor, almost covering it. The floor is what we stand on. Could this signify my standpoint—my beliefs and conceptions? Or is it signifying something deeper which is foundational to all experience? Ashishda asks me to 'sort them out'. So that they may find a connection to my life and are grounded in my understanding. Also, if much had been given because of Ashishda, the Mandir, and Mirtola, then all of myself had to be offered (prasad), so that I become more rooted within that which is Real, the underlying principle of all life.

The dream, by suggesting more offerings (experiences) might come, was emphasising that further work had to be done. Only when the earlier experiences were fully grasped would new ones come. To be honest, I could understand and absorb only in the measure of how much of myself I knew and had unravelled. It also struck me that the injunction to sort out perhaps also applied to earlier dreams too, whose full import may not have been fully integrated.

These earlier dreams had initially been viewed as a

comment on what was happening in my outer life. Now when I look back, they were relating two stories. At that point in time my emphasis in deciphering them had been to garner enough strength to cope with my outer circumstances. Most likely, the other story in those dreams was in congruence with my later dreams after I had left the Ashram. Why had I limited their meaning mainly to outward events? Is it because the inner dimensions are complex, having impact at varying levels, and therefore more difficult to fathom? In comprehending dreams, it would be a mistake not to pay attention to their tangible aspects, but it would be a graver mistake to ignore the immensity of their deeper, universal content, merely because it is intangible. Ashishda had emphasised how dreams can be the switch-points on the journey.

After we left the Ashram, in a dream Ashishda tells Rajeev, 'When you are a little more mature you might understand my dictates!'

In the chapter 'Get Out of the Way', Rajeev, in a state of 'wakefulness', had seen birds flying high in the sky. This was followed by a-month-long period in which his mind had been cleared of all its clutter like a table-top is with one sweep of the hand. The clutter, however, returned after that month. Over two decades later, he realised he had been privy to a state of being that was free and in which only calmness was.

Perhaps that was what Ashishda had hinted at when he had asked for maturity, and for me to sort out the prasad. I realised the intent in his taking us into the temple was not merely about acceptance or rejection. That is a very preliminary and soon-to-be-left-behind-stage. All along he was drawing my attention to the core of the inner life, hoping I would make the shift away from the ego—my significance, its bruises and pains. That I would learn from the inscrutable face of the dream mirror with its capacity to reveal states of consciousness which are shorn of all outer struggles. The imperatives of our participation in everyday life compel us to look through consciousness but never squarely at it. Meaning that there will be states when consciousness can be known by itself, and perceived as such. Only we have to be ready to give cognisance to it.

Perhaps the dream of 'death-dhyan', by abandoning the personality, was alerting me to these possibilities. I felt the message of the recent dreams was that the hidden treasure is the impersonal consciousness. Not as a personal possession but as a principle. We all embody that principle, but the more a person accepts it, the more its foundational aspect shines forth. They were calling upon me to see that all that happened was an unfoldment, an understanding of the nature of that which is deeply impersonal.

A part of this process had started while we were in the Ashram, where my mind could envisage the actual message of the dreams but my heart could at best very slowly metabolize my perplexity of those years. Perhaps, emotionally I found it difficult to fully transcend the binaries of good-bad, sin-virtue, right-wrong, fair-unfair, and the implacable judgements that arise from them. Now viewed with the eye of distance, I was being asked once again to sort out the 'gifts' given to us. My current dreams had awakened an impersonal level of consciousness, free from the horizontal plane with its inevitable joys and sorrows of the everyday. Now I appreciate that the challenges we had faced had not effaced our confidence, instead strength had been gained, which had sustained us. Wasn't this the treasure the dragon of suffering was guarding?

Was this what Ashishda had hoped for when he asked

me to 'sort out'? I strongly sensed that my dreams, earlier and current, were asking for a shift from participation to sheer observation, and this could not be done with a clenched fist or by taking a deep breath. In time I realised the 'big fight' lay in the training and shifting of attention. In doing so, a significant amount of energy locked in my personality and its concerns would get released. The real shift, however, could take place only because of these transpersonal experiences. A profounder mode of knowing had been activated which in turn carried me further into 'being' than would normally have been the case. The more I tried to understand and give significance to them, the more the personal concerns began to recede.

As the dream of sorting out the prasad had stated, more was to come. And, more came...

One night, I became aware in sleep; I had gained lucidity. For some moments there was nothing except the awareness of the quiescence of sleep. Then:

> *I saw a spinning top of concentrated light, a pure focus of joy, dancing, whirling and then spinning out into manifestation in myriad directions. It was full of some ineffable delight, as though spinning with a rapture it could not contain as it sought expression in creation.*

So far, what I had been shown was an impersonal, featureless, implacable awareness. Here in this instance, it was seen as the essence and source of joy. In another instance when I was taking an afternoon nap in the study, a stream of love welling and radiating seeped into my being. Every pore of my body was soaked in Love itself. Just an unalloyed state, blissful and boundless, attached to no one, belonging to nothing. Perhaps, love in its essential nature.

Much later, I was given a different perspective to this puzzlement. It came against a background of emotional fatigue. Compounding this was an exceptionally hot Indian summer where repeated power cuts added to my discomfort. I emerged from sleep hearing the following words:

That comes to birth, That experiences and That goes out in death.

As I came awake, my thoughts completed that which was left unstated—I had nothing to do with 'That'.

It bluntly stated: That comes to birth, not you. Why? Because 'That' wishes to experience. What remains when every bit of my uniqueness, every identification is dropped cannot be 'me' but an impersonal 'That'. It was not my story, but 'I' was part of 'ITs' story. Any residual feelings that the impersonal awareness had something to do with me, were blown away by the utterly impersonal statement in the dream of 'That'. Having known this presence in my dreams wiped away all my ideas of idols, images, and holiness. Were these dreams asking me to dive deep into myself; into that which matters, and, finally, into that which *alone* matters?

I was repeatedly being told—'Everything is That.' Something whose essential character was not a 'thing' assailed with attributes. This is probably one of the hardest perceptions to assimilate.

I constantly pondered on why it is so difficult to see that everything comes from 'That', the one source. And that each one of us, like glow worms, carries that light.

Gradually came burgeoning perceptions that I was not my feelings of pleasure and pain, or my desires, or the fears, anger, and hurts. They were all part of me, but that I was not wholly them. No longer were they my sole yardsticks as they did not completely describe 'me'. Of course, I mostly participated in life as earlier—and often forgot this other 'presence', yet, in a few instances I was able to learn that I am separate from what I watch, and the greater the separation between the watcher and the watched, the greater the freedom. I also sometimes perceived that rare neutral space within, biding its time to be permeated by something other than myself. The result was I began to measure my life against a much wider canvas in which the 'me' and 'mine' were reduced to anomalies against some measureless backdrop. There is now a reference point in dealing with the vagaries of the mind, with its insidious power of projecting what lies within me as belonging to the 'other'. And, when I felt I was not hearing the right note, in those moments I would open my cache of precious experiences and take heart again from that which had been shown as the invaluable measure of all things, as the unity in the diversity.

Letting go

A last dream which, for me is the essence of all that I learnt in Mirtola. Many years after Ashishda's death I had dreamt of him:

> *I am on the banks of the Ganges, maybe in Benares. There is no one there but him. Tall, thin, with greying shoulder-length hair, his all-too familiar faded gerua robe tied with a similarly dyed cloth around his waist, his eyes shining with a light I had seen more than once when he was alive.*
>
> *In his hand he holds a cloth like the one he is wearing. He gives it to me and says, 'Wear it.' I climb the steps of the ghat and go to a room. First, I tie it as a lungi. It does not work. Then as a saree. That too does not work. Finally, I wear it as an alkhela (robe) and go down the steps to meet Ashishda. I think my head is shaven; maybe a stubble remains. The setting sun streaks the sky with*

orange and lights the waters. I touch Ashishda's feet. He raises me by the shoulders and says, 'Remain still. Work unobtrusively and die to your former life.'

He looks at me for a long moment. I feel overwhelmed. The next moment, he has gone.

I sit on the banks of the river not knowing what to do. I watch the sun set.

And now, many, many years later, the colours of renunciation appear once more before me—sanyas. Was the dream indicative of the future? If not, what could it be? A wish fulfilment? Sanyas represents a wandering mendicant detached from wealth, property, family—a wish many Hindus harbour as a cultural ideal.

The shade of the cloth given by Ashishda suggests that this may not be the meaning of the dream. It was not dyed in the usual saffron of a sadhu's garb. Could the dream be nudging me towards an aspect of his teachings, and not towards traditional sanyas? His own journey as a novice had begun with the death of the smaller self. Possibly, the dream was not about leaving the world, staff and bowl in hand, but about going 'still' on one's smaller self. A different order of letting go than the traditional one. Sanyas is not an outward giving up of things or relationships, or a ritual ceremony—it is primarily a giving up of the mind.

The way I tried to wear the cloth also made me reflect. Not as a saree (feminine), nor as a lungi (masculine). It worked as an alkhela, devoid of gender distinctions. Mystics of every tradition assure us that in spiritual awareness, we gradually dis-identify from everything that normally constitutes identity—body, gender, mind, intellect, ego. It is said that by the time we reach the threshold of full spiritual potential, all dualities are left behind: no more are we black or white, old or young, learned or ignorant. No more you or me. So, was the reference to dying in the dream urging for the dissolution of all distinctions—the true sanyas?

But hadn't my entire life been a letting go, a relinquishment of one sort or another?

When we left our Delhi life for the Ashram, it was a letting go of all former representations of myself—work, family, a familiar lifestyle and all the aspirations of the culture we lived in.

But what we had relinquished outwardly had to be dealt with inwardly: the struggle to let go of the 'self'. In the Ashram, your personal identity or 'you' did not count, only service did. The constant submission was to the deities in the Temple, represented by surrendering to the will of the Teacher, seeking inspiration from who he was, and which was often resisted by who I was. He maintained that for a new centre to form, the present integration needed to be dissolved. A shift away from one's desires, opinions and comforts. The existence of this new centre of consciousness had to be taken on trust. And a sustained effort had to be made to live by it. Perhaps the effort to sense it and live by it became an invocation. A renunciation of the personal so that Reality could reveal itself. Ashishda never failed to emphasize that the search is an enquiry and not merely a following of disciplines. 'Follow that enquiry back beyond your identifications,' he would urge us.

Yet another kind of renunciation followed when we left the Ashram. A reluctant leaving behind of a life that we had adopted, and more than that, the moving away from the Teacher.

Gradually, the old voices, which had not been silenced by my shift to the Ashram, raised their head again—voices affirming personal identity. Juxtaposed against this were values from the Ashram where we tried to self-remember, be watchful of ourselves, still the mind and go beyond. In time I discovered that the old voices need not be trampled underfoot but transformed. A letting go of that which was unexamined. Time to seek the truth from an unborrowed self—something which is completely my own and matches with who I truly am.

When I had first met Ashishda, I asked him how I would find my true identity?

'By keeping still.'

'What does that mean?' I asked.

'Watch, observe, don't identify with your thoughts. The effort should be to try and stem the flow of thoughts. There is a quiet place within, that is not fussed about by people, things, hurt feelings and unsatisfied desires. When the mind is quiet only then can the true identity be found.'

Was this what was being affirmed in the sanyas dream? Remain still.

And would remaining still lead to working unobtrusively? Perhaps each supports and fulfils the other. When we work unobtrusively, we let go of self-affirmation. And wouldn't that, in turn, help in remaining still? Half of one's life is spent in building up one's identity and the other half in defending it. Perhaps, this statement demanded a sloughing off of all that constituted 'me'.

And wouldn't that be linked to dying to my former life—my individual biography or the way I viewed it? After all, traditional sanyas hopes to find meaning by radically removing the structures of life. But before doing that, one has to develop a sufficient amount of personality to gain confidence. Ashishda had likened this dismantling to the scaffolding that must be removed once the building is complete. 'If one has worked on oneself, age helps one to see the scaffolding for what it is: a necessary but temporary structure.'

I did discover something. If I managed to stop my thoughts, even momentarily, in that infinitesimal pause, the slate would be wiped clean, the person that I habitually was would become absent. In fact, for that duration, this untidy world would dissolve. Yet an awareness remained, an attentive awareness—self-existent, featureless, unbounded. Observation suggests some sort of involvement in what is observed. But this state is unconcerned with what it is observing. It felt like a presence, glimpsed when thoughts were not eclipsing it.

Was I being reminded by the dream of this state? Or was it asking for a more direct approach to the source of this awareness? Religious symbols stir feelings and act as vehicles to affirm the sacramental nature of that awareness. However, the rituals must be internalized. One must find within oneself the states of being which they outwardly represent. Sanyas is lighting one's own consciousness with a new fire.

Ashishda had once asked, 'Whose are these pleasures and pains?'

I felt the obvious answer was 'me'—what my body experiences.

He then said, 'It does not take very long to realise that the body is not the same as "me".'

'Why?'

'Because I observe the sensations provided to me by the body. So, the "I" or the "me" must be separate from the body. But what is the nature of this "me"?'

'Isn't the "I" my thoughts and feelings, my personality?'

'Again, you can be aware that you observe all your thoughts and feelings. Doesn't this suggest that the observing "I" is apart from the "me"?' he asked.

'Are you suggesting that the ability to see, hear, or sense cannot be the "I"?'

'You may have to enquire: Which "I"? The "I" that participates in activities, or the "I" that observes?'

I was silent, trying to digest his words.

'I am only suggesting an obvious fact, that the "mind" has two aspects—it can see objects in the outside world, and it can also see itself. This ability is possibly what distinguishes us from animals. But what is the nature of this observing "I"? Is it identical with the personality, or is it distinct?'

Was my dream a call to seek in the direction Ashishda was suggesting? Perhaps it would be a dual relationship. I would begin to own myself, my thoughts, my perceptions. And in owning them, I would begin to watch them as though they were separate from "me". And maybe, just maybe, in the space between the two, I would begin the journey from the circumference to the centre. A sanyas where the measure of one's absence reveals glimpses of an ever-present awareness.

Epilogue

The seasons had run their course once again. Winter, a charcoal etching; spring, a hue of watercolours; summer, a dry-eyed glance, firefly lit nights followed by monsoonal dark, foreboding skies, and then sepia toned autumn, a mosaic of all seasons.

Once more it is monsoon, the twilight hour in August. The grass gleams damply in the garden. Water is slowly dripping off the deodar trees, fresh from rain that had drummed on them. The scene from our room overlooking the Sattal lake and the surround of reserved forest, is an ever-changing tableau. A white mist is descending, blurring the distant mountains, their outline barely discernible.

I turned away from the window and thought, soon it will be autumn. The autumn of my life. Why did I feel all the seasons, my beginnings and ends were present in just this moment, a pause that contained my whole life. I felt I was standing in my own presence and that of none else. Can a life be measured by a moment in time? Perhaps it can when it contains all its essence, when speech borders on silence, when memory, the world and my experiences in it suddenly feel pristine, as they would to a new born. As though time itself was unwinding all that had been done and then asking: What remains?

I thought about the three weeks I recently spent in Delhi. I was just someone rushing around, ticking off the chores on my list. I don't remember being very conscious of myself. Except for a mild dissatisfaction lurking somewhere in the background that I was living an average day with average pursuits, held ransom to a state of mind which was fleeting, distracted, aware merely in a functional, surface way. Like an old pair of slippers that are comfortable in a sloppy worn-out way, I had slipped back into my standard responses to standard situations. Where had I disappeared?

In Sattal, I feel a shift in my centre of gravity. There are few distractions here, there is a natural return to an inner stillness, a return to myself. In Delhi I seemed to have been caught in the vortex of living, without being present to that living. Here my senses are more acute, my thoughts clearer, instinctively slowing down, so that I can keep pace with them. I have learnt to take note of the small movements of the mind, its various voices and tried to distinguish between those that I had borrowed along the way and those which are truly my own. It was not always a simple process, but in the course of it, I learnt to hear better the silent spaces between my story, especially the inner one.

Rajeev and I stood together at the window watching the silhouette of the distant mountains with their steadfast stillness dissolving into the oncoming dusk. The mist was threading itself through the trees, shrouding them in a white diaphanous veil. The dimly visible lake below, its waters green, peering through the mist was like an eye, watching the dissolving landscape. Such beauty!

It was here that I recognised that the physical body is closely connected to the mind and its emotional content. Everything that transpires in the mind, has a parallel in the body, and vice versa. I had begun to understand the outer events in my life by their inner resonance and the inner movements as the source of everything outer. As though a seamster had taken all the disparate patchwork pieces of my life and sewn them into a quilt that brought warmth from some unknowable abundance. I turned to Rajeev. His smile gentled as though he had picked up my unexpressed thoughts.

With this came the capacity to acknowledge and allow feelings and experiences which I had overlooked, or brushed under the carpet as uninteresting or undesirable aspects of myself to come to the foreground. Once faced and examined, they could then be set aside. Just to articulate one unadmitted thought into words, liberated the thought. This I realised led to an ability to direct my attention onto any aspect of myself, unafraid at what I may unearth. And this in turn would channel my energies on how to deal with it. Unexpectedly, and to my delight this situated me in a place where I could choose between the helpful movements of the mind and those that were obstructive. I began to notice what arose from long-grooved, unquestioned patterns of thought that always narrowed my thinking instead of creating a wide-angled perspective. Then increasingly I began to pay less attention to these distinctions in the currents of the mind. Now I would sit on the banks of the river of the mind seeing it rushing forth, just watching its flow. I had been quite at sea about how to live my life till I had learnt to make this conscious gesture of separation which enabled me to stand aside and observe my experience.

Going inwards also made me closer to nature and its rhythm. When I climb up the hill, I climb not only in body but in spirit also. The rumble of thunder, dark clouds, belly full of rain, the sudden streak of lightning, all merge and seem one. My being mingles with all that is around me—the bird, the tree on which it is perched, and its interrupted song as it hears the thunder and gives pause, like me, to the moment.

The magpies, with their very conspicuous long blue tail, radiant orange-red beak, a black head, neck and breast, contrasting with a white underbelly, often visit our garden. They bathe in the clay pots, feed on the grass, mimicking a variety of sounds. In the hills they are sometimes called lampuchia, the long tailed. Then, one nesting time, a male began pillaging our garden shamelessly. With his beak he first untied the string that tied the dahlias and flew off with it to his companion, carrying the first building blocks of their nest. The arch above our gate covered with a mass of entangled climbers was the chosen site. Then he sat on the gate and surveyed the garden and swooped down for twigs and leaves. He settled at the edge of the water-filled clay pot, peering intently into it, and triumphantly ferreted out a maroon, water-drenched leaf, brandished it in his beak and hopped onto the cobble stones, preening with his prize. Suddenly he dropped the leaf and for a brief moment turned towards me. In that moment, we communed over a very fragile nest-in-the-making.

'You call this garden and house, your home. For me it is just a way point on a journey,' he said.

'And your nest?'

'A temporary address in an onward journey.'

I felt my sense of place and home shifting. Is my notion of home anchored to this house, to my body, my mind, the people I love, the things I care about? Or is it the memory of a state of being, over which often a veil or mist falls? I skid upon the surface of time yet I know that it is the remembrance of a timeless self that redeems transiency and mysteriously becomes my coming home.

The bird shook his feathers restlessly, flapping his wings as if ready for flight. Then he darted a sidelong glance at me. The divide between us was bridged. My world expanded or rather deepened as he flew away on his way elsewhere, without a backward glance. Let go, let go, the rhythm of his wings sang.

This communing and oneness with nature was part of me when I was about five years-old. I perceived shapes that were familiar and sounds that hummed within me. The evening light slanting on the trees, the scent of damp leaves, the cicada's chorus, a sweet blackbird's song were my companions. The luminescence of the setting sun was not saluting the day's end, but coursed right through my body and nothing marked the boundary between the light and me. My 'I' at that moment knew no boundaries, and what was inside and outside felt one.

Gradually, growing up meant being woven into the web of the world where my body imprisoned me, my mind began to speak a different language and my senses learnt the vocabulary of fear. My ingrained habitual reactions now prevented me from seeing the myriad joyous epiphanies in the book of Nature and in the surrounding world. An impoverishment occurred.

And now to feel that once again, to see the world through those eyes, to hear the humming of the wordless song of the universe. Nature is not some remote abstraction but an ever-present presence here, giving solitude a different texture, an alternative vision. Everything seems to open a door to the beyond.

The mist has now covered the lake. Much of the landscape has disappeared from all around me, only the outline of trees near the house glimmers occasionally through the mist. I moved onto the terrace seeking out what had remained.

The beauty without, slowly became the quiet within. It did not happen automatically. Sometimes it happened spontaneously, this void in involvement with any thought, pleasant or unpleasant, allowing me to stay in a non-involved zone. Then to hold it there as long as one can is the hourly, daily endeavour.

And this holding back from mental action brought about an accumulation in energy, raised potency and intensity. The energy, no longer continually ebbing away in noisy streams of purposive effort, began to be contained in silent pools of clearness. And this silent, clear space, is not personal, not the 'me' as I ordinarily know myself. But the calm fullness of a presence which had chosen to make itself felt, according to its own will.

Somewhere down in the village a temple bell pealed. A call to prayer? The mist hid its cultural vestment, the whiteness draining it of its local colour. Just a bell pealing, returning anybody, anywhere to the centre of their being.

In the early evening hour, the mist shimmered silver or was it the lights of the village peeping through? Through this misty veil why did I feel, somewhere, a ship had come to harbour?

At around eleven o'clock that night I heard a rasping, hoarse cough, then a guttural roar of a leopard. I listened intently, to ascertain whether the sounds were coming from the forest behind our house or from the one to the right? Essentially a solitary creature, was he making his presence known to another approaching leopard? With this nocturnal hunter on the move, the web of the jungle felt the impact of yet another cycle of rupture and renewal. I went to the balcony behind our house overlooking the forest, to hear better. A pause and then he gave a distant call which sounded like someone sawing wood. The mist had cleared.

A full moon bathed the forest, the night, the earth. A few stars twinkled for recognition under its searchlight beam. The moon's smile was whimsical as it gave recognition to my being a single thin, fragile strand in the skein of this cosmic web.

And in this web the more I tried to hold onto reality, the more unreal and paradoxical it became. I came to see that the reality of the world out there is ever in motion and changing shape. Nothing is as it is for even a moment. And no two moments are similar. In this transiency what future do I pursue when the past is already speeding by, leaving scarcely any time to greet the present? My memories, my past become the warp and woof of my perceptions that weave an illusion of continuity in my blind search for identity. An identity that is hardly stable in the passage of my transient existence. The forest grew grave and I felt all that I believed I am, recede, merging into the darkness in deference to the ever-extending vastness of the landscape.

'Nature does not hurry yet everything is accomplished,' Lao Tzu had said. In nature, the process of becoming is continuous, and an enduring certainty of the eventual completion of the process inheres within it; if interrupted, it will begin anew. Perhaps, true solitude means you have grown quiet enough to know that the process is underway. That you are part of it and are capable of watching its unfoldment.

Solitude, then, is an unfolding relationship with yourself, of how well you know yourself and how much of the unknown 'other' within you still needs to be discovered. Gradually an awareness comes of the fullness of your own presence rather than the absence of others.

And then to dive deeper into one's own depths. And wait, and wait for life to quietly disclose its secrets.

The next evening, the trees curving down the ridge of the green mountains were once again threaded by mist. An anchor-shaped presence, it lurched down towards the lake to disperse over it.

The mist had a dream-like quality. It made me feel my life was like a very vivid dream in which I had been stirred by the richness and variety of the world, dazzled by the dizzy heights of hope and anguished by the hard bite of despair. Where my attention had snagged on everything transitory, infatuated by all that passes in the march of time. Yet in my lifetime, in the ever moving 'now', the veils lifted, and I felt the pause, sensed an ever-present presence. Was that me or another? Or both, in the now and forever? Who was it that had watched this dream I call my life, or more likely dreamt this dream, and yet was not itself the dream?

By now the mist had covered the whole lake. The birds vanished from the sky, the cloud and mist became one. Then even the foreground of the trees, near the house, vanished. Everything disappeared and I too dissolved in some trackless, measureless, immortal white. The dream was gone. Did the dreamer remain?

Glossary

Arati: Ritual offering to the deity or guru; the offering is usually made by circular movements of a panchpradeep and is accompanied with the ringing of a hand-bell

Ashram: Retreat; Abode

Chamar: White bristled whisk

Chula: Wood or coal fired cooking stove

Darshanarthi: People who visit a temple to pay homage to the deities

Dhikr: Recollection; Contemplation of God

Dhyan: Inward contemplation

Fana: Merging; extinction

Ghee: Clarified butter

Griha Pravesh: Ritual ceremony before entering a new home

Hamam: Wood-fired water heater

Haveli: A large house designed along traditional lines

Hayrangi: Perplexity; bewilderment

Janamashtami: Hindu festival celebrating the birth of Lord Krishna

Jannat: Heaven of Islam

Japa: Repetition of a sacred mantra often with the aid of a rosary

Lungi: A Sarong-like garment tied at the waist

Mahout: Elephant keeper

Mantra: A religious incantation

Panchpradeep: An oil lamp with five wicks

Parabrahman: The Supreme; The Absolute

Roti: Unleavened bread

Sadhu: A religious ascetic

Sahib: A European male, usually with a social or official status

Samadhi: Cenotaph

Sanyas: A form of asceticism marked by the renunciation of material desires and prejudices in pursuit solely of the spiritual goal

Saree: A traditional garment worn by Indian women

Sevak/Sevika: A male (Sevak) or female (Sevika) devotee who serves in the temple

Thakur: Literally the head of the family; also used by Vaishnavs when they refer to Lord Krishna

Vaikunt: Paradise of the Vaishnavs

Vaishnav: Follower of a devotional Hindu religious sect which worships the God Vishnu, whose incarnation was Lord Krishna

Yogi: Ascetic

Acknowledgements

My special thanks to those who were significant contributors in shaping the earlier version of the book.

Namita Unnikrishnan, who revised, changed and edited significant portions of the manuscript by unstintingly giving of herself in time and effort. I cannot think of the book without her.

Pratima Mitchell, who always believed I had a story to tell and helped in every stage of its telling.

Malashri Lal, for her perceptive and defining remarks in the earlier book as also her comments on the new material added to this book. In fact, her suggestions guided my hand in writing the last two chapters.

Alok Bhalla, who read the raw initial draft of the penultimate chapter of the current book and still had words of encouragement!

Robey Lal and Vasundara Bhalla, for always being there.

Mohit Satyanand, for reading the original book and the new additions with care and empathy, giving me valuable feedback.

Reba Som, Rajni Sood, Anjana Pasricha, Jasjit Mansingh, Punam Sikka Khanna, Richa Singh, and Chitra Iyer, for reading the additional material in the book.

Ravi Singh, for seeing this book anew and agreeing to meet me yet one more time to clarify the direction the new material could take.

Dyuti Roy, my editor at Speaking Tiger Books, for empathetically sharing the journey and for her questions that helped clarify things I had written earlier.

Purnima Mehta, for her inexhaustible energy in editing, commenting, rereading the book several times so that nothing slips her vigilant eye. Her giving is humbling as is Rajeev's whose involvement helped shape the book.